MULTIMEDIA

Gateway to the Next Millennium

MULTIMEDIA
Gateway to the Next Millennium

EDITED BY

Robert Aston

AND

Joyce Schwarz

AP PROFESSIONAL

Boston   San Diego   New York
London   Sydney   Tokyo   Toronto

AP PROFESSIONAL
955 Massachusetts Avenue, Cambridge, MA 02139

An imprint of ACADEMIC PRESS, INC.
A Division of HARCOURT BRACE & COMPANY

United Kingdom Edition published by
ACADEMIC PRESS LIMITED
24–28 Oval Road, London NW1 7DX

Library of Congress Cataloging-in-Publication Data
Multimedia: gateway to the next millennium / edited by Robert Aston
  and Joyce A. Schwarz.
      p.   cm.
    Includes index.
    ISBN 0-12-065625-6 (acid-free paper)
    1. Multimedia systems.   I. Aston, Robert, 1945–   . II. Schwarz,
Joyce A., 1946–
QA76.575.M832   1994
006.6–dc20   94-22329
                                                   CIP

Printed in the United States of America
94 95 96 97 IP 9 8 7 6 5 4 3 2 1

Contents

Preface

BOLDLY GOING...
WHERE?

BRANNON BRAGA
CO-PRODUCER, STAR TREK—
THE NEXT GENERATION

As a *Star Trek* writer, I spend a great deal of time conceiving a future where human beings and technology have achieved a perfect balance. Technology is pervasive, but not intrusive—a harmonious presence in the human landscape. This was a conscious choice by the show's creator, Gene Roddenberry, who believed that futuristic technology should not overshadow the characters of the Next Generation. We tell stories about *people*, not gadgets.

This smooth relationship between humanity and technology is a fine ideal for a television show, but what will the future really be like? How will people interact with technology? We are very different from people before the advent of television. . . or before the printing press. . . or before writing was invented, when people lived in purely oral cultures. . . and a new breed of human beings will exist fifty or a hundred years from now. As we discuss these potentially strange and profound new technologies that will comprise the "information superhighway," we have no sense of how they might change the culture and the human psyche—for the good or the bad.

If only we could travel through time and glimpse the future. Unfortunately, this isn't *Star Trek*, where people jump through time like it's a jaunt to the corner market—but you do hold in your hands the next best thing. *Multimedia: Gateway to the Next Millennium* explores the future of telecommunications, film, and broadcasting and the impact of technology on education, entertainment, and the world at large. It is a seminal book. Never before has such a comprehensive range of multimedia technologies been covered in a single compendium, their relationships explored and potential clarified in a timely manner. And thank God for it, because never in the history of humankind have so many technologies emerged all at once, all with the potential to redefine the way we live and think— for the good or the bad.

Will the real future be like *Star Trek*? I hope so. The moment we lose sight of our humanity and the idea that multimedia technology should enhance our existence but not replace it, is the moment we're in danger of becoming a new and disturbing animal...at worst, an interconnected mass of mentalities like the "Borg," to put it in *Trek* terms. And if you have no idea what I'm talking about, you will very soon. Just start reading. . .

Tables

Figures

Contributors

Robert Aston, Market Vision, 326 Pacheco Avenue, Suite 200, Santa Cruz, California 95062

Frank Biocca, Center for Research in Journalism and Mass Communication, University of North Carolina, Chapel Hill, North Carolina 27599-3365

Roger L. Fetterman, 2245 Laurelei Avenue, San Jose, California 95128

Stanley Klein, S. Klein Communications, Inc., 730 Boston Post Road, Sudbury, Massachusetts 01776

Kenneth Meyer, 1810 1/2 North Van Ness Avenue, Los Angeles, California 90028

Mark Radcliffe, Gray Cary Ware & Freidenrich, 400 Hamilton Avenue, Palo Alto, California 94301

David Rosen, 345 Union Street, San Francisco, California 94133

Joyce A. Schwarz, Joyce Communications, 1714 Sanborn Avenue, Los Angeles, California 90027

Robert Yadon, Center for Information and Communication Sciences, Ball State University, Muncie, Indiana 47306

Chapter 1

INTRODUCTION
THE JOURNEY BEGINS

ROBERT ASTON
JOYCE A. SCHWARZ
EDITORS

More than 500 years ago, Christopher Columbus stood on the edge of a new continent and gazed at the unknown horizon with both anticipation and fear. He had set off to prove that the world was not flat and he had navigated across oceans of difficulty to accomplish his goal.

We too now look into the unknown of a new world and even a new millennium where distance and time are compressed to the speed of light. With both naysayers and advocates viewing our progress, we begin our voyage into our new world of digital visual communications.

Multimedia: Gateway to the Next Millennium is not just about the destination but about the journey and the many paths and people that are forging this new industry.

As we drive along the electronic highways and byways, some ramps will lead us nowhere, while others will launch us onto the superspeedways.

This collection of works by some of today's most thought-provoking leaders in this emerging industry strives to bring you an overview of the many accomplishments, issues, and concerns in this evolving technology. The authors combine their perceptions of to-day's visions with the perspective of the past and preview the future.

Our goal is for this volume to serve as a resource for you whether you're developing new products or just interested in learning more about the multimedia medium.

You'll find an overview of multimedia applications and market developments and trends.

Whether you're a media communications executive, an industry strategic planner, a lawyer, an agent, a broadcaster, a hardware or software developer, a multimedia maven of any level or just inter-ested in what the information highway holds for you and your busi-ness, you'll find a wealth of information. As *Star Trek* originator Gene Roddenbury has said so poignantly, we endeavor to "go where no man has gone before," to a new millennium with new technolo-gies and a new paradigm for working together internationally. . . and perhaps even beyond the boundaries of what we know as our world today.

Multimedia applications and developments cross many disci-plines, and the authors discuss in detail the impact that these changes have on each of their respective areas, including the telecommunications industry, the film arena, broadcasting bands, intellectual property problems and challenges, virtual reality, and marketing applications. Brief descriptions of the chapters follow.

Multimedia Will Carry the Flag

Robert Aston and Stan Klein demonstrate the impact of unleashing digital power. The reinvention of multimedia is covered from the various aspects of market sectors, end users, and revenues. The authors express hope for consequent quality education in the evolv-ing era of interactive television. As a reader, you'll be able to go behind the scenes of the building of a digital market infrastructure sector by sector.

Who will be the winners (and the losers) in the digital turf wars? What platform will win out? From broadcast to narrowcast, what will be the power of advertising in these new mediums? Who will be the content owners and how will intellectual property rights be determined? This chapter endeavors to answer more questions than it asks and to find a glimmer of the light at the end of the tunnel leading to the multimedia future.

Hollywood USA: Creative Approaches to New Media Production

As a Hollywood film, television video, and new media analyst, Joyce Schwarz explores digital production and the new paradigm of "the creatives" working in teams with the "techies" that is virtually re-inventing Hollywood as we have known it.

Powered by new developments in computers, digital film and video, compact discs and new delivery systems, a new Hollywood is developing that is more a state of mind than a geographic location. The convergence of consumer electronics, publishing, the computer industry, the film, television, and cable environments, and the telecommunications arena is designing a new Tinseltown for tomorrow's audiences guided by the holy grail of instant access to the consumer at any time and any place.

The leaders of the "New Hollywood" come from a vast variety of fields—theater, television, movie studios, independent production companies, Silicon Valley, telephony, and start-up operations in garages and garrets from London to Louisville.

Multimedia and the Phone Companies

Author Roger Fetterman chronicles technology advancements and regulatory shifts in multimedia-based consumer services. From the Baby Bells to the interexchange carriers, how will they ring in the new millennium? The new networks, media server suppliers, and revenues are surveyed in terms of cooperation and competition. Across the country and around the world, cable and telephone operators are designing trials to determine the outcome for their future and consumer and corporate challenges in the new information infrastructure. Fetterman analyzes the advances and the retreats of the failed phone/cable mergers and alliances.

Broadcasting in the Information Age

Robert Yadon, co-director for the Applied Research Institute at Ball State University, retraces the evolution of broadcasting from its technical, economic, and creative origins. He cites critical factors in the future of the now-burgeoning broadcasting arena, including cable television, Video-on-Demand, asynchronous transfer mode (ATM) technology, transactional TV, satellite delivery systems, and video dialtone. Where there were once only three major networks, now there are promises of 500 channels and a network for almost every imaginable niche audience. Yadon explores the role of the Federal Communications Commission (FCC), the broadcasting and cable leaders, and the upstart newcomers with gleams in their eyes that may evolve into the next MTV or Home Shopping channels.

Legal Issues in the New Media World

Mark Radcliffe, Harvard Law School graduate and partner in the Palo Alto, California law firm of Gray Cary Ware & Freidenrich, wends his way through the complex legal issues arising in the creation and publication of multimedia. Serious legal challenges face developers and publishers regarding copyright issues and ownership in music, film, video, and creative concepts. The scope of protection, the quantum of copyrightability, fair use, and other topics are detailed on levels that both the professional and lay multimedia maven will value now and in the future.

Patents, trade secret law, ownership, derivative work, and more issues are discussed in this section. Specific examples and multimedia production case studies are detailed for ease of reference. You'll even find valuable tips for working with partners and your own legal counselors. This complex terrain of legal issues must be traversed by every multimedia developer whether you're a home user or a high-level corporate client.

Virtual Reality: The Forward Edge of Multimedia

Dr. Frank Biocca, director of the Center for Research in Journalism and Mass Communication at the University of North Carolina, and Kenneth Meyer from *CyberEdge Journal* join together to guide us through the virtual world of products and services evolving on the new simulated panoramas of tomorrow. Take a peek inside the Pandora's box of developing VR technology and systems. You'll discover that VR is not just a medium; it's a destination involving immersion, presence, and yes, telepresence.

The VR industry is just beginning to emerge and could expand at twice the pace that the computer graphics arena grew in the 1970s. Everything from the Navy's ocean experiments to garage VR setups, vehicle designs, through-the-window operations, and mirror worlds to the whole new range of VR paraphernalia options such as head-mounted displays, 3D monitors, haptic (tactile) displays, and even olfactory options are detailed in this section. You'll even discover how soon you may be able to buy VR at the retail level.

The three significant applications of teleconferencing and virtual communities (virtual news environments and entertainment and interactive narrative arenas) are explored. The authors delve into the ultimate communication interface that virtual reality can offer in terms of collapsing time and space and modeling ordinary and extraordinary experiences.

Multimedia and Future Media: 2000 and Beyond

Multimedia is the next step in the social and technological evolution of publishing and sets the stage for even more profound means and experiences of communications, according to author David Rosen, principal of Praxis and previously Commodore's international marketing director. Rosen surveys the role of multimedia in United States households today. He shows us the next stages in communications. Valuable timelines plot pivotal product introductions and services in the multimedia arena. The history of the evolving compact disc is discussed along with the role of artificial intelligence (AI) as our navigator on the new digital highway.

Rosen's business-like survey of the communications industry's restructuring and reengineering gives perspective to dice rolls and deals that merged and purged the 1980s and 1990s. The National Information Infrastructure and the role of public policy and the private market are explored in depth. The evolution of television, especially high-definition television (HDTV) and other technological developments, is surveyed in this section. Rosen moves to the forefront of the industry as he confronts the issues of visual literacy—communications in the 21st century, universal access, and new media initiatives.

A Final Editor's Note

How digital technology will permeate and alter all these businesses, individual activities, and communications, is the focus of this anthology

Multimedia and digital communications are also about wealth and power. As those with vision and technological ability go forth to chart this new world, so do those ready to capitalize on this new opportunity.

We have started down the path to an integrated digital world and there is no turning back. There is much to learn from the hundreds of years of building an analog world, but we are in uncharted digital waters. The next 10–15 years will set the boundaries for a new world for good or bad. What is exciting is that we are at the beginning of this journey, with a new chance to avoid the same old mistakes.

Chapter 2

Multimedia Will Carry the Flag

Robert Aston
Market Vision

Stanley Klein
S. Klein Communications

It is January 15, the year 2010, and as you awake to your morning toast and coffee, a personal digital "accountant" on your computer TV appliance informs you via voice response that a tax refund has been credited to your account and the annual surplus was transferred to the retirement fund.

It is snowing heavily outside, and your driveway has not yet been plowed, so you have no choice but to stay home and meet your clients via telecommuting hookup, including a desktop video conference with some key clients who need to sign off on a revised gizmo design. But before doing so, you want to tend to some personal errands. So, you click on your computer TV appliance for a visit to the video shopping mall. Here, you enter a Macy's ski department to order up a training video that you and your teenage son will work with later this evening; you will also put through an order for ski boots, and receive confirmation on the screen that they will be sent to you directly from the factory within two working days.

As you complete the transaction, a message comes in on your personal communicator; it's one of your analysts, whose car has broken down in Timbuktu on the way to the airport, saying that he'll probably miss his flight, and, therefore, a customer meeting. To save his time, he requests that you let the customer know about the mishap, adding that he will fax a backup schedule from a later plane, and could they confirm its okay prior to his arrival in Moscow.

Oh yes, one final personal chore is to review your stock portfolio, so again you turn to your computer TV appliance to call up a list of your holdings, whose values have been automatically updated based on last night's closing prices. You've decided to give up on your IBM stock, no longer believing that the once-giant company will turn around, and so you program in a sell order at $2.75 a share directed to your on-line brokerage firm.

Now, as you wash up to get ready for the day, you turn on that same computer TV to watch the *Tomorrow Show,* only to be bored by yet another segment on a sports personality. Using keywords selected for your personal interests, you switch on the channel that you programmed to watch yesterday's congressional hearings on the automobile highway system that has fallen into disuse, supplanted by the information superhighway infrastructure. The auto and oil industries want the government to support a campaign to encourage driving to work.

Such is the world, admittedly some of it tongue-in-cheek, that is held out by the emergence of digital technologies coming together under the aegis of "multimedia." This is a world where all information, activities, and communications are connected through a single, seamless combination of wired and wireless links. It is a world where information, including one's own personal records, is maintained in central storehouses. Such information utilities are accessed and massaged by "home management systems" and also connected to other households and businesses through one's own mobile "personal transaction system."

The first baby steps toward this vision—the so-called interactive, multimedia future—will be taken over the next three to five years, following the multimedia capabilities that have been developed on stand-alone platforms over the past half decade.

Before this full power of digital technology can be unleashed, however, new standards must evolve that bridge the ways that traditionally disparate industries born of the analog era communicate with one another. These are the current mega-industries—computers, print/publishing, film/videotape, TV/radio broadcast media, as well as telecommunications and consumer electronics—each catering in its own way to people's needs for information, education, communications, and entertainment.

These six industries collectively generate revenues in excess of one trillion dollars annually, but this sum will be small when compared with the opportunities for digital multimedia to serve all commerce, information, communications, and personal needs. For this reason, each mega-industry is poising itself to exploit the conversion now underway from an analog to a digital world. How such digital technology will permeate all these businesses and society as well are what this chapter, and, in fact, this anthology is all about.

DIGITAL UNLEASHED

The Path from Analog to Digital

A fundamental fact of nature underscores the arduous and costly undertaking that lies ahead in moving out of an analog and into digital information handling: in the analog environment, the processes that make up information capture, processing, and output depend on the media format, i.e., whether it be print, video, film, audio, etc. As a consequence, separate and disparate mega-industries have grown up around the different communication modes, each sporting its own unique identity and infrastructure, such as differences in distribution channels, labor forces, craft skills and knowledge bases, jargon, and culture.

Moving from one of these formats to another is difficult and costly, frequently requiring specialized equipment and skill to go, for example, from videotape to high-quality prints. The high cost of conversion of images with high resolution and visual quality tends to preclude the use of the same source material in multiple media.

In the digital world, where all information is reduced to zeros and ones, it makes not one bit of difference whether the information represents a word, number, sound, still image, video or whatever else. In essence, digital entails one common standard that enables the data and information to be output onto any format and, even more important, enables the different data types such as audio, animated graphics, alphanumeric text, and video to be combined and displayed in a seamless manner.

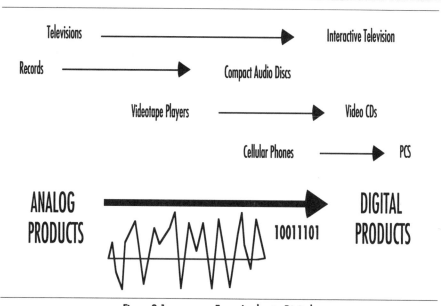

Figure 2-1   From Analog to Digital

Source: Copyright © 1994 Market Vision. Used with permission.

Thanks to digital technology, we have already witnessed the shortening of product cycles in manufacturing. As the multimedia revolution takes hold, product cycles are likely to become even shorter as design and manufacturing techniques rely more heavily on digital-based communications and information technology. However, the pace of such technology adoption will be determined not only by technology per se, but, perhaps more so, by social, economic, and political forces such as labor unions, government regulations, and the pool of relevant skills.

Digital know-how has been around for a long while, so it is fair to ask, "Why now the multimedia revolution?" The answer is simple. Only recently has digital technology, especially the microprocessor, become powerful enough to set the stage for putting all information into a single digital format. Doing so also entails a host of other electronic devices—storage systems, high-resolution displays, server hardware, lightweight, portable devices—all combined with sophisticated operating systems, advanced user interfaces, abundant application software, and broadband communications. Improved manufacturing processes are making such powerful integrated hardware/software implementations available for the first time and at ever-decreasing costs.

The commercial products emerging from this technology avalanche promise to give users a significant reason to reinvest in what are already installed applications. Consumers, for one, only replace, upgrade or acquire appliances when such an expenditure is deemed worthwhile...or when a desirable device breaks. An existing television set, for example, stays put unless a new one comes equipped with digital stereo, a large, high-resolution screen, and interactive controls.

Sales of multimedia-ready personal computers featuring built-in CD-ROM drives and sound boards are already sweeping into the marketplace. This, in turn, is setting the stage for mammoth business opportunities for entrepreneurs as well as the conventional mega-industries. And egging on all of this change is the computer industry itself, whose own business health is tied tightly to multimedia and the phenomenon of digital convergence.

Nor will the new digital technology have an impact on just the existing mega-industries. On the contrary, multimedia promises to spawn entirely new ones, perhaps best exemplified by CD-ROM publishing. Here, all the media types—narration, music and other sound, written text and numbers, still images, graphics and animation, and video—are combined onto a single recording disc. These are then replicated en masse, converted into other formats, including some yet to be invented, and sold as if they were ordinary books.

It is not hyperbole to say that the world storehouse of knowledge and learning—as well as information and entertainment—is now in the process of being converted to such multimedia CD-ROM formats. Discs already on the market cover subjects ranging from encyclopedias to travel journeys and dramatic presentations and to other reference, educational, and entertainment titles.

Defining Multimedia

The uses for multimedia are so vast that the term eludes definition. In brief, multimedia may be viewed as applications that operate within a media-rich, digital environment on the desktop, over local networks via telecommunications or in mobile milieus. As a result, the term "multimedia" takes on vastly different meanings to different groups of people. The real value of the term is that it serves as a common vision for the direction of new visual communication opportunities and markets—a vision where the barriers to communication and self-expression in media have been removed.

Yet, it is important to lay out a working definition of multimedia to ensure that this common vision does not get confused with the larger, more natural process underway—the simple conversion of all information into the digital realm. Hence, "multimedia" does not pertain solely to multiple media types stored and distributed as digital data, but also implies a high degree of structure in the data that permits access by users as well as a high level of interactivity. In addition, multimedia data, because they are essentially high bandwidth digital data, require supporting communications technologies that can handle such broadband information with acceptable performance.

Multimedia will not supplant the need for passive communications and entertainment that are not part of our definition of multimedia. "Video-on-Demand" movies are not a multimedia application, because they are simply a "start–stop" delivery of sequential information.

By our definition, multimedia must contain interactivity whereby a user becomes a participant in the communications, even a director or creator. This leads to an additional requirement not normally associated with multimedia: the content in the new media must have an entertainment quality or intellectual level that compels a user into an interactive involvement. Of course, this interactive nature of multimedia is both a redeeming quality and, because at times one wants simply to be a "couch potato," also a major drawback.

An extreme example of this strict definition is that fanciful application referred to as Virtual Reality (VR). Through the use of VR interfaces, a person actually "merges" into a computer-generated scene to roam through a synthetic environment such as Chicago's BattleTech entertainment booth that serves as a simulation ride. Indeed, VR's biggest use currently is for entertainment, although the technique is also used in architecture where "walk-throughs" can be conducted in buildings still on the drawing board.

If this controversial VR concept materializes to its full potential, it promises a new dimension in entertainment, providing joy seekers with amusement park thrills, more realistic violence, and even virtual sex, thus perpetuating—and enhancing—our fascination with vulgarity. On a more positive note, VR may even find usage in medicine where a surgeon, for example, can practice an operation before actually performing it.

Yet, even with all this remarkable digital technology, not everyone will be able to craft visually stimulating and high-quality messages like those of professionals working in advertising, entertainment, and other artistic-oriented businesses. In the forthcoming digital millennium, however, messages of such complexity and high visual impact may become more doable by reasonably talented and highly motivated individuals, given the likely availability of adequate expert software tools that can guide and assist such efforts. Sadly, though, it may never come to pass that just anyone will ever be able to create a commercial rock video from a pickup school band using out-of-pocket funds.

Wrapping up this definition or description, of what multimedia is and is not, it should become clear that the term will eventually be rendered meaningless, since it is all encompassing. Nevertheless, in the interim, "multimedia" as a term currently serves a truly worthwhile purpose when applied to the marriage of computing, communications, networks, entertainment, training, i.e., all information endeavors. The expression serves to unify all participants in the common goal of bringing a new level of human communications into being through the deployment of digital technologies, one that is highly visual and engaging.

Will Videogames Lead the Way to New Media?

Having said all this, the main money-making opportunity today in multimedia outside of the industrial and business sectors lies with entertainment in the form of interactive CD-ROM titles and new-generation videogames. In 1992, home videogames generated $6 billion in revenues, arcade games, $12 billion. Nintendo alone had sales exceeding $6 billion annually, while runner-up Sega doubled its U.S. business in 1992 for the third straight year.

For the most part, videogames are packaged as cartridges that plug into game devices. CD-ROM discs and high-resolution, real-time graphics and video are only now beginning to play an important role, which, along with 32-bit processors and VR-like interfaces, portends games with cinematic quality, photorealistic imagery, and compact disc-quality sound.

Beyond the stand-alone device, videogames lend themselves to interactive play, especially with the advent of the Sega TV Channel that will make videogames available through the telephone network and television screen. A similar implementation will be found in hotels where LodgeNet Entertainment Corporation. has teamed up with Nintendo to supply videogames to guests via their in-room TV sets. The fast track taken by the videogame industry puts the companies in this sector in the lead as the largest and most important players in multimedia. Videogames, they say, will pave the way to other consumer applications in education and learning.

REINVENTING MULTIMEDIA

While the process of converting information from analog to digital began about 50 years ago with the introduction of computers, multimedia technology began at the commercial level only some eight years ago when laserdiscs were used to provide instruction under computer control.

In the late 1980s, several authoring systems emerged enabling audio and video with graphics, text, and animation to be combined. As more sophisticated multimedia authoring tools came on the market, led by MacroMind Director, applications in desktop video and interactive presentations grew increasingly abundant. As early as 1990, the research firm Market Vision had identified and classified more than 100 potential multimedia applications.

Also out of the early mainframe environment run by highly trained experts, there has emerged the personal computer of today, operating not only stand-alone, but also strung out locally and remotely in diverse, distributed networks. Now these networks, which are hybrids, with only portions of the backbones being digital, are being connected together to create a network of digital networks. This is epitomized by the Internet, which, though confined for the most part to noninteractive, alphanumeric data, promises to become a main channel in the eventual electronic distribution of multimedia content. As the leading edge, the Internet and other commercial on-line services such as Prodigy and America Online will help to forge a structure for the new information superhighway by shaping its network architecture, economics, and social, political, and moral fabric.

This new "internetworked" world promises to give rise not only to another generation of multimedia tools, products, and services, but also to new venues for doing business, especially retail merchandising à la television home shopping. One will be able to "go" to an interactive, on-screen video department store like the one alluded to at the beginning of this chapter.

In fact, digital multimedia is already giving birth to many new patterns of retailing, merchandising, and entertainment. Apple Computer, for example, distributes a CD-ROM disc containing fully functional computer programs for sale, including all regular features and documentation. Prospective buyers "try out" the different programs also provided as sample segments. Want the disc's complete version? Then, the buyer calls an Apple 800-number and "plunks down" credit card information, whereupon the telephone order clerk supplies a code for unlocking the program.

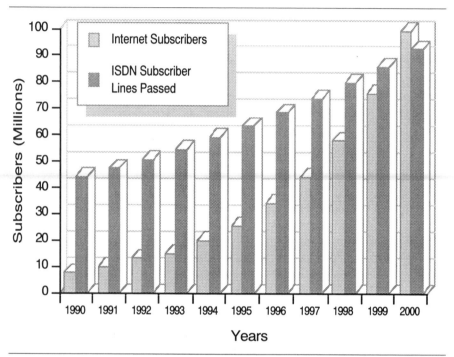

Figure 2-2   Multimedia Network Growth
Source: Copyright © 1994 Market Vision. Used with permission.

In a somewhat different vein, Apple expanded this marketing concept by creating a general merchandise CD-ROM catalog, akin to an L.L. Bean or Sharper Image print version, but employing audio and video in addition to text and still imagery. In this case, a customer calls an Apple 800-number to order the merchandise, which is then physically delivered to the customer's home or office.

In both cases, Apple serves as middle man and collects a sales commission. It does not take much imagination to envision the next step: ordering merchandise of all kinds via an interactive television service where even the "catalog" is distributed electronically.

Here's another example of the marriage occurring between electronic and physical delivery of information. Today, you can file your federal income tax by computer, but when it comes to submitting the supporting W-2 documents and signature, paper delivery is still necessary through the U.S. Postal Service.

In the future, the operation of devices for accessing interactive services via the television set will be greatly simplified, which was the goal of Philips Compact Disc Interactive (CDi) players. Some industry observers believe that such dedicated boxes will be the principal way that the home television set will deliver interactive information, instruction, communications, and entertainment. In essence, a wireless remote control will enable a consumer to navigate through menus and execute push-button commands just as is now done in on-screen VCR programming by remote control.

Another school of thought—held largely by the computer industry and the telephone and cable industries—insists that a control device called the "set-top-box" will in essence be a computer, i.e., a microprocessor to handle the data married with a monitor whose high-quality resolution lends itself to text display as well as picture presentation.

With tens of millions of boxes waiting in the wings, traditional "cable converter" box manufacturers such as General Instrument and Scientific-Atlanta are scrambling to align themselves with the telephone, cable, and computer companies. At the time of this writing, the jury is still out as to whether it will be Apple Computer, Hewlett-Packard, Silicon Graphics, or Intel who wins this "box" race against the videogame companies who view their control boxes as evolving into the interactive consumer appliance of tomorrow.

Market Sectors, End Users, Revenues

A fundamental question emerges from all of this transitional turmoil. How do we organize, i.e., rationalize, the businesses or infrastructure that make up so-called multimedia? One way is to

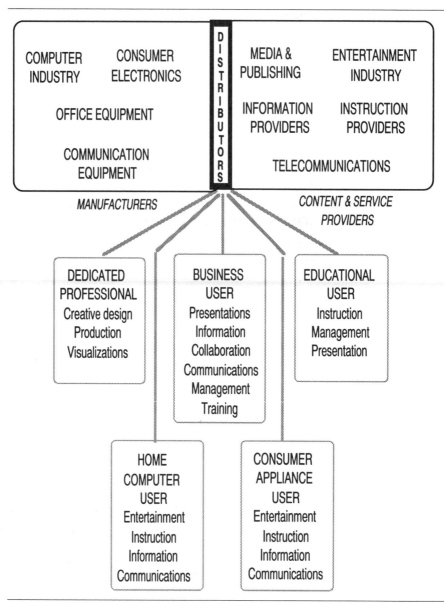

Figure 2-3   The Multimedia Application Model

Source: Copyright © 1994 Market Vision. Used with permission.

look at multimedia users, who can be placed into one of five separate categories:

- Dedicated Professionals;

- Business;

- Educational;

- Home Computer; and

- Consumer Appliance Users.

Each of these can be further subdivided into 20 different application categories as depicted in Table 2-1. This scheme can be readily expanded as cheaper and more effective technology and tools come on to the market to support additional applications.

An alternative classification is to divide multimedia into application segments or market sectors. The ten listed in Table 2-2 below cover three different consumer categories (information, entertainment, and communications), six business categories (presentation, information services, data management, collaborative work, training, and communications), and education.

According to Market Vision studies, revenues from multimedia-based products and services covering the categories itemized above for the computer industry alone will total $9 billion by the year 1997, and for consumer products, nearly $15 billion, excluding videogames. Consumer players, alternatively referred to as multimedia appliances, will dominate the multimedia market by then. Their annual shipments will total 7 million devices made up of consumer players, TV set-top interactive control boxes, and videogames. By 1997, the total $24 billion revenue stream will account for 10 percent of the worldwide information industry, with networked multimedia, accounting for four of these percentage points. Clearly, multimedia even three years out will still represent an emerging market despite the heady growth between now and 1997.

Here are a few more examples in business news and information delivery that illustrate the persuasiveness of the infrastructure changes that are underway. Field trials have begun only within the last year or two:

MARKET SEGMENTS & CATEGORIES	APPLICATION EXAMPLES
DEDICATED PROFESSIONALS	
Creative design	Advertising, graphic art design, music composing, scripting
Production	Art & entertainment, desktop video production, music production, theme park entertainment
Visualization	Design visualizations, simulation & modeling, diagnosis and forecasting
BUSINESS USERS	
Presentations	Corporate communications, desktop presentation, product/sales, direct promotion, trade shows
Information	Executive support
Communications	Mail/facsimile/data/voice
Collaboration	Telecommuting & videoconferencing
Management	Cataloging & archiving, office document management & workflow
Training	Customer training & support, interactive learning & training, performance support, personnel performance evaluation
EDUCATIONAL USERS	
Instruction	Higher institutions, primary schools (K–12), vocational schools, distance learning
Management	Libraries, museums, research
Presentation	Libraries, museums, research
HOME COMPUTER	
Entertainment	Adult & child entertainment, interactive books
Instruction	Adult self-improvement, special group learning
Information	Home shopping, personal data, reference
Communications	Digital answering, personal communications
CONSUMER APPLIANCE USERS	
Entertainment	Adult & child entertainment, videogames
Instruction	Adult self-improvement, child learning
Information	Home shopping & reference
Communications	Digital answering, personal communications

Table 2-1   Multimedia Applications and Markets

Source: Copyright © 1994 Market Vision. Used with permission.

MARKET SECTORS	DESCRIPTION
Consumer Information & Instruction	A suite of consumer information services delivered to the home, displayed on a television or computer display, employing interactive navigation and using a return data path. Applications include: electronic home shopping, banking, and reference.
Consumer Entertainment	A suite of consumer entertainment services delivered to the home, displayed on a television or computer display, employing interactive navigation and using a return data path. Applications include: movies, video, sports, special events, and guides.
Consumer Communication	A consumer service that permits the transfer of documents in electronic form. The only consumer communication application is consumer e-mail.
Business Presentations	Delivering multimedia data as packaged media for a wide array of internal, sales and marketing activities. Applications include: Interactive publications, retail merchandising, product promotions, and consumer education.

Table 2-2   **Multimedia Market Segments**

Source: Copyright © 1994 Market Vision. Used with permission.

- IBM and the National Broadcasting Company teamed to introduce an on-line information service, called *NBC Desktop News*, targeted at corporate executives. Via desktop PCs, they receive late-breaking financial, business, and industry-specific news on demand, as well as other information personalized via keyword profiles to specific interests. Material is delivered in multimedia formats—video, audio, text, and images. All of this is put together by the NBC news-gathering staff, utilizing IBM digital handling and delivery capabilities. After making a splashy announcement, news of this pilot program has subsided, suggesting that this innovative multimedia news-on-demand scheme may be beset with technical or market difficulties.

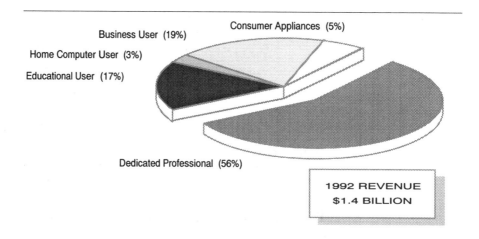

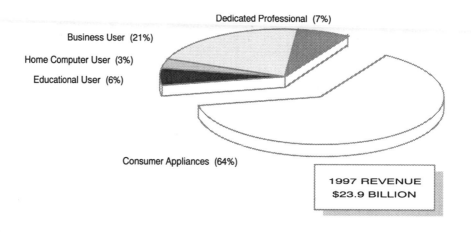

Figure 2-4   Multimedia Market Shares

Source: Copyright © 1994 Market Vision. Used with permission.

- To serve the consumer arena, NBC has also teamed with two on-line services, Prodigy and America Online, to deliver interactive databases, information, and advertising to their sophisticated Information Age customers. Various bulletin board services enable subscriber/viewers to "talk" to NBC personalities and executives directly and to receive schedules and information on NBC personalities and programs. Also, logo'd merchandise related to NBC sports coverage will be merchandised through the on-line medium. This venture represents a pioneering effort by the broadcast industry to become a major contender on the emerging information superhighway that until now seemed to be the sole preserve of the telephone and cable technology communities.

- Multimedia as a stand-alone format is represented by *Newsweek Interactive,* a quarterly multimedia "magazine" published by *Newsweek* on a CD-ROM disc and sold on a subscription basis. Besides housing recycled articles from the print version of the news weekly, each interactive edition incorporates two or three exclusive "take-outs" covering technology and science, sports, the arts, politics, and whatever. The discs also incorporate interactive multimedia advertising on an experimental basis to assess the opportunities and pay-off for this facet of the multimedia world.

New Hopes for Quality Education

Multimedia's ultimate meaning implies more than videogames and entertainment, even more than business, commercial, and industrial applications. A generally positive attitude also surrounds multimedia's use in education. Many school administrators, teachers, and parents are enthusiastic about digital interactivity as a way for students to prepare for the 21st century.

Such an educational transformation—whereby students pace their own learning via computer-based, multimedia lessons—promises a lucrative opportunity. According to 1993 statistics from the U.S. Department of Education, one out of every three people in the United States is involved in education. These data suggest that the kindergarten to twelfth-grade education market alone accounts for nearly five percent of the gross national product.

Instructional technology has already penetrated deeply into school systems, via Apple II and Macintosh computers, laserdisc players, and CD-ROM drive.s The labyrinthine U.S. school system houses 4.5 million computers all told, while some 40 percent of the nation's school districts also make use of integrated learning systems. Much of this installed equipment, however, is becoming rapidly outdated, prompting school districts, teachers, and parents to look into networked interactive multimedia instructional services as a more cost-effective way to use educational technology while remaining within shrinking budgets.

A networked solution is exemplified by the interactive multimedia offering from Jostens Learning Co., a supplier of educational software to elementary school and high schools. Jostens markets a system that enables many classrooms through their desktop PCs simultaneously to access full-motion video, color imagery, and other resources housed on a central server. Moreover, Jostens has expanded its networked program to incorporate take-home computer software that encourages parents to become involved with their children's learning processes. Preliminary "report cards" from schools participating in Jostens' high-tech approach to education give the company excellent grades. The Pemberton Township public schools in New Jersey, for example, find that Jostens' take-home computer program "does improve the overall mathematics achievement and critical thinking skills" [of students] while also "increasing [their] self-esteem, closer communications with parents, and success in the regular classroom."

All of this, however, represents only the beginning of an educational trend to multimedia learning. Only 20 percent of the computer population in schoolrooms can be classified as multimedia-capable, a proportion that will increase significantly over the next few years. These local systems serving school districts will be supplemented by on-line service, such as the Internet and the National Research and Education Network (NREN), now under development.

Other supplementary technologies that are likely to invade the home will include interactive educational tools from the likes of Broderbund. Such products will come from Dorling-Kindersley Publishing and Microsoft in support of both the home personal computer and dedicated multimedia players from Philips, Sony, and Commodore.

Beyond these well-understood desktop trends, our educational future also holds out the promise of distance learning. Utilizing the information superhighway, interactive and canned lectures from super teachers will be used to deliver knowledge and information, perhaps even reducing the need for rural schoolbuses as students log in on such virtual classrooms from home.

The concept extends beyond the use of superstar instructors working with groups of students via distance learning technology to groups of students who are located remotely from one another and have different cultures participating in school projects and exchanging ideas and opinions that result in their learning from each other as well. This is undoubtedly one of the highest forms of education.

Interactive TV—More than Entertainment

In the forthcoming millennium something new under the sun will emerge in the area of multimedia. Once information and entertainment can be delivered electronically and be price-competitive with packaged media, the format for its delivery will become irrelevant. Owning personal copies may be part of human nature, but just as ownership of movie tapes has been superseded by short-term video rentals, so, too, access to programming via a computer TV appliance will become more important than physical ownership. For this reason, interactive television holds out the potential to transform the chaos of today's confused multimedia play devices into a single, unified delivery mechanism.

Moreover, interactive TV in time will deliver more than Video-on-Demand (VOD), sports, special events, and videogames. True, most new title releases, particularly the big successes, tend to be fast-paced "fly-shoot-kill" themes. A few, nevertheless, do provide noteworthy interactive family entertainment. *Twisted* by Electronic Arts for the 3DO Multiplayer is a parody of a TV game show where contestants solve puzzles and challenges. *Twisted* represents an example of a new breed of title intended to appeal to the entire family, not just the traditional videogames market, namely young boys and men.

Beyond fun and games, television home shopping, already a three billion dollars-a-year business dominated by the QVC and Home Shopping channels, is another natural interactive multimedia application. Though a seemingly big number in absolute terms, this dollar amount represents noise-level—one percent of all retail sales in the United States. Its rapid growth and profitability in recent years, however, suggests a happy future, particularly as established, top drawer retailers, such as R.H. Macy and Co., for one, bring more appealing merchandise into play. Extensive market tests of home shopping technologies and concepts are underway by Time Warner, Telecommunications Inc., AT&T, and a host of other potential information superhighway suppliers who are now furiously partnering to defray the expense and acquire the expertise necessary for these home shopping pilot activities. As interactive TV shopping becomes the norm by the next century, technology may once again serve to alter individual lifestyles. For this to happen, however, it will take effective marketing, competitive pricing, and liberal return policies at least so that the net result is a pleasant home shopping experience for consumers.

Building a Digital Market Infrastructure

Development of a multimedia infrastructure will proceed along five overlapping paths. The first requires that desktop computer hardware be integrated into complete multimedia systems at ever-diminishing price levels. Simultaneously, operating system software must be continually extended or redesigned to accommodate audio, video, and other time-dependent data appropriate to more and different types of evolving multimedia applications.

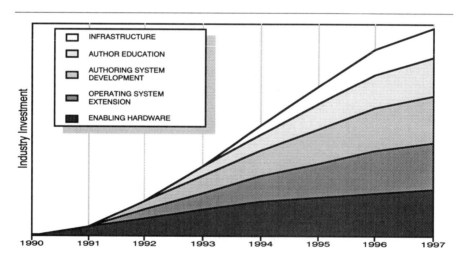

Figure 2-5   Multimedia Development Timeline
Source: Copyright © 1994 Market Vision. Used with permission.

The third path requires that advanced authoring tools be developed to support the creation of media-rich titles. Here, new cross-platform scripting environments, such as the Apple/IBM ScriptX and General Magic's MagicCap, once completed, will enable multimedia producers to "repurpose" existing material into multimedia titles as well as to create entirely new works, all across different brand computers.

All of this hardware/software effort will come to no avail unless a sufficient pool of multimedia-capable authors are trained simultaneously to produce state-of-the-art multimedia titles and business applications. This constitutes the fourth requirement to achieve a meaningful multimedia future. Whole generations of graphic designers, film and video producers, script writers, photographers, and other creative types need to learn how to use the new digital multimedia tools as they become available. Unfortunately, no more than 3,000 multimedia specialists will undergo formal training in multimedia programs in 1994, such as those put on by San Francisco State University. This number is minuscule when compared to the hundreds of thousands of skilled people necessary to create and use multimedia applications. Business establishments must support training efforts, with the goal of matching the level of quality in multimedia works that is routinely attained by professional TV broadcasters.

The fifth pathway necessary to usher in the multimedia age entails establishing distribution channels. On the one hand, sales staffs in traditional consumer retail, mail order, and specialty stores will need to undergo special training and support in multimedia merchandising, a requirement made necessary by the complexity of products incorporating the new digital technology.

Just as important, consumers, too, need to be educated on how multimedia works through packaging messages and advertising. As electronic distribution techniques take hold, perhaps displacing traditional retail outlets, consumer end-users will once again need special support to help them use the new media effectively. For economies of scale to take hold, a multimedia-literate populace becomes essential. Unlike the current environment, where an individual who cannot program a VCR wears the failing as a badge of honor, individuals must not be leery of using the latest interactive

TV tools. Such an attitude could ring a death knell for interactive multimedia applications and any attempts to have them ride the information superhighway.

Through many years of trial and error, each mega-industry has evolved separate business models pertaining to the product design, distribution channels, consumer support, and whatever else they do. With the advent of digital multimedia standards that enable information to cross these industry boundaries, it becomes imperative that the affected big industries evolve new business models. The need to do so, in fact, underlies the numerous alliances currently underway by the industry players to improve their strategic position in the multimedia milieu. This, of course, is certain to lead to permanent infrastructure changes that alter the operations and makeup of these industries.

An example would be the videogame industry whose "toy" business model will become too simplistic, thereby forcing a more mature business model to be formulated. As another example, the current business model for electronic publishing, namely that of computer software, is likely to be replaced by a publishing business model. As for the delivery of movies and other interactive TV programming, use of the telephone industry model will likely stand the players in good stead as opposed to, for example, their adhering to an entertainment business model. Tracking multimedia markets will require an understanding of these shifting business models.

WINNERS (AND LOSERS) IN THE DIGITAL TURF WARS

Interestingly, the fierce race sweeping through the multimedia-enchanted landscape is taking place within the context of what are in reality largely unproven markets (the exception being CD-ROM title publishing, which is just beginning to prove itself). Once secure in their traditional competitive positions by holding markets captive, the regulated regional telephone companies, over-the-air broadcasters, and cable companies now find themselves chasing about to find suitable venues to offer in the new multimedia millennium. Cable companies want to be free to supply telephone connections, telephone companies hunger to supply video dialtone services, and broadcasters seek to use a portion of their spectrum allocation to transmit data as a new business offering.

Entertainment companies, too, want in on the interactive future, as do retailers. As they all jockey to stake out a position in the emerging marketplace, these companies are betting billions of dollars to protect themselves from becoming suppliers of "horse and buggies" in the space age.

While the likes of TCI, Viacom, Bell Atlantic, and Time Warner race out of the multimedia starting gate, some of even the biggest contestants fail at times to perceive limitations and thereby risk falling into market traps. Understandably, the computer industry especially seems to violate consumer market principles, since this is a new target market for these players. The various companies within this sector, for example, continue to develop incompatible platforms and media formats, something that is anathema to consumers and is becoming so for the business community as well that now wants "open" systems. One standard that defines a basic CD-ROM platform configuration handling multimedia discs, for example, fails to be compatible across Apple, Dell, IBM, Windows, and other platforms despite the standard having been promulgated by an industry trade association.

The seemingly endless introduction of different standards for doing digital video compression compounds the CD-ROM dilemma. Take Philips Electronics. With support from the major movie studios, it has introduced a video-CD format and player based on the MPEG-1 standard, although an MPEG-2 is in the works as well. This new format requires that full-length movies be played on not one, but two compact discs, an approach that market history tells us does not work in consumer entertainment. It is unlikely that Joe or Jane Couch Potato will give up his or her VHS tape until a full-length movie can be fit on a single CD platter at reasonable cost.

The workstation vendors fare no better. Suppliers such as Digital Equipment Corp., Sun Microsystems, IBM, and Hewlett-Packard, in fact, view workstation multimedia differently from that of PC multimedia. These niche players focus on multimedia as a videoconferencing application where desktop workstations do audio/visual communications in addition to traditional alphanumeric computations and graphics. Put another way, this group of vendors envisions the day when computers will routinely process all multimedia data types.

One indication that the public is already warming up to the idea of an information superhighway is the tremendous surge in the usage of existing computer-based public networks, such as Internet, Prodigy, America Online, and CompuServe. Since late 1992, Internet alone has been expanding at the rate of 15 percent per month. The information and bulletin boards made available by these services provide catalog shopping, flight information and ticketing activities, and other business and consumer applications.

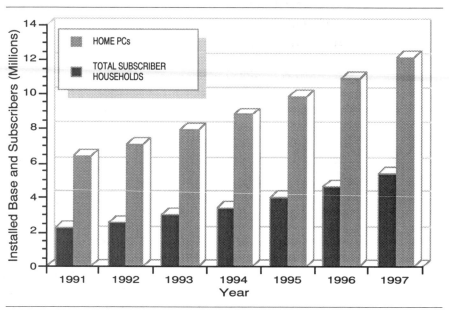

Figure 2-6   Growth of On-Line Services
Source: Copyright © 1994 Market Vision. Used with permission.

Competitive Wired Communications

An even larger battlefield takes place in the telecommunications realm where terrestrial-based communications have long been the most reliable form compared, for example, with wireless broadcasting. Because the transmission and delivery of multimedia services to home and office promise to become such a pot of gold, the telecommunications industry continues to deploy large amounts of fiber optic cable, much of which remains unused. That's come about because the Federal Communications Commission permits telecommunication companies to transport video into the home and even to deliver program content outside of their own service territories.

In addition, common carrier electric and gas companies that own large stretches of right-of-way access are also deploying fiber when upgrading their trunk systems. Out of all this activity, an almost unlimited amount of bandwidth available for communication and multimedia applications will emerge.

That's but one phase of the coming revolution. Building on its understanding of the ins and outs of switched media, the telecommunications industry is beginning to deliver personalized, point-to-point communications as well. In doing so, the two wires entering the home and office may be fine for voice and, with advanced digital processing techniques, may also lend themselves to handling two video channels. But a big question remains as to whether this "plain-old-telephone-service" (POTS) will be sufficiently robust to meet the demands of advanced interactive video services.

In this quest to build multimedia transmission facilities, the telephone industry faces off against the cable operators whose relatively wide bandwidth wires pass some 90 percent of U.S. homes, of that some 60 percent subscribe to cable service. But, the cable companies are at a competitive disadvantage in lacking the switching capabilities necessary to deliver interactive TV services. And as a relatively lightweight $20 billion-a-year (revenues) business vs. $200 billion a year for the telephone industry, the cable companies also lack the financial leverage to obtain the necessary switching technology. As a result, the two industries are attempting to combine, at first by merger and acquisition, but now through alliances and joint ventures such as US West's $1.5 billion investment in Time Warner.

The goal is to create a so-called "information superhighway" that can be used to interactivate and transmit multimedia data in two directions. The federal government, particularly the Clinton Administration, has lent support to this concept by proposing funding to help create such a data superhighway, independent of the programming control of the commercial cable companies or any other industry group. Congress made a start in this direction by authorizing $80 million to upgrade the Internet into a fiber-optic-based National Research and Educational Network (NREN) by 1996. The purpose is to enable multimedia data in digital format to be distributed to universities, schools, and research institutions nationwide utilizing radio and infrared wireless links in the network as well.

From Broadcast to Narrowcast

After a long day at work, most people want to be entertained by watching a programmed or videotaped movie or just "vegging" in front of the boob tube. Some may opt to visit a video arcade or play a videogame on their televisions. The role of broadcast television today serves one primary purpose: to provide an environment in which people can relax and diffuse their hostility and frustrations by being mindlessly entertained.

Interactive multimedia turns this laid-back purpose for TV on its head. The principal idea in the new digital environment is that consumers will interact with their TV sets, participating in sports games, political polls, and the like over an information superhighway connected to "warehouses" of information or voluminous databases put up on servers.

What's overlooked in this vision, however, is that, long before such an interactive mode of TV comes into the home, narrowcasting will have arrived, i.e., the broadcasting of special-interest programming to highly selected groups of viewers. For example, in the motion picture *Wayne's World*, a local television show is broadcast from Wayne's basement over a public local access cable station. This is what one will come to expect from an amateur production broadcast over the Internet or the information superhighway, where the charm of the broadcast is derived not from professional skill, but rather from the chemistry and wit of the two hosts. It's a forerunner of what we will get in the way of lay programming as the cost of television production declines and bandwidth becomes virtually limitless.

Narrowcasting enables us to select only programming of interest and will be made possible as the 30 or so network channels now available expand more than tenfold. With this increase in diversity, more effective ways will be required for "surfing" through the channels to select pertinent programming, a need that will become even more intense when interactivity comes to the tube as well. Such navigational aids take the form of on-screen TV guides employing Macintosh-like computer interfaces to simplify program selection, such as those under development by StarSight Telecommunications, Inc., e•on, Microsoft, Intel, Apple, and News Corp.

As for the TV broadcasters, over the long term, their destiny appears linked to digital communications via high-definition television (HDTV). According to Federal Communications Commission (FCC) plans, digital signals in commercial broadcasting will supplant analog frequencies by the turn of the century. That forecast appears overly optimistic, however. Short-term, the broadcasters want to offer data communications and other messaging services using a portion of the HDTV frequency allocated to them and have petitioned the FCC to do so.

Until now, the broadcast industry appeared to have been left well behind in the multimedia era where interactivity seems dependent on wired communication, not wireless transmissions. The broadcasters, on the other hand, enjoy a rich programming background such that they are certain to be big players in interactive multimedia, either through partnerships and alliances, mergers and acquisitions or, as the ultimate protection, by Congressional fiat.

Moreover, even in a full-blown interactive era, there will still be need for truly mass communications and distribution of information, be it presidential election returns, the outbreak of a war, the death of a movie star, or the results of a World Series. Here, network broadcasting even as we know it today will remain a mainstay of the emerging digital world.

The Power of Advertising

Also critical to any discussion of interactive multimedia is the question of who will pay for all the programming. Traditionally, advertising largely has done so, but, with so much channel fragmentation taking place, what will become of advertising as a revenue source that typically relies on mass audiences? As noted, mass programming will always remain viable, and products suited to universal use, such as soap, after-shave lotion, cars, stockings, and the like, are likely to continue to use such mass communication outlets.

Market fragmentation will instead divert more specialized advertising, such as ship cruises and vacations, fishing, guns and hunting, sports equipment, and the like, to narrowcast channels that offer better-defined and targeted audiences. Revenues for this, however, will primarily be siphoned off from the specialized magazines now on newsstands, at least where channels are created that go head-to-head against print editorial.

But multimedia life is not simple, and anything may happen. A cartoon channel, for example, could siphon off advertising from the children's TV ghetto found on network TV on Saturday mornings. Educational channels, on the other hand, may lend themselves to entirely new advertising opportunities for those businesses otherwise cut off from mass-scale TV advertising.

In any case, to reach these fragmented user groups, new interactive tools have to be developed. Some attempts are underway, such as that by Interactive Network, which is putting together a consortium of advertisers for its interactive TV game system experimenting in Chicago and northern California. Time Warner and other cable companies also plan to test interactive advertising as part of their full-service networks now under development.

Meanwhile, on the CD-ROM front, *Newsweek Interactive* has begun to incorporate interactive advertising into its quarterly multimedia CDzine. While it is too soon to report any results, one major expectation is that interactive advertising will result in immediate feedback from consumers. This should provide advertisers with valuable market information that can help them to target and merchandise their products in addition to a learning what interactive advertising can do.

Before multimedia can find its way onto the information superhighway, two major impediments must be overcome. Achieving data security, for one, is essential, both to protect content owners whose information can be pirated, as well as the recipients of data signals containing confidential information, especially those entailed in interactive financial transactions. Consumers are unlikely to utilize these advanced two-way transaction schemes unless the encryption applied to the transmissions and signature authentication procedures that accord access to transactions are in place and proven to be fail-safe.

Publicity surrounding security breaches could doom, for example, interactive banking and even home shopping transactions were the public to worry about such transgressions. This obstacle would further complicate the new lifestyle adaptations that are concomitant with use of the information superhighway.

Fortunately, these security needs, though complex, present primarily a technical challenge, with some of the techniques already in place thanks to the 500 million credit cards in service that already benefit from sophisticated authorization and transaction tracking technologies. However, since most of these systems are based on document image capture and processing, not character recognition, more advanced forms of electronic monetary control systems still need to be developed if the growth of consumer on-line services dealing with sensitive information is to accelerate.

A second challenge facing the future of interactive multimedia speeding along the express lane of the information superhighway is seldom discussed in either the public media or in the trade press. This entails the humdrum stuff—the accounting, billing, and transaction monitoring schemes that would be necessary on a global basis. Again, technologies derived from pay-TV, satellite TV signal distribution, and other existing services lend themselves to use in interactive television applications as well. Here, too, the technology will capitalize on what is now used to serve credit card, banking, and public utility businesses. But when it comes to interactive television, the smorgasbord of current services will need to be consolidated into two or three national billing systems at most. This is essential if the interactive information superhighway is to be a seamless carrier that is simple enough to have universal appeal.

None of the aforementioned barriers pose insurmountable hurdles, although the effort required to overcome them will take years and hundreds of millions of dollars more than what is currently envisioned by multimedia enthusiasts and boosters of the information superhighway. These are merely the growing pains that must be endured early into the next century while interactive multimedia reaches maturity.

Competitive Wireless Communications

Even wireless communications, which can serve as yet another pathway into the home, are getting into the multimedia act. For this purpose, the House Telecommunications and Finance Subcommittee recently voted to free up 200 megahertz of government frequency. This will permit wireless modems to transmit full-color images and digital video to office, home, and mobile receivers. Although such radio modems cost about $1,000 today, eventually they should come down to the price of a telephone.

Another contender for a place in the multimedia sun is the emerging direct broadcast satellite (DBS) services beginning with Hughes Communication's DirecTV small-dish home antenna system that deciphers compressed digital signals. As a result of this cornucopia of wireless, terrestrial and satellite systems, communications devices of all kinds—stationary, mobile, and personal—will have several alternative ways to be connected. This, in turn, will lead to a more competitive communications infrastructure, hence lower prices, that will render advanced broadband telecommunications applications more and more affordable to more and more people and businesses.

Demand for wireless, mobile communications seems insatiable and it, too, plays a role in the interactive world of tomorrow. With more than 27 million cellular subscribers worldwide currently, the number continues to grow at a rate exceeding 25 percent per year. Such technology encompasses DBS, Personal Communications Services (PCS), Global Positioning Satellites (GPS)—all new technologies distinguished one from the other by the frequency allocated to each—with broad deployment anticipated by 1995.

Wireless communications has already found a home in fleet management where trucks deploy two-way wireless message transmission and position reporting systems. Despite its proven success here, the market potential is barely tapped, with not even 15 percent of truck fleets using this technology.

Nevertheless, there is even a larger market for wireless access, one that simply entails substituting radio frequency transmissions for copper wire "loops" to connect telephone switching centers to homes and offices. Where geographic coverage is precluded by terrestrial barriers, satellites, too, can augment this communications to provide seamless global coverage. The Loral/Qualcomm Global Star joint project and the Motorola Iridium Consortium are both intended to provide a constellation of low-orbiting Earth satellites that will extend communications—multimedia communications at some point in the future—to remote locations virtually anywhere in the world... and beyond.

Content Owners—Hollywood Lessons Learned

There is a wealth of information awaiting use by multimedia producers. Years of production of film, video, photography, illustrations, recorded voice, music, and the printed page provide a ready source of materials for conversion to digital. Several problems prevent its use.

Content providers are involved in the creation of information (also called software by the entertainment industry). These include content creators such as publishers, producers and artists, content owners and distributors. Traditional print publishers such as Time Warner, McGraw-Hill and The Wall Street Journal are investigating new forms of electronic distribution. Suppliers of educational software are moving quickly to adopt multimedia delivery approaches.

The entertainment industry consisting of film, video, broadcast, cable, and videogames software is exploring digital delivery. With an enormous archive of commercial film, Sony, MCA, Disney, and others are seeking new ways to distribute and "repurpose" libraries. Owners of large archives of images and audio are beginning to realize the business opportunity. Ownership of content with high entertainment value is shifting. Content providers will deliver on platforms developed by computer hardware vendors, whereas information distributors provide the delivery infrastructure for content providers.

People pay for value but won't change unless there is a compelling and exciting reason. Significant market development has to occur before the value of the technology is clear. Success depends on determining what users really need and are willing to purchase in the near-term.

The publishing industry started in churches and schools and then moved to the masses with the invention of the Gutenberg printing press. The tools and economies involved required a sufficiently long time to develop the market. In the 1930s the movie industry lacked infrastructure and had limited production expertise. Studios grew up, combining resources and developing financing and distribution channels. The studios had the power, not the artists that were paid by the hour.

Today, production expertise is widely disseminated, with investments coming from many sources, mostly private. Production facilities are now rented to artists. The power shift from studios back to artists has led to skyrocketing costs for the studios.

The rapidly emerging multimedia industry is creating a shortage of creative expertise. Limited projects and funding may force content providers and independent producers to join large production companies. Regardless of the economic model selected, it is clear that there is a shortage of talented individuals with sufficient multimedia skills. Multimedia success will depend on the direct support by manufacturers for each of these groups.

Intellectual Property Lost (and Found)

Intellectual property (content) is also valuable and has been protected to insure a fair compensation for the authors. With the advent of electronic distribution, there are well-founded fears that such protection will be lost, leading to a reduction in the amount and quality of new ideas. As seen in the computer software industry, with an easy way to copy software, more software is distributed illegally than through normal sales channels. Creators and owners of content must be assured that their work is protected and that they will receive a fair compensation for its use. This will allow for the funds to continue the stream of quality content.

Considering all of this tumult, only one outcome remains certain. The owners of multimedia content—the publishers, book companies, film and videotape title producers, still image banks—are in the "catbird seat," for it is they who possess what, in essence, multimedia is all about: the content!

Besides using freshly created materials, multimedia works draw on the archival wealth that already exists as film, video, still photography, illustrations, magazine articles and books, works of art, and recorded voice and music. Just as television breathed new marketing life into old movies, and then the VCR made possible yet another lucrative market opportunity, so, too, multimedia will accord all these content owners, not just the film and video industries, the opportunities to recycle their archival libraries.

Some individuals and companies have already begun to act on this business insight. Billionaire Bill Gates of Microsoft Corp. fame again shows his prophetic powers by being among the first to aggressively buy up digital reproduction rights to museum works and other image collections.

Eastman Kodak has also responded to the opportunity by recently acquiring the Image Bank and its collection of hundreds of thousands of images as 35mm slides that are to be digitized into Kodak's PhotoCD format. PhotoCD provides amateur and professional photographers with both digitized versions of their pictures on compact disc as well as conventional analog prints. It represents Kodak's last-ditch effort to reap the market for traditional silver halide-film, while buying time as this giant company prepares for film's eventual— and inevitable—long-term displacement by the electronic image.

With regards to yet another data type, audio, Time Warner seizes another historical business opportunity wrought by multimedia. Currently, CD-ROM titles typically use generic music by relatively unknown artists. But, now, the Warner Special Products unit offers a new alternative. It makes available segments of musical recordings by 50 top stars, including Kenny Rogers, James Taylor, Judi Collins and the Electric Voice.

Because Warner wants to encourage such recycling of its musical libraries, referred to as "repurposing" by some industry gurus, the company has set a very attractive licensing fee: $300 per 30-second segment. This compares to hundreds of thousands of dollars, for example, for use of a song in a movie trailer.

Other content suppliers are investigating new forms of electronic distribution as well, including *Newsweek*, which in 1993 launched a quarterly interactive CD version of its weekly magazine. To differentiate it from the print edition, the so-called *Newsweek Interactive* also contains articles from its sister publication *The Washington Post*, supplemented by custom-prepared content not found in the weekly.

And, of course, this multimedia vision where content is everything reached a pinnacle of sorts with Sony's acquisition of CBS Records and Columbia Pictures, Matsushita's purchase of MCA, and other combinations of this kind.

For many of multimedia's creative types, however, the ownership of content through copyrights has a downside: the legal restraints they face concerning use of third-party materials. Given the myriad data types that go into a multimedia production, gathering permissions can be frustrating and expensive as well as administratively complex.

Digital Equipment Corp. (DEC), for example, recently introduced its own multimedia authoring and development software, called Media Impact, and found out first-hand how copyright issues can be a major problem transcending the mere legal hassles. It acquired rights to art images from The Voyager Co. but for use only to demonstrate the new package. DEC application developers acquiring Media Impact may also license the use of these images from DEC, but again only for demonstration purposes.

Content creators face another expensive challenge: choosing from among the myriad platforms on which to run their entertainment, educational, and other software products. It is this costly inconvenience that prompted Trip Hawkins, founder of Electronic Arts, to launch 3DO as an enterprise intended to create a universal home entertainment player. The device hooks up to a TV set to play computer software, music compact discs, and PhotoCDs initially, to be followed by video and other advanced services eventually. So appealing is the 3DO concept that Hawkins has obtained the backing of Time Warner, AT&T, and Matsushita, whose MCA unit owns Universal Studios.

Also, in a stroke of organizational genius, Hawkins brought into the enterprise Kleiner, Perkins, Caufield & Byers, a venture capital firm. Its neutrality and objectivity should counter any vested interest impulses by the other partners. Such creativity beyond technology innovation itself will undoubtedly determine which companies achieve long-term success in multimedia. Nevertheless, 3DO's approach will encounter considerable competition from the PC manufacturers, videogame vendors, and others who also want to stake a claim in this exploratory business.

Indeed, toward this end, the equipment vendors will woo the content creators and owners intensely. For example, despite its digital savvy, IBM teamed up with NBC as the program supplier for what is to be an on-demand news and information service delivered to executives via their desktop PCs.

One thing appears certain. When it comes to digital media, the standard legal models for copyrighting film, music, prints, photographs, and the like will have to be revised. Otherwise, progress in multimedia may be stymied by a litigious environment, which is certain to delight lawyers, but will retard industry growth.

BEYOND THE LIGHT AT THE END OF THE TUNNEL

As noted throughout this chapter, the market for multimedia products and services is only now emerging. The conversion from analog information to digital data streams already affords many business and employment opportunities. Even more jobs and start-up companies are likely to be created in the future, resulting from the significant industry investments over the next 10 to 20 years necessary to bring on the transition to an all-digital information world. A major impetus for growth in this new field will come not from new applications alone, but rather from standard applications that have been enhanced with multimedia capabilities in word processing, spreadsheet, database, and presentations.

As this multimedia world unfolds, each subsector that makes up the overall market (depicted in Figure 2-7) will follow its own evolutionary path to critical mass as an attractive and lucrative business arena. As the graph depicts, consumer appliances used in interactive activities, for example, will begin to surge towards the end of 1994, led by videogame devices; business applications do not take off until some two years later.

Also evident is the remarkable potential for consumer networks, whose tenfold growth in revenues to $50 billion by decade's end can be accounted for by the success of on-line services, i.e., the oft-mentioned information superhighway. While the growth of each sector can be depicted separately, interplay between them will be profound and will have a significant impact on each other's rates of growth.

The large economies of scale afforded by consumer multimedia markets will serve to drive many professional, business, educational, and government markets. Conversely, knowledge workers in these commercial and professional environments will demand state-of-the-art technologies, and their willingness to pay up for the performance sets the stage for these products to enter eventually into the consumer domain.

The first to feel the impress of such change will be the telephone and cable companies. They are firing on all cylinders to deliver Video-on-Demand, home shopping, and interactive TV shows into the home environment. Nevertheless, the demand is not likely to have a significant impact until 1997 when a nationwide digital-communications infrastructure of critical mass can be expected to be in place.

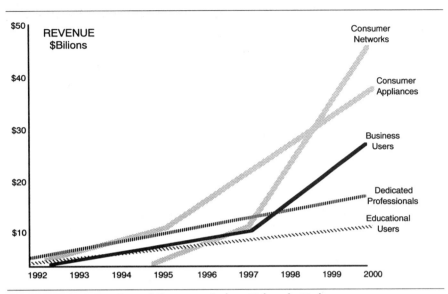

Figure 2-7   Evolving Multimedia Markets
Source: Copyright © 1994 Market Vision. Used with permission.

Large investments also will be required to establish the necessary infrastructure that will permit widely deployed on-line consumer products and services. Deployment at the consumer level will have a positive effect on the rate of growth of dedicated professional, business, educational, and government applications.

Because of this technology blitzkrieg that surrounds applications in multimedia and digital communications, their markets are destined to account for an increasing portion of all information and communications, attaining a dominant proportion by early next century. While the exact time frame for this reversal to happen is unknown, certain surges along the way can be pinpointed. In CD-ROM publishing, for example, this will happen when the price of consumer CD players drop below $300 and when large numbers of quality titles become available priced at less than $40 each. Given these parameters, by 1997, the sale of TV-based multimedia players, portable information devices, and communications hardware will exceed 20 million units for consumer markets alone.

Multimedia packaged as discrete CD-ROM discs is just an initial step towards a digitally integrated information universe. Sometime in the future, broadband communications will be sufficiently widespread to enable the multimedia material now housed on a disc to be retained remotely on servers in an information utility. From here, multimedia data will be transmitted upon customer request to business, home, or school without any of these uses having to be cognizant of the delivery mechanism. At this juncture, when information content of all kinds is widely available at affordable cost, the world will experience new levels of productivity and creativity.

The digital gate has been opened and we have entered the path to multimedia and communications convergence; there is no turning back. The once autonomous mega-industries taking refuge in analog standards no longer have a choice. Digital changes everything for them forever. Whether one is a manufacturer, retailer, or consumer, it is advisable to embrace this social change that promises to usher in a new pattern of communication in the fabric of society. Regardless of whether this volatile period in information and communication technology that we now embark upon is self-induced or part of our human nature, it is our choice either to go boldly into this next millennium or to be swept into oblivion.

BIOGRAPHY

Stan Klein is a multimedia industry analyst. His firm, S. Klein Communications, Inc., based in Sudbury, Massachusetts (508-443-4671) provides writing and marketing services and conducts

4671) provides writing and marketing services and conducts seminars for professionals and executives on writing for publication and career advancement. Mr. Klein, an M.I.T. graduate, is an accomplished author, having written extensively on advanced technology and trends for such publications as the *New York Times* and *Business Week* magazine.

Recently, he sold to Macmillan all of the computer graphics publishing properties that he had founded, including *Computer Graphics Review Magazine* and the *S. Klein Newsletter on Computer Graphics*. Currently, beside writing for *New Media* magazine, *Computer Pictures, AV Video, Multimedia Producer,* and others. Mr. Klein teaches a course for technical and executive professionals on writing for publication and career advancement.

Robert Aston is the president of Market Vision, a consulting firm and a publisher of multimedia research since 1988. He has founded two leading-edge software companies in computer graphics and desktop publishing. He is the author of *Multimedia Defined, Multimedia Applications and Markets—A Five-Year Forecast* and the recently released *Multimedia Applications and Markets—1994 Annual Forecast.* He is a frequent contributor to books and magazines on multimedia.

Chapter 3

HOLLYWOOD, USA
CREATIVE APPROACHES TO NEW MEDIA PRODUCTION

JOYCE A. SCHWARZ
JOYCE COMMUNICATIONS

By the year 2015, Hollywood as we knew it in the 1990s may have undergone a change so profound that its impact will be equivalent to the advent of "talkies," television, and home video combined. A major paradigm shift in Hollywood film, television, and video production is evolving, powered by new technologies in computers, digital film, compact discs, interactive multiplayers, and new delivery systems including fiber optic cable.

To most of Hollywood, "multimedia" is still a computer nerd term. However, mention the word "interactive" and talk bottom-line numbers and you've captured a share of the more adventurous Hollywood dealmakers and their Silicon Valley counterparts. According to Joe Miller, Sega of America's senior vice president, the interactive business toted up revenues of $4.5 billion last year, rivaling the theatrical box office numbers of $5.2 billion. The interactive business has garnered not only a financial niche but new respect as the Hollywood studios form their own divisions and begin to produce a multimedia product that complements box office hits.

Speaking at Hollywood's ShoWest industry trade confab, Columbia Pictures Chairman Marc Canton said, "In the future we won't just see the movie, we will interact with it, feel it, play it and ride it." He also added that, without significant improvement in the way theaters present movies and a much greater commitment to making quality entertainment and more diversified films, the theatrical business as Hollywood knows it could be replaced by the end of this decade.

So is it any wonder that in May, 1994, Twentieth Century Fox became the last major studio to form an interactive division? Paramount and Universal announced similar divisions in 1993. Universal came out with its first release, *Jurassic Park*, in the spring of 1994 on the 3DO platform.

Warner, Sony, and Disney have had new media, computer software, and interactive divisions for several years, producing and licensing products for various platforms. In April, 1994, MGM surprised the entertainment and computer industries by signing a coproduction deal with Sega of America Inc. to produce television shows, games, and movies.

To date, however, major studios and traditional Hollywood have not been able to rival the success of independent game developers such as Acclaim and Electronic Arts, which generate about $500 million a year. As Jeff Berg, head of ICM's talent and literary agency, said recently, "Sega and Nintendo last year outgrossed the motion picture industry. And that's just two companies."

Studios want their "fair share" of the burgeoning multimedia marketplace and see other potential money-making arenas in "edutainment" (education and entertainment intertwined) and "infotainment" (entertainment-oriented information presentations) for homes, schools, workplaces, and the general public. Multimedia and its by-products may literally create an electronic landscape that brings the glittering touch of Hollywood to all aspects of our lives.

For almost 100 years, film has reign supreme in the kingdom of Tinseltown. For the past 50 years, consumers have lived in the age of television with videocassette tapes and cable enhancing those powerful formats rather than replacing them in the marketplace.

Between 1992 and 1994, a virtual cinematic multimedia panorama of technological and creative developments began to bridge the gap between Hollywood and Silicon Valley. Every day, Hollywood film and trade papers abound in stories about new technological advancements and multimedia deals. But it is stars and films that will continue to advance the medium to the big money-making level Hollywood is best known for producing.

The "star power" of multimedia continues to heighten weekly as slates of new products featuring stars are announced. High-rated "TV Q" (a measure of television audience recognition) names that are on or coming to your computer screen or set-top-box (STB) include Jason Hervey of *The Wonder Years,* currently starring as the evil Troll Leader in Activision's *Return to Zork.*

Popular action heroes Wesley Snipes and Sylvester Stallone filmed extra footage of *Demolition Man* for Virgin Interactive's 3DO version of the movie. Many Virgin aficionados are familiar with Donald Sutherland as a former KGB agent who fights evil, corruption, and lies in *Conspiracy.*

Sega has attracted its share of stars too: Deborah Harry, the former Blondie rocker, stars in *Double Switch* for Sega CD. Lots of stars' voices can be heard via soundblasters in the game world on such projects as the CD-ROM version of *Gabriel Knight: Sins of the Fathers* where you can hear Tim Curry, Mark Hamill, Michael Dorn (of *Star Trek: The Next Generation* fame), and Efrem Zimbalist Jr.

Other stars you'll find on upcoming CD-ROM discs include Brian Keith, Margot Kidder, Grace Zabriskie, Kirk Cameron, Hulk Hogan, Chris Lemmon, and even supermodel Carol Alt.

For the most part, until now multimedia's featured actors have been unknown or little-known performers. And many develop their own following in the game or cinematic experience arena. Robert Hirschboeck, a well-known Shakespearean actor, has captured many new media fans as the evil mansion owner in Trilobyte/Virgin's *The 7th Guest* and *The 11th Hour.* Videogames have served as a connecting point between the "Old Hollywood" and the "New Hollywood."

The boundaries of Hollywood's landscape are fast-forwarding action beyond even what digital animators could fathom. The "New Hollywood" is developing not just hundreds of miles north of Los Angeles in Silicon Valley or San Francisco's multimedia gulch but across the United States and around the world. The national and international impact is almost impossible to measure, but the media is certainly charting a fascinating future. In what *Business Week* magazine is terming the "entertainment economy," Hollywood will become more a state of mind than a place in any particular country or state.

The Wall Street Journal called this new vision "Hollywired" in its special National Association of Broadcasters (NAB) spring 1994 supplement. And Northern California pundits referred to their arena as "Silliwood," thumbing their noses at the potential merging of Hollywood and Silicon Valley and the other signing alliances and deals that may or may not materialize.

But economists and other experts are welcoming the changes. According to top industry advisors, since the economy turned up in 1991 in the entertainment and recreation industry, not health care or autos, it has provided the biggest boost to U.S. consumer spending— a documented $20 billion increase between 1991 and 1993, not including home computers. A stunning 12 percent of all net new employment (more than 200,000 workers) in 1993 were added in the entertainment and recreation industries.

The entertainment economy and the best of the "New Hollywood" are contributing to prosperity in pockets across the country. From Branson, Missouri to Las Vegas to Orlando, to Shea Stadium, Disney, Blockbuster, Matsushita's MCA, Paramount and Viacom have broken ground for a staggering array of theme parks, theaters, casinos, and ballparks. It's estimated that more than $13 billion in big entertainment projects will be in the pipeline by the mid-1990s, with more planned.

Will couch potatoes accept the new media in every walk of life on the road to the electronic highway? Yes, if Hollywood has anything to say about it. Hollywood will use its star power to dominate the

500 channels, move into prominence in the games world, and claim a strong stake in the new arena of location-based entertainment.

Remember that Hollywood has a century of experience on its side. The early film pioneers such as Edison tinkered in laboratories, but their early "flickers" were destined to fascinate only a privileged few. It took marketing prowess and creative genius combined with technical innovation to form the building blocks for the ivory towers of the Hollywood studios that have dominated the world's entertainment market during the past century.

At most multimedia industry conferences, moderators seriously announce "We're all here looking for the next Chaplin." For like early Hollywood, today's multimedia world is led by great innovators who are designing today's on-ramps to the new electronic highways of tomorrow.

The digital revolution of the early 1990s dramatically changed the relationships of the consumer electronics, computer, entertainment, and recreational industries. The much-talked-about convergence of technologies was echoed over and over at computer and new media conferences and confabs at the beginning of this decade.

One of the early innovators to prognosticate on what Hollywood's future would hold came not from the studio system but from the "New Hollywood." Silicon Valley guru Trip Hawkins, former head of the successful game firm Electronic Arts, left to helm 3DO, the controversial multiplayer and software developer firm that was formed back in 1992.

As Electronic Art's head, Hawkins guided that firm to the $200 million level. So it is no surprise that he garnered headlines from both the Hollywood trade press and business sections of major consumer papers when his 3DO company was announced, especially since he crafted his product launch to attract major acclaim. He masterfully chose to reveal at the 1993 Consumer Electronics show, in a much-ballyhooed press conference, that his partners were a collection of entertainment industry heavyweights including Matsushita, AT&T, Time Warner, MCA, Electronic Arts and one of Silicon Valley's leading venture capital firms, Kleiner Perkins, Caufield & Byers.

Hawkins's 3DO press event attracted not only print attention but attendance by such Hollywood kingpins as Sid Sheinberg, President and Chief Operating officer of MCA, Inc. The industry trade paper *Hollywood Reporter* carried the story on page one—one of the first new technology stories to make headlines. The surprise of the 3DO launch was that it was one of the first visible alliances between Silicon Valley and Hollywood other than videogames licensed previously from Hollywood movies.

Hawkins promised that his firm would license both hardware and software technology so that its partners could market its new interactive multiplayer (that tied in with the TV set top) and that it would become the de facto worldwide consumer electronics standard, much like the VHS format for videocassette recorders. (Matsushita is well known for having been on the VHS leadership side versus the Beta format, so its involvement added a halo of electronic brilliance to the venture.) And the Kleiner Perkins venture capital company involvement buttoned up a pinstripe Wall Street vestige of respectability.

Until the 3DO deal, multimedia was seen by many Hollywood players as a vague term for computer nerds and cyberpunks. The beep, gong, quak, ding tada of the video arcades and game industry was eyed as a peripheral nuisance that the kids or grandkids played, not as the nascent entertainment megalopy it was amassing.

They don't call it show business for nothin'; show 'em business and they'll go after it. After all, as one studio executive said, "Stamp my passport Hollywood and I can make a deal anywhere—Russia, China, and even with Eskimos—remember Nanuck?"

Hawkins insisted there was big money to be made in the new media. For many new Hollywood minimoguls and groupies, Hawkins became an evangelist of the new economy. He said that the impact of the new technology and the national information infrastructure would change our lives. He talked about $3 trillion of bottom-line business.

Later, John Sculley, still in his role as Apple's chief, noted at the National Association of Broadcasters Convention that by the year 2000, the three industries of telecommunications (at about $1.2 trillion) and the media (at about $1.3 trillion) and the combined industries of consumer electronics and computers (at $1 trillion) would add up to an amazing $3.5 trillion worldwide (our 1992 U.S. economy was only $6 trillion).

Only a few months earlier at a San Jose trade conference called Intermedia, Hawkins was joined by a quartet of VIPs that mesmerized the media and finally made the Hollywood mega- and minimoguls begin to take notice. An impressive dais included Ray Smith, Bell Atlantic; John Malone, TCI; Barry Diller of QVC, and Hawkins.

On the Silicon Valley side, major computer leaders such as former IBM proxy Jack D. Kuehler were telling trade show audiences, "In the eyes of the consumer we are both consumer electronics and computers—not separate industries anymore. Technology has allowed our two streams to form a very powerful river. It has opened up enormous opportunity for us and those we serve. Just how well we exploit that opportunity is up to us. But one thing is certain—customer demand is insatiable."

The times they were achanging. Many Hollywood insiders were reminded that at the 1939 World's Fair (just about the same time that Dorothy walked down the yellow brick road to Oz) no one had ever envisioned the personal computer. Strategic planners at studios put on their thinking caps and the antennas were adjusted to see what might be ahead on the digital highway to the new electronic Oz.

HOLLYWOOD AND THE NEW INDEPENDENTS

Back in 1992 and 1993, most Hollywood studio business affairs executives, lawyers, and agents were still mostly concerned about the potential summer blockbusters or who would have the best parties at Cannes or what independent filmmakers were to be discovered at Sundance or Telluride or the IFP market in New York.

For the independent film world was suddenly in Hollywood's traditional face with films such as *El Mariachi* (made for $7,000) and grossing a seeming zillion times that and others such as Quentin Tarantino's now camp classic *Reservoir Dogs* made for less than $2 million. *Sex, Lies and Videotape* had catapulted the upstart distributor Miramax to the headlines of the trade pages.

Meanwhile a new breed of "independents" was developing in the Multimedia Gulch south of Market Street in San Francisco, in garages in Silicon Valley and in the SIGs (special interest groups) of such national "new media" organizations as International Interactive Communications Society (IICS).

Not surprisingly, many financial analysts see the independent film business dynamic as the prototype for the new media business. Others predict that the studio business model or publishing world system will gradually take hold in the game and CD-ROM worlds.

MULTIMEDIA AND POSTPRODUCTION

To date, the most measurable impact of multimedia on Hollywood has primarily been in the areas of postproduction and special effects. There technicians and creative types have worked together to redesign the way the work is done and the results that appear on the big and small screens.

In the early 1990s, despite the threat of 500 channels, broadcast television was still hot and even new media gurus such as Stan Cornyn, former head of Warner New Media, were quoted as saying that "Television is here to stay." Yet today, Cornyn is deeply involved in multimedia and new media project development.

So although a few avant garde leaders—many of them too young to have learned to disco—were doing the technodance at interactive conferences such as Home Media, Multimedia World, and Digital World, most of Hollywood was playing the sidelines and sending the "kids" out to test the virtual waters of the new technology.

Most of Hollywood still saw films and television as the ultimate multimedia. And the studios and production companies not only owned the rights but had proven they had the savvy to produce the best software programming in the world. From the ivory towers of the Century City and Culver City lots, minimoguls and the industry megastar agents and wheeler-dealers looked askance at this thing called multimedia. Even when the word on the street was that the ultimate big wheel, Mike Ovitz, head of Creative Artists Agency (CAA), was rolling out groundwork for the new electronic highway with matchmaking alliances, eyebrows, not toasts, were raised by most Hollywood VIPs.

Barry Diller, the former head of Twentieth Century Fox and Paramount, was the personification of the "great man theory" influencing multimedia history in Hollywood. He invested $24 million of his personal fortune in this "thing" called QVC—home shopping. The Monday-night Morton's Restaurant Hollywood "in" crowd was abuzz.

Diller, after all, was the guy who had created the Movie of the Week and later Fox TV, a fourth network, when everyone knew that Hollywood was designed to have only three majors. He had also headed not one but two studios—Paramount and Twentieth Century Fox.

When *The New Yorker* and *The New York Times* published articles quoting Barry as stating straightforwardly that this new medium of interactive television was a business about the convenience of "buying underwear in your underwear," Hollywood started to go topsy turvy because many of the baby boomers suddenly remembered that was the lure of television—to be able to watch a movie in your pajamas and grab a beer when you wanted.

About that same time, the venerable trade paper *Variety* started to cover the technology beat with a regular column. *The Hollywood Reporter* published its first special interactive media supplement.

Financial analysts swarmed like bees learning new buzzwords at the new media trade shows. And a "gold rush" fanned excitement in San Francisco's multimedia gulch where a flurry of fledgling multimedia companies began to paint a new landscape dotted with developers and high-definition pixels.

Still, many Hollywood executives, producers, and directors were skeptical at best and oblivious at worst. When this researcher called the top studios and networks in preparation for a special book *Multimedia 2000* for the National Association of Broadcasters in the Spring of 1993, the most frequent answer to the question "Who handles your multimedia?" was "What is multimedia?" and the second was "You need to talk to our MIS" department or our "computer people. "

Those were the days when, if you said "CD," the first thing a Hollywood mogul thought was that it was time to roll over his $50,000 certificates of deposit, and television anchors were voicing amazement about the rise of the CD-ROME (sic) market. Many Hollywood VIPs thought that a CDi was a music compact disc personalized (like a license plate), not the compact disc interactive multiplayer then being launched by Philips in Blockbuster's 2000 stores nationwide.

Even today, confusion abounds about what the difference is between multimedia, new media, virtual reality, and 500 channels. And if you're not a member of IICS (International Interactive Communications Society) or haven't signed up for the new media expos or read *Multimedia Week* or *WIRED* or a postproduction journal such as *Film & Video* or *In Motion* or the Hollywood trades and *Byte* and *Personal Computing* and aren't in a SIG group (special interest group) on-line on Prodigy or America Online or a subscriber to the newly popular *Hollywood On-Line*, you may still be waiting for more visible signs of a multimedia revolution. Dollar deals in multimedia are figured in hundreds and thousands, not the millions that Hollywood studios thrive on.

For many on the "cutting edge of multimedia," the new world is as open as the Wild West. If you work for Introvision or ILM or Iwerks or Rhythm & Hues or Pacific Data Images or at Kodak's all-digital Cinesite, then you see daily the impact that multimedia has on both bottom lines and meeting tight schedules.

Despite all the hubbub about multimedia, it was only when the terms "interactive television" and "interactive movies" started to be used by the media, that traditional Hollywood started to understand what these platforms were about. But in the postproduction departments of studios and at postproduction houses around Hollywood and across the nation in the early 1990s, it became apparent that multimedia was big and getting bigger.

According to analysts, the interactive multimedia industry will swell to some $10 billion by the end of this decade.

Ten years ago, in 1984, in the days before notebook PCs, VGA graphics, fax modems, 2400 bps modems, and desktop publishing, when the Mac was still vaporware, much of Hollywood was still using Selectric typewriters, and some executives still hired secretaries based on their legs and dictation skills, 80 percent of all postproduction for television was done on film. Today, 90 percent of it is done on tape.

Most Hollywood studios didn't even get PCs until 1988. Yes, there were a few first-generation 8086/88 systems around, but those were in the MIS departments or left to the mavericks such as Robert Abel, a renowned leader in the world of special effects, noted for designing some of the best scenes for *Star Wars* and more. Techies were for the most part left outside the studio gates. Many studios had long ago disbanded their cohesive in-house production departments.

If you saw the film *Chaplin*, you know that there also were many naysayers when talkies first came to Hollywood. While some people rambled nonstop for two years about the wonders of Quadras and the mystery of "multiple platforms," only about 40–60 percent of Hollywood was even computer literate according to industry consultant Ray Solley of The Solley Group. "But that's better than the average consumer base where 99 percent of the homes have television but about only one quarter have computers (now it's 34 percent)," added Solley.

In some areas of Hollywood, like music and postproduction, computers invaded earlier. MIDI was developed in the early 1980s as an industry standard. Todd Rundgren came out with an early audio CD constructed in multilayer segments that home listeners with CDi or with CD-ROM players could manipulate.

Former ITS President (International Teleproduction Society—the people who own most of the postproduction facilities) Linda Rheinstein said, "The largest part of multimedia until recently was basically post; perhaps that's why people are becoming increasingly high-tech oriented."

A report called *Creating Multimedia: Hollywood Goes Digital* by Volpe, Welty & Co., a San Francisco-based investment banking firm, caused some waves and brought their analysts to the forefront as predictors of the future. The report forecast that the Hollywood post-production market would increase by 16 percent or more than $3.5 billion in the next three years and that the market would zap up to 825,000 customers—more than 10 times the current postproduction client numbers. Volpe analyst Charles Finnie was quoted as saying that he believed that trend alone would rewrite the rules for Hollywood's postproduction community.

A good example of that change was the fact that Industrial Light and Magic (ILM) did its Oscar-quality special effects for the film *Death Becomes Her* on a Silicon Graphics Inc. workstation that sells for less than $100,000. "People aren't going to be able to spend $1 million on a single machine in the future," Rheinstein predicted.

But postproduction houses were not the only ones embracing multimedia during the past three years. Commercial production companies were making "moving storyboards" with it, directors and camera operators were editing their reels, set designers and art directors were "walking through" their 3D designs in advance, and photographers were creating interactive PhotoCDs. Stock film archives, books, music, children's stories, and more were being developed on CD. And of course, the world of special effects was being forever changed by its entwining with multimedia and computer-generated effects. Word on the street was that some top studio VIPs were actually viewing their dailies for major films on Apple QuickTime systems, perhaps adopting the "quick peek" permanently and banishing the stuffy, cigar-smelly screening sessions forever.

GUILDS AND MULTIMEDIA

Hollywood power has traditionally been centered in the unions or guilds for writers, actors, directors, and postproduction personnel. By 1993, the guilds were beginning to take notice of the impact of technology.

Joyce Communications attracted an audience of several hundred directors when it was asked to give a retraining session for underemployed directors. Instead of encouraging them to sell automobiles or Amway on the side we instituted the DGA's (Director Guild of America's) first workshop on multimedia.

Just showing videotapes on Voyager interactive books and Showscan and Iwerks location-based entertainment and Quantel's paintbox postproduction promotional tapes had directors ready to reel into a new multimedia milieu.

The promotional visuals, coupled with the information that the director for the first Jane Fonda video wasn't covered by the guild, created a real buzz. What, no residuals! Just flat fees? In an economy where the feast-or-famine work style was dependent on repeat performance, ancillary rights, and the "aftermarket," the new media was a new opportunity and one that directors were not going to let pass them by. Days after the DGA West Coast seminar, the New York DGA division called and sent an airline ticket and an invitation for Joyce Communications to talk to East Coast VIP directors.

A similar seminar was done for the California Film Commission (CFC) regional film liaisons. Since that time, technologically savvy CFC director Patti Stolkin Archuletta has led the way to the future by applying for a federal grant in connection with the commission's new high-technology library system being developed jointly with NASA's Jet Propulsion Laboratory in Pasadena and Kodak. Stolkin has been quoted as saying, "California recognized that the entertainment industry and information technology will together facilitate our economic comeback." It's said that the CFC's program eventually will result in more than 300,000 color images being stored electronically with background information. The system is planned to be a public access on-line network.

About the time of these first industry multimedia seminars, the CMAT (Creative Media and Technologies Committee) of the Writers Guild published its own supplement listing writers prepared to enter this new realm of multimedia. Today, in 1994, less than 18 months later, all of the guilds—AFTRA, SAG (Screen Actors Guild), WGA (Writers Guild of America), and DGA (Directors Guild)—have interactive multimedia agreements.

Actors, writers, directors, and voice-over experts want their piece of the new multimedia pie. They all now have subcommittees watching the growth and creating outreach programs looking for work for their members. And classes and seminars are being held to upgrade computer skills for IATSE and "below-the-line Hollywood personnel."

Figure 3-1   Digital Pencil Sketch from *Ride for Your Life*
Provided courtesy of Interfilm Technologies, Inc.. © 1993 Interfilm Technologies

Shortly before this book was published, The Writers Guild of America West (WGAw) signed what it calls a "first-of-its-kind" deal with New York-based Interfilm Technologies (which develops interactive cinematic experiences for theatrical viewing nationwide). WGAw Executive Director Brian Watson has been quoted as saying, "This agreement sends the message to this fast-growing new industry that the WGA is open for business in new technologies."

Interfilm COO Bill Franzblau has noted in the industry newsletter *Interactive Update* that the deal is significant because the WGA gives it access to the Hollywood writing community. The deal covers compensation, credit determination, dispute arbitration, and residuals for certain uses. Since Interfilm is based in New York, far from Silicon Valley and Hollywood and the other new media mecca of the Northwest, it is further evidence that the New Hollywood is where the talent or their laptops are located!

On this topic, Min Yee, former number-two man at Microsoft who established the Multimedia Publishing division there and is now head of his own new media firm *riverrun*, claims that he goes to the trade shows to find that one special new developer. At Digital Hollywood, he said "I think I found Hollywood in Charlottesville, Virginia," since he met a developer from that city attending the conference who impressed him.

"Hollywood will definitely play a major role in the growth of multimedia," forecasted Jeannine Parker, former IICS president (under her auspices, this trade group has swelled from 200 paid members to a mailing list of 3000). "Our tastes in film have been defined by Hollywood. Film-resolution, film aesthetics, film motion are all important. It's mind boggling how fast Tinseltown is actually moving into multimedia. Voice recognition, intelligent wireless communications, and even nanotechnology are next."

Summarizing what is really happening behind closed doors in Hollywood studios regarding multimedia, virtual reality, and holograms is all but impossible. In the past year, a score of major multimedia developments and new media deals have begun to sculpt the digital diagram of the New Hollywood.

Barry Diller, Barry Diller, and Barry Diller

Yes, QVC and QVC 2, the spinoff channel, are what Hollywood moguls are seeing as the wave of the future. Although not truly multimedia now but rather transactional in approach, Diller hints that multimedia developments will appear in the future on his channels and in his productions.

Al Gore Information Highway Summit

The prestigious Academy of Television Arts & Sciences (the Emmy people) held a conference at UCLA that changed the way that many Hollywood and Washington VIPs viewed the new industry. C-Span covered the sessions live and later sold the videotapes of the conference for $300. The imprimatur of Vice President Al Gore's featured address ushering in multimedia and the new Hollywood was significant. Gore was later named one of 1994's 100 influential people in Hollywood by the slick *Premiere* magazine's April issue. The conference attracted major leaders in the telecommunications, film, and television industries along with an audience of 2000 entertainment and media professionals.

Figure 3-2   Lily Tomlin Surprises Al Gore
Photo by Craig T. Mathew/ATAS

Vice President Al Gore gave the featured address at the Academy of Television Arts and Sciences' "Superhighway Summit" in January, 1994. Lily Tomlin was a surprise guest, as shown in Figure 3-2.

The Admission of Videogames into Hollywood's Inside Circle

The revenue of video and arcade games at $14 billion has suddenly become hard to deny compared with $5 billion for film. Disney's success with *Aladdin* as a Christmas 1993 videogame paved the way for more videogames based on films and even television show spinoffs. Aftermarket rights for videogames and movies took on a new dimension when Disney announced a new *Aladdin* video cassette with new footage to be released following the successful Christmas launch of the videogame.

Studio Home Video Division Entering New Media

Xiphias, an entrepreneurial developer headed by new media opinion leader Peter Black, stunned many moguls by capturing the new media rights to the high-rated children's television spellbinder *Power Rangers*. Black first announced an agreement to produce a CD-ROM program based on Saban's Entertainment's the *Mighty Morphin Power Rangers* TV program. Only weeks later, Paramount Home Video (PHV) announced an agreement to market and distribute Black's CD-ROM *Ranger* multimedia programming.

Paramount's announcement was significant because it was underscored by the well-respected video division head Eric Doctorow. The Domestic Home Video president said in *The Hollywood Reporter* that, "Just as I believe video and record stores will be a natural place for the evolution of CD-ROM products, I also believe there is an opportunity for computer specialists to move into linear video. " The deal is seen as an early foothold for PHV. Many forecasters agree with Doctorow that the 5-inch disc will replace the videocassette over time and become the common carrier.

The Bell Atlantic/TCI Deal or Misdeal

The phone companies have big money and big money is what Hollywood likes to play with—so the talks go on. And the Baby Bells such as NYNEX continue to move into multimedia and interactive test markets.

The Viacom/QVC Parry for Paramount

How and why would anyone pay so much for Paramount? The question lingers on as the stockmarket scurries in disarray in spring of 1994 prior to publication of this book. The Viacom/Blockbuster misdeal (estimated to be at a $275 million failure rate) adds fuel to the frenzied gossip and guestimates of what the future holds.

Time Warner Orlando

The Time Warner Orlando test has been postponed to the end of 1994. Real interactive TV! Even if it's only 4,000 households. Even if it costs $5,000 to install in each household! Look—you get a color printer to work with your television set!

Proliferation of the Black Boxes

3DO, TVAnswer, Philips CDi, Nintendo, Sega, Sony—new boxes are announced quarterly. Experts say the average home has an average of 2.2 videogame players. And new MPEG (Motion Picture Experts Group) video cartridges offer consumers the quality of video they are used to demanding from TV and film.

Location-Based Entertainment

Is location-based entertainment (LBE) just a fancy name for theme parks? Then why is Paramount so involved? Why did this stock called Iwerks open at 10 and close at 37 during its IPO day? And just what are all of those experiences that my kids are enthralled with at the Luxor Hotel in Las Vegas? And what is this thing called Cinetropolis that my cousin experienced in Connecticut? And why is everyone flocking to Universal City Walk and wanting comp tickets to the *Back to the Future* "ride" at Universal Studios?

Multimedia and the early stages of virtual reality have found a home in LBE even if it's most visible in simulator rides revolving around movies that are not truly interactive. LBE is still an entertainment venue that sells more sizzle than steak even to many aficionados. But as in real estate, LBE's promoters know the value of location, location, location and being out first in the marketplace.

Multimedia and interactive TV and film production is finally covered in Hollywood contracts. Most Hollywood literary agencies have assigned a new media agent to place its top writers into the inner circle of the new media and to put together the megadeals for the electronic highway of the new millennium.

According to *Variety*, interactive agents Alan Gasmer and John Massof of the William Morris Agency have secured the rights to all titles from computer game manufacturer Sierra On-Line. The first franchise that they will take out for possible film deals is the hit

Leisure Suit Larry. They've attached screenwriter Tim Kelleher (*First Kid*) to write and are currently pitching the project. Casting suggestions for the lovable Larry nerd include Bill Murray!

Suddenly Hollywood moguls have taken notice and they are asking, say, couldn't we turn that CD-ROM stuff into a movie? Or what about all that old stuff we have in our vaults? Couldn't we repurpose it? Get me an agent please! And call my lawyer, I want to know about my intellectual property rights. And by the way, when is the next IICS meeting or the next new media conference—get me on a panel. Let's announce a New Media Division, let's get some game developers in here. Let's add a third camera to the shoot on location on our next film.

Philips Interactive Media of America launched their own interactive cinematic experience called *Voyeur* that featured Robert Culp and used a Hitchcock "rear window" type approach to disguise the fact that the experience is not truly full-screen. Shown in Figure 3-3, *Voyeur* director Robert Weaver showed actors the delicate art of dealing with the "blue screen" to create the drama he wanted for the PIMA adventure. Interfilm's *I'm Your Man* pilot interactive cinematic game launched in 1993 in New York and LA was a consumer and media sensation. Thousands of consumers got to experience interactive film in movie theaters on both coasts.

Now Bob Bejan and his COO Franzblau are preparing new Interfilm cinematic experiences following a sensational multimillion-dollar IPO. Dozens of movie theaters will be retrofitted with pistol grips to add the necessary interactivity of the Interfilm experiences.

As shown in Figure 3-4, Writer-director Bob Bejan from Interfilm utilized a bike-cam and virtual reality goggles to shoot bike racing scenes in *Ride for Your Life*, an interactive cinematic game with up to 400 scene variations.

The "500-channel marketplace" will also be affected by Hollywood's involvement in new media. DirecTV, the GM Hughes Electronics-owned direct broadcast satellite programming service, has signed a pay-per-view distribution agreement with Warner Brothers pay TV. The agreement will allow the company to offer 40 channels of pay-per-view movies on its Direct Ticket Near-Video-on-Demand system with start times every 30 minutes.

Figure 3-3   Scenes from *Voyeur*

The Hughes satellite service has already inked agreements with Paramount, MCA, Sony Pictures Entertainment (including TriStar, Columbia Pictures, and Sony Pictures Classics), and Walt Disney Television, including Touchstone Pictures, Hollywood Pictures, and Miramax. So far, there are no interactive elements to the programming announced for DirecTV, but experts feel that the satellite-based system is poised for new technology ventures including multimedia spinoffs and interactive programming.

Hollywood wonders what is beyond multimedia, CD-ROM, electronic publishing, Video-on-Demand, pay-per-view, and these early interactive film pilot programs. What about a phone company developing its own Hollywood studio? That was the question this writer was asked by the *Multimedia Week* newsletter editor weeks before it was announced in Spring, 1994, that Bell Atlantic had formed a relationship with the advertising agency network the Interpublic Group to team with two Silicon Valley venture capital firms entrepreneurs for funding interactive multimedia television producers and suppliers. The Interpublic program is purportedly more a creative incubator for the combined talents of Hollywood and Silicon Valley.

Figure 3-4   Scenes from *Ride for Your Life*
Provided courtesy of Interfilm Technologies, Inc. © 1993 Interfilm Technologies, Inc.

What makes the Bell Atlantic project different is that in most cases, Hollywood creatives have been guided by a guild and union economy where you may get not what you deserve but what you negotiate. In the new media, creatives are increasingly being included in the back end of the deals.

Back in 1993, John Sculley told *The Hollywood Reporter* that "If Hollywood doesn't get in on the ground floor and get some experience with talent (and) understand how you begin seeing in new ways, it's going to be hard to catch up once the momentum gets going." Developers, writers, and producers are important to the new media, but it may be the big-name studio players in new cable and telecommunication and wireless joint ventures and alliances that move the process forward with greater momentum.

Many Hollywood companies are reengineering for the new millennium. Sony USA Vice Chairman Michael Schulhof announced that Sony was being forced to "redefine" itself. In fact, Schulhof finds that new technology and developments will prompt Sony to merge its electronics, movie production, and music divisions sometime in the foreseeable future.

Director Paul Schrader made headlines in the DGA newsletter in early 1993 by labeling today's films very antiquated, at least as theatrically exhibited, and underscored the view that only now with digital technology is the future of film truly coming into focus. The advent of digital technology will not only redefine movies but also the essential idea of the visual image itself.

In Schrader's view, digital technology is not only transforming film exhibition, it is transforming the very notion of the video image. Schrader went on to suggest that digital technology will challenge the traditional relationship between the artist and the viewer/listener.

Top-level corporate financial planners have their eyes on the bigger profit pies. The $100 to $500 billion reported by the *Los Angeles Times* that the nation's telecommunications industry can look forward to in fresh investment in the 1990s has attracted the big alliances.

THE ENTERTAINMENT ECONOMY

About 20 percent of all U.S. discretionary income is spent on entertainment and recreation. Let's look at where the $341 billion entertainment dollars are today according to the U.S. Commerce department (Table 3-1).

Hollywood wants a piece of every part of this pie and sees multimedia and interactivity as an entree into the new economy. For example, ESPN is said to be strategizing how to enter the multimedia business to capture more of the $6 billion spent on spectator sports. According to *Interactive Update*, ESPN has been working on two multiple-platform videogame releases with Sony Imagesoft, baseball and football games that will recreate the atmosphere of an ESPN telecast.

ENTERTAINMENT CATEGORY	REVENUE (BILLIONS)
Toys and sporting squipment	$65
VCRs, TVs, consumer electronics,	
recorded music and videotapes	$58
Books, magazines, and newspapers	$47
Gambling	$28
Cable TV	$19
Amusement parks and other commercial	
participant amusements	$14
Movie admissions and video rentals	$13
(Note: $5 billion is movie admissions)	
Home computers for personal use	$8
Personal boats and aircraft	$7
Live entertainment except sports	$7
Spectator sports	$6
Other recreation and entertainment	$70
Total	$341

Table 3-1   Entertainment Economy for 1994

Source: U.S. Department of Commerce

The first title, *Baseball Tonight,* features video and audio of ESPN baseball commentator Chris Berman and was set to be released in June, 1994. Other games on auto racing and another based on the National Hockey League franchise are planned. ESPN will release the multimedia products themselves at a suggested retail price of $69.95. And ESPN is also venturing into the instructional arena with sports CD-ROM discs with Atlanta-based Intellimedia featuring such sports pros as tennis's Tracy Austin and St. Louis Cardinals shortstop Ozzie Smith.

But to most of Hollywood and to many consumers, the ultimate multimedia is still the movie. PIMA's video cartridge for its CDi player allows consumers to see full-screen, full-action video on a television set-top multiplayer. And the firm has signed agreements with many of the top Hollywood studios to show its films. *Top Gun* was one of the first titles to hit the Blockbuster and Virgin megastores.

The film industry may just be healthier than ever before. Wilkofsy Gruen Associates Inc., an economic consulting firm, estimates that domestic spending on filmed entertainment (box office admissions, home video, and television) will total $30 billion in 1994, up 7.4 percent. In 1994, Hollywood studios are estimated to produce 198 films, up 10 percent from 1993.

VIDEOGAMES: AN AMAZING MAZE

To the next generation of filmgoers, games are probably the first place they saw video—not on television or in movie houses. If you're reading this book, chances are that you're part of the 34 percent of adults who are hooked not on phonics but on multimedia "multiplatforms."

And if you live in the Midwest, maybe you traded in your bowling ball for a CD-ROM so that you could go on-line with your pals and play Wargames via modem on Tuesday nights when it's 20 degrees below zero outside. An expert at a recent trade conference pointed out that 2000 bowling alleys have closed in the last decade alone. Yes, indeed, Americans are playing more games than ever before, and many of these are on computers and television sets.

A *USA Today* survey of 10-year-old boys showed that 32 percent knew who Mickey Mouse was versus 54 percent who knew who Sonic the Hedgehog was (Sonic is a videogame character).

Videogames sales rose by 18 percent to $14 billion. Schulhof of Sony says that's because the big leaders such as Sony are rolling out new products such as multimedia videogames and competing with the individual video entrepreneurs who used to rule the roost in the video barnyard. Nintendo and Sega would probably contend that they set the stage and the studios are indeed the media neophytes.

And some videogames have been made into other forms (see the case history on *Carmen San Diego* in the Edutainment section of this chapter). Some experts feel that the licensing and merchandising potential for videogames has just begun. Many comic book companies are now forming alliances with videogame companies. Malibu Comics has an interactive division and Voyager Communications was just bought by Acclaim to bring even more comic book heroes to our arcades and homes in the next year or so.

But what people really want is MPEG 64-bit games—the holy grail that many top experts such as Trip Hawkins believe will skyrocket videogames to the top of the charts.

Still other experts feel that adding celebrity names and Hollywood film title variations and virtual reality experiences to the game world are what the designers must create to keep pace with the demanding 10- to 16-year-old male audience who dominates the game market demographics.

And then there are those exhibitors at the Las Vegas Sahara Hotel's Consumer Electronic Show who believe that it is softcore porn that will really propel the game and CD-ROM market. After all, they say, isn't that what really made videotape fast forward into our households?

Some softcore pornography developers maintain that the original paradigm for home video was 80 percent softcore and 20 percent children's videos. There are many CD-ROM and software manufacturers who claim those statistics compare favorably with what is being sold in the new media today.

And why is this so shocking? After all, you can't watch a "dirty" video in full view on the living room VCR but you can revel in *Virtual Valerie* or *Penthouse On-Line* or *My Girlfriend's* exploits in the privacy of your den or bedroom on your personal computer. And if anyone peeks in the door, with just a flick of a key you can have your income tax spreadsheet back on screen or be deeply involved in a search for dinosaur trivia.

Traditional Hollywood has always tried to distance itself from the softcore market. Many leaders breathed a sigh of relief when games makers voluntarily decided to go to a rating system. At this time, most of the Hollywood-related videogames have been family fare. *Voyeur* by POV, a division of Philips, has a sophisticated and sexy approach, and Trimark's proposed *Evolver* film promises a bit or byte of more than just gams.

Although no one's making public announcements, it's possible that just as Hollywood creates a different, more erotic version of many films for the foreign marketplace, X-rated videogames may find a place in the marketplace. Many of the depictions of virtual reality in Hollywood films have involved sex (see earlier references to *Lawnmower Man* and *Demolition Man* scenes).

What effect will all of these new services have on each other? Traditionally, in Hollywood adding new delivery systems has only enhanced the ancillary rights or aftermarket for current products. A certain percentage of the market will wait to see *Batman V* on home video rather than at the theater; more will see it one way or the other. And many would like to see it both ways. And pay-per-view experts contend that some viewers (like this author) will pay big bucks to see it first in their homes in a pretheatrical window.

How about it? Would you prefer to have an opportunity to see an interactive *Batman* at home with your friends where you can choose your own point of view, bring up information on how the film was made, and maybe even reorganize the scenes yourself or even select a different ending? Pay-per-view and Video-on-Demand aficionados say that is what the future is all about: having it your way—not the way of the studios.

And for many adults the best interactive entertainment experience is not films, video, or television; it is gambling. Virgin Atlantic

Airways LTD has installed gambling machines on international flights on which you can play poker or slots and the limit is skyhigh. The GTE Imagitrek system in Carlsbad allows you to "gamble" interactively now.

Many a Hollywood executive attending a new media conference in Las Vegas has been mesmerized by the video poker or video craps machines. Maybe it's that yen to beat out the Silicon Valley types face to face or man to machine? Or maybe it's that quest to see how to cash in on the $28 billion spent on gambling nationally.

Still other leaders feel that it is the educational and informational marketplace that is Hollywood's next arena to conquer. Edutainment and infotainment are concepts that multimedia people love to hate and Hollywood seems ready to cash in on.

EDUTAINMENT AND INFOTAINMENT

Many of Hollywood's "working" actors, writers, producers, and directors long ago learned the secret to getting a regular check in Tinseltown—and it isn't just marrying the studio executive's daughter or son! No, if you want regular work, you learn fast that 70 percent of all television work is in the industrial fields: educational films, television shows, videos, and, in the past decade, a growing number of infomercial and informational programming.

Now new terms have evolved for this work that is fast deleting the demarcation of what is entertainment and what is "edutainment" (educational programming with an entertainment slant or vice versa) and "infotainment" (informational programs and even documentary-type shows that have real entertainment value to the viewer).

Hollywood deals in the multimedia arena to date are peanuts compared with the estimated $4.5 billion foothold of the current educational publishing industry. The educational software business is already growing at a rate of 40 percent per year. Add multimedia and interactivity to the mix and you have potential for exponential growth beyond what the traditional math teacher could pinpoint on graphs of the past.

Pressure from parents groups and the FCC has literally changed the look of shows on Saturday morning TV. And technology is literally reshaping the way we learn at home, school, and work. In 1992, home learning software programs increased almost 50 percent to about $150 million according to the Software Publishers Association (SPA). Sales in 1994 will approach $250 million says San Francisco brokerage and research firm Volpe Welty & Company, which estimates that by the new millennium parents will be spending $1 billion a year on software for at-home learning.

In the workplace, training is now estimated at a $42 billion industry (and informal training—one worker training another to use software etc.—is estimated at about $80 billion).

One CD-ROM manufacturer estimates that there are 80,000 players in Florida schools alone. *The Wall Street Journal* recently headlined that CD-ROM publications were virtually replacing the college textbook. And a new publication, *T.H.E. Journal* (Technological Horizons in Education), featured ads by all of the top hardware companies, including Digital, Canon, AT&T, Hughes Communications, Pioneer, AT&T, NCR, Prodigy, Sony, Intel, and a special IBM supplement in its February, 1994 issue.

So how is Hollywood affected by or affecting this learning revolution? A $50 million joint venture between Paramount Publishing and Palos Verdes independent developer Davidson & Associates is said to put Paramount on the inside edge in electronic publishing.

According to the *Los Angeles Times* and the trade press accounts, Paramount plans to spend $50 million to co-develop titles in the educational field with Davidson based on its library of reference works, how-to titles, and children's books.

Paramount's VP of communications, Andrew Giangola, says that the overall strategy is to work with well-established "creative and efficient partners" as an express route to make its own mark in the business. This co-venture could be a signifier of more new joint ventures between studios and independent developers. According to executive recruiter Neal Fink at Fink & Blakely in Northern California, many of the top software companies are also looking to acquire or "co-produce" with firms who have a ready-made product and teams of experts available to joint venture with them. Witness the Electronics Arts deal with Northern California-based PF Magic.

Some major studios such as MGM are just tapping into the true potential of "repurposing" their current libraries for "educational" or "informational" purposes. Can an interactive James Bond or Pink Panther CD-ROM be ready for Christmas 1995?

With 5 million multimedia PCs already in the home according to *Multimedia Business Report* and another additional 4.5 million machines set to be sold in 1994, the market for educational or informational CD-ROM alone is significant. The Philips CDi slate offers families, classrooms, and offices opportunities for experiences that they might never have otherwise.

Visit the Louvre, play golf on the finest courses in the world, or challenge the crap tables at Caesar's Palace. Is that education? Is that training? Is that information? And what about the kids in schools in Carlsbad, California using GTE Imagitech's on-line, interactive video poker games to learn math?

Hollywood—especially its writers, directors, and actors—want a piece of this action. And they feel that they are best suited to add an entertainment slant to materials. The Writers Guild established a Creative Media and Technologies Committee (CMAT) and published a directory of those members whose backgrounds include traditional industrial work, Hollywood titles, and new media experience.

Even the big guys are interested in the educational market. Producers and distributor of many movies of the week, television shows, and such movies as *Schindler's List* have distributed behind-the-scenes video footage and curriculum guides to schools and libraries across the country.

It is said that George Lucas took a year off to work in educational programming development along with North Carolina schools. And Viacom officials have visited the "all-wired" school in Oxnard, California. CCI, a division of Paramount Interactive, is working with a school in Pasadena and numerous other pilot learning programs are being developed by Hollywood producers and PBS executives. *Scholastic* magazine is even starting its own channel.

Millions of people pull college-level courses off of satellite programming each year. An interactive encyclopedia such as Encarta is just a hint of what is still to come. CD-ROM discs are already a real threat to the college textbook publisher. When Hollywood enters this arena you can ask Schwarzenegger to teach you Austrian and Princess Di to guide your on-screen tour of London.

But Hollywood is not leading this field at this time; it is the smaller companies that have captured this early sector of the multimedia edutainment and infotainment marketplace. And these companies are booming. Here's how the top six companies in educational software rate at this time according to a recent review in *Business Week*:

Broderbund Software had 1993 revenues of $95.6 million. The firm was subject to an astounding $400 million buyout from Electronic Arts but then backed out as EA's stock dropped.

Best known for their hit title *Where in the World is Carmen Sandiego?* the firm was started by two brothers in a garage. Now *Carmen* is not only a best-selling CD-ROM and a hot software item but also a top Saturday morning animated TV show after being an award-winning live-action PBS show. Broderbund, as with many firms, is using top Hollywood children's screenwriters to create its newest adventures.

Prior to its new joint venture Paramount announcement, California-based Davidson & Associates was already a force to be reckoned with. Davidson grossed $59 million in 1993 and just went public less than a year ago at 13 and traded in Spring, 1994 at 22 3/4. It's said that Jan and Bob Davidson's stake is $290 million.

Compton's New Media hit $41 million in 1993 revenues, and its Interactive Encyclopedia includes live-action film clips. Its other titles include a *Lifestyles of the Rich and Famous Cookbook* and *Library of the Future II and III* that brings thousands of books into your house on one CD-ROM.

The Learning Company at $27.5 million in revenues has attracted kids with its *Reader Rabbit* and *Treasure Mountain* titles. Maxis has made a name for itself with *SimCity* and *SimAnt* and mounted more than $20 million in sales for 1993 too.

One of the hottest companies to watch in this edutainment arena may be Knowledge Adventure, with 1993 sales at $18.5 million. The firm's president Bill Gross was the author of Lotus Development Corporation's Magellan program. Gross's investors are AT&T and Paramount Communications. (At press time, Steven Spielberg and Gross were in joint venture discussions.)

7th Level, another very hot edutainment and software developer, was launched by George D. Grayson, who left Micrografix and, with his brother Paul and partner Scott Page (a former saxophonist with the rock group Pink Floyd), set up shop in Los Angeles. Their first product, which shipped in early 1994, was Howie Mandel's *Tuneland* an interactive animated storybook with 42 sing-along public domain songs.

A Canadian company, Sanctuary Woods, attracted lots of great press and recognition when actress/producer Shelly Duvall created *It's a Bird's Life*, a best-selling title for that firm. The British Publisher Pearson paid $462 million in March, 1994 for Software Toolworks, which has systems that teach piano and typing.

Why all of this emphasis on edutainment? Because backers of these products see the programming as the gateway to planned interactive cable channels. In fact, one of 7th Level's biggest investors is Michael R. Millken, the junk-bond king who is developing programming for his new Educational Entertainment Network.

Micrografix developed a deal with Hallmark Cards' Binney & Smith subsidiary to develop Crayola-brand drawing programs, and Sega Enterprises showed up at the Toy Fair in New York in February 1994 with Pico, a $160 million home computer that hooks up to the television to deliver early learning exercises to kids.

Many manufacturers see edutainment and infotainment as a definite inside track to the information highway. Norman J. Bastin, executive vice president of Compton's New Media Inc. in Carlsbad, has been quoted as saying, "You might say we're all getting cable ready."

Hollywood isn't just sitting and watching the new infotainment and edutainment entrepreneurs cash in at their ATMs. Asked at a recent seminar what kind of entertainment programming Time Warner subscribers will have available to them in Orlando, an executive pointed to the new interactive animated version of *Peter and The Wolf*.

Animation director Chuck Jones and *Bugs Bunny on Broadway* creator George Daugherty are combining their talents to create this project. Jones will design the characters, Daugherty will direct and cowrite the script with Janis Diamond of *Sesame Street* and *The Electric Company*, and actress Kirstie Alley will provide voices of the characters.

Children watching will be able to interact directly with the characters, play a variety of computer/videogames and even see a minidocumentary on Jones and composer Serge Prokofiev. A Time Warner Symphony Orchestra performance of the score will be released as an audio compact disc with the CD-ROM disc. IBM and Apple versions of the game will be out for Christmas, 1994, along with a related coffee-table book.

The ancillary rights of these edutainment projects could be worth millions and millions more than the initial product line alone. Take *Carmen Sandiego*, for example, first issued in software and then CD-ROM and then a live-action TV show and then an animated Saturday morning series. Can the theatrical film version be far behind, and what about merchandising rights and licensing? The success of Mickey Mouse gives some idea of what could happen if Hollywood agents and studios joined forces with these talented entrepreneurs to exploit these new digital stars.

Direct Response Television (DRTV) has ceased being a market controlled by a few companies and become fertile soil for Hollywood and the ad world. At the spring 1994 New Media Expo, the highly respected trade magazine *Advertising Age* announced its first awards for transactional programming.

Integrated media experts (the new phrase for the combined fields of advertising, PR, promotion, and direct response) say that the playing ground has been leveled. Hollywood multimedia and new media involvement could add that magic touch. Hollywood's special effects concept of "morphing," first introduced by Michael Jackson in his *Thriller* video, inspired hundreds of commercials that morphed their America's homes.

Personally, this author's bets are on underwriting and sponsorship as the wave of the future replacing the 30- and 60-second commercial spot by the year 2010. Sponsorship has a strong track record in Hollywood. Examples of this are the acclaimed *Hallmark Hall of Fame* television series and the General Motors-sponsored PBS *Civil War* series by filmmaker Ken Burns. And as noted earlier, every producer in town is trying to bring back *Playhouse 90* live theatrical productions sponsored by alliances of major corporations.

Many roadshows of plays and major art museum exhibitions are underwritten by companies such as JC Penny, RCA, Sony, etc. Why not sponsored multimedia and virtual reality programming for home, school, and business? Hollywood's involvement would be a keen incentive to sponsors seeking celebrity involvement and endorsements.

As you scroll up the offerings on your telecomputer in the year 2015, will you really stop and discern what is edutainment, what is infotainment, and what is entertainment? If your seven-year-old nephew is visiting, you may want to pull off the latest segment of *Where In the World is Carmen Sandiego*. If you're preparing a presentation for your telecommuting colleagues in Paris on the future of doing business in LA, you may want to download a low-priced 30-second clip of *Blade Runner* to open your video demo. And if you're bored working outside on your beachfront cottage in Maine, you may want to search behind the scenes in *Singing in the Rain* to see how the choreographer created certain dance sequences and revitalize your own creative juices so you can develop your next on-line project for your Digital Widget company.

With the help of Pacific Telephone's Virtual Studio, you'll be able to download the video and public domain artwork and tap into a Hollywood screenwriter for an opening segment, pick up some music from the Warner library for less than a grand, and sell your new real estate development project with an on-line presentation that will wow them from Peoria to Paris.

Or you may be able to show your own multimedia production on the video wall at your local shopping center. New media consultant James Alexander sees the nation's ATMs as potential infomercial outlets on every corner. Public venue video access should be as available as billboards in the next millennium and moving video billboards (now already available in Japan) may just clutter up what open space is left on the freeways and autobahns around the world.

Today, the number one videogame genre is flight simulators, so it makes sense for Hollywood to use its celebrities and key talent as entree into the world of education and training. In the year 2015, I'll hopefully be able to sit in my in-house or in-office simulator with ergonomic hydraulic seating and virtual reality movement-sensitive gloves and make the following infotainment or edutainment selections from my "telecomputer":

- Race cars with Tom Cruise (*Days of Thunder*);

- Update my makeup with Max Factor's great grandson;

- Fly to the moon with Leonard Nimoy of *Star Trek*;

- Play virtual volleyball with Tom Selleck's 1994 hologram; and

- When no one's looking, I can even sneak a kiss by projecting myself on screen in any scene from Kevin Costner's *The Bodyguard* while listening to the soundtrack of my choice.

Now that's really Hollywood at its best: fantasy, adventure, drama, and comedy at my fingertips. Not mentioning the body heat I could generate from my Cybersex dildonics telecomputer peripheral if I tune into an X-rated program or two. And if anyone's looking, I can punch up a screensaver that shows that I'm learning French from Maurice Chevalier!

Mostly advertising agencies stayed away from the multimedia marketplace until recently. The best videogames have been advertised by word of mouth. Only recently did companies such as Sega and Nintendo launch major consumer advertising campaigns.

But if you look back, it was advertising deals such as the Pepsi Cola/Paramount *Top Gun* deal that really helped consumers cash in on buying videotapes. The rebate from Pepsi made the purchase of tapes much more affordable than ever before. At $19.95, it was within what the retailer Sears had always called "impulse" purchase price. And McDonalds' holiday deals that offered special movie videos at the unheard-of price of $5.00 made buying them almost as irresistible as a hot Big Mac smothered with cheese.

Advertising on CD-ROM discs? Not too likely, but advertising is already visible on Prodigy and America OnLine and other systems. And hospitality game networks such as NTN (which says that it has more than 2 million bar and restaurant patrons that play its trivia and QB 1 football games) have found that advertisers are increasingly interested in getting a share of their patron's time and direct response. Early advertisers for NTN's interactive games have been Miller, Chrysler, and Chevrolet. A Chevy truck commercial is said to have driven in more than 128,000 instant responses from viewers.

The NTN playmaker (a freestanding remote hand-held device) allows an opportunity for players to key in their names, locations and other information, giving advertisers what they have always wanted—instant access any time and any place.

Even better of course for multimedia fans, games players, and interactive film and video aficionados, will be the development of sophisticated Personal Digital Assistants that play MPEG-2-quality video. *The Wall Street Journal* estimates that 6 million Personal Digital Assistant (PDA) devices will be sold by 1997. It seems hard to fathom with the Apple Newton's poor word of mouth and its current market price of $595. But wireless could indeed create not only excitement but jobs. It's estimated that 300,000 jobs will evolve from wireless alone by the year 2005.

George Lucas says that we are at the cutting edge of an era that will have the impact of the industrial revolution. Many other commentators believe that life will never be the same and that the only thing we can predict is change and more change.

So just how many quarters do you have that I can use in the video arcade of tomorrow? Or will you lend me your smart card for your telecomputer instead?

BEYOND MULTIMEDIA AND THE 1990S

New theatrical delivery systems such as the Pacific Telephone system and the Sony satellite delivery system and DBS could literally change the way films and video get to the viewer. HDTV could change the quality of video we view.

The forecasts for Hollywood's future are as varied as multimedia platforms and programs, including on-line casting, distribution of films and press kits, Video-on-Demand, Near-VOD, interactive MTV, edutainment, and cybersex.

But technology is not the silver bullet; it is human psychology that will plot the path to progress. Speaking at the 1994 USC Graduate School of Business, Sony Pictures Entertainment chairman/CEO Peter Guber reminded us that the new technologies should enhance rather than replace interpersonal relationships: "In our pursuit of revolutionary new ways of communicating powerfully and resonantly, on a global scale, we must never loosen our grip on the face-to-face, one-on-one communications that are the touchstone of human experience," Guber stated.

On the broader perspective, he noted, "You can build the largest format screen that ever existed, create a 500-channel universe or construct a supercomputer network that instantaneously accesses a vast array of people and information, but our communications technology will be soulless and will create nothing of enduring value unless it nurtures, cherishes and preserves contact among human beings."

Two classic Hollywood sayings developed during the past century are "I'll have my people contact your people" and "Let's do lunch." In the new millennium, we must make time to have lunch in person and to reach out and shake hands flesh to flesh, not just via simulated characters, holograms, or virtual reality.

Ten Showcase New Hollywood Multimedia Projects

Picking ten top multimedia projects to represent the "new Hollywood" is a challenge for any new media expert. Yet, the following meet these three criteria: they have some degree of interactivity, they are controlled by the consumer/viewer/operator, and they are in public operation—not just vaporware or smoke and mirrors.

- IWERKS *Virtual Adventures* is described by the company as the world's first high-capacity virtual reality attraction and offers high-resolution, 3D computer-generated, real-time graphics by Evans & Sutherland. The interactive attraction allows each participant to affect the outcome of the experience. Also upcoming is *The Loch Ness Adventure*—an underwater journey to save Nessie from extinction.

- *Vactor Performer*, the SimGraphics Engineering/Iwerks interactive animation performance system, premiered at IAAPA (the amusement park conference) in 1992 in Dallas. It has been used by the Philadelphia Spectrum along with the 76ers and Flyers, and was featured at several new media conferences operated by such celebrities as Sly Stallone.

- Cinetropolis is a location-based entertainment attraction at the Foxwoods Casino in Ledyard, Connecticut. It is said to attract 10,000 people daily. Foxwoods is owned and operated by the Mashantucket Pequot Indian Tribe. *Luxor Hotel* LBE is actually three different attractions—holograms, hydraulic seating, and audience participation—that have a common thread of action adventure with a repertory group of actors and a classic villain versus the good guys in a cross between an *Indiana Jones* and a *Blade Runner* storyline. Theater One is the best: Try the first two rows and you'll feel like you're part of the action (I mean the movie)!

- *I'm Your Man* is the world's first "interfilm," a term that the makers use to distinguish the project from "normal" movies. It premiered December 18, 1992 at the Loews Theater in New York. The interactive movie was shot for $350,000 on 16mm film and transferred to two instant-access video discs and is shown on a projection screen. Audiences control the 50 branching points including multiple-choice endings via Nintendo-like pistol grips. The audience thus "votes" and the majority rule on the next path or plot decision. Created by Controlled Entropy, it ran for six weeks in New York and had a brief run on the West Coast. Watch for new projects from Interfilm, which recently went public. Significantly, Controlled Entropy's founders Bob Bejan and Bill Franzblau bypassed traditional Hollywood distribution channels and shopped the project directly to the Loew's chains. Sony paid for theater retrofitting that amounted to about $70,000 per theater. Company executives forecast new "cinematic experiences" aimed primarily at the MTV generation.

- *Voyeur* from POV, a division of Philips Interactive Media, was the first cinematic interactive "film" on CDi (compact disc interactive). The "film" featured Robert Culp in a "rear window" type mystery story produced by Dave Riordon.

- At publication time, the Time Warner Orlando full-service network was rescheduled for Fall, 1994. Warner New Media has produced such interesting titles as *Seven Days in August,* a *Time* magazine joint effort about the building of the Berlin Wall that mixes education with entertainment, and the CD-ROM *Clinton, Portrait of Victory* done in conjunction with Warner Books. *The Orchestra* and *Funny* remain Warner New Media classics as well as *How Computers Work* and *Hellcab,* a game that pits an unsuspecting New York tourist against a cabbie who has Satan for a boss.

- From MCA Universal and Universal Studios, *Back to the Future* is the best ride there, or is it the *Jurassic Park* experience now? Or what about the 3DO *Jurassic Park* game?

- Paramount has *The Busy World of Richard Scarry* and Great America's *Top Gun* ride. Trekkies can't wait until they see the joint venture that Paramount is preparing with Silicon Valley's Spectrum Holobyte that is rumored to be the ultimate *Star Trek* virtual reality-like attraction.

- Viacom's Castro Valley fiber optic test system will offer 12,000 subscribers true Video-on-Demand and maybe interactive MTV and interactive Nickelodeon. MTV's popular *Get Out the Vote* project was tested by teens regionally in an unusually popular pilot project. MTV's worldwide tour of the rock and roll band U2 called *Zoo TV* was essentially a large-screen, high-fidelity, digital interactive broadcast of a live concert where audience members could provide their own direct video feeds into a large, multicell videowall.

- Peter Gabriel's simulation theater has been traveling across country. The *Mindbender* storyline calls for the classic frog meets princess scenario. It is directed by Brett Leonard, who did *Lawnmower Man*. What makes this project special is that Crystal Pepsi sponsors this "rock motion theater" experience.

Other New Hollywood Multimedia to See or Watch for

- *Forever Growing Garden* is an interactive edutainment project produced by Arboressence for Media Vision and told on two levels for adult and child, using real actor voice-overs and 300 screens of animation.

- *Carmen San Diego—The Series* can be seen on Fox TV on Saturday mornings. Watch for updated versions from Broderbund.

- *Digital Beethoven on Speed* by KAT is billed as the first hyperspeed-metal classical music CD-ROM combined with interactive multimedia, which performer The Great Kat calls "MultiMusic" (KAT's multimedia personified);

- An upcoming interactive music video project on CD-ROM from ION takes us "into" David Bowie's musical world and even has room for product placements.

- *Lawnmower Man* or *Demolition Man* on home video provide a comparison of the "virtual reality" cybersex experiences in both films.

BIOGRAPHY

Joyce A. Schwarz is one of the nation's foremost speakers and consultants on Hollywood and the new media. Her firm, Joyce Communications, is based in Hollywood, California, and she specializes in new product launches and start-up consulting for Hollywood studios, independent production companies, and advertising and public relations agencies.

Joyce, who has been termed a "futurist" by industry leaders, has what she claims is the ultimate multimedia background, including training and high-level experience in publishing, education, advertising, film, television, and new media. She combines her more than two decades of experience in promotion, marketing, advertising, and CEO consulting with her masters degree in cinema from USC's Professional Writing Program. Schwarz is also past president of the USC Cinema/TV Alumni Association.

She is also well respected for her guidance as a career packager. The author of the best-selling book *Successful Recareering: When Just Another Job Is Not Enough* (Career Press, 1993), she has instituted seminars on careers and the future for more than 50 corporations and organizations.

She also hosts and produces her own cable television show called *Turned On Hollywood: Bridging the Gap Between Hollywood and Silicon Valley*. The corecipient of two NEA grants, she has another proposal pending for a project called *Silicon Soul Watch* for her upcoming books on *How to Break into the New Hollywood* and *Hollywood USA: Life Beyond 500 Channels*!

Chapter 4

MULTIMEDIA AND THE PHONE COMPANY
TECHNOLOGY ADVANCEMENTS AND REGULATORY SHIFTS

ROGER L. FETTERMAN
MAST

Technology advancements and regulatory shifts are prompting the development of a robust set of multimedia-based consumer services. At last, the Baby Bells will likely be freed from the tyranny of regulatory and legal restraints that prevented them from entering the entertainment and consumer information services businesses. The question that immediately arises is "What will the smart telephone companies do to ensure success in the emerging multimedia-based services market?"

The shift to digital technologies opens the door to an interactive entertainment and information services universe where consumers will be able to get what they want, when they want it and where they want it. However, the technologies mentioned in Figure 4-1 will be available to all of the players in the long run so it behooves the smart telephone company to acquire all of the resources necessary for success in new entertainment and information services ventures.

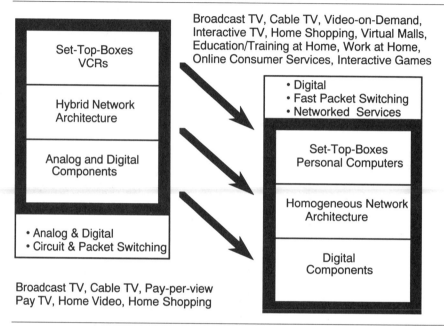

Broadcast TV, Cable TV, Video-on-Demand, Interactive TV, Home Shopping, Virtual Malls, Education/Training at Home, Work at Home, Online Consumer Services, Interactive Games

Set-Top-Boxes
VCRs

Hybrid Network Architecture

Analog and Digital Components

• Analog & Digital
• Circuit & Packet Switching

Broadcast TV, Cable TV, Pay-per-view Pay TV, Home Video, Home Shopping

• Digital
• Fast Packet Switching
• Networked Services

Set-Top-Boxes
Personal Computers

Homogeneous Network Architecture

Digital Components

Figure 4-1   Technology Shifts in the 1990s

Regional Bell Operating Companies (RBOCs) and GTE want access to new revenue streams to offset competition in their traditional businesses and to stimulate growth at a level that will support the capital expenditures needed to deploy the information superhighway. Holding the line won't do it since earnings from Plain Old Telephone Service (POTS) are likely to grow by just 4 to 6 percent a year. Before the RBOCs and GTE can proceed, they need to find new profit centers that will provide double-digit growth.

Telephone companies have the networking expertise but they do not have experience as entertainment programmers/exhibitors or information service providers. Cable operators have the programming/exhibitor expertise but they are not networking or technology gurus. The time for cooperation may be at hand.

American regulatory/legal constraints will likely be relaxed given the push by the White House to establish the information superhighway. Although this may open the floodgates for an array of new services—entertainment-on-demand, interactive TV, interactive home shopping, multimedia-capable information services, etc.—it is important to remember that consumers have demonstrated limited willingness to pay.

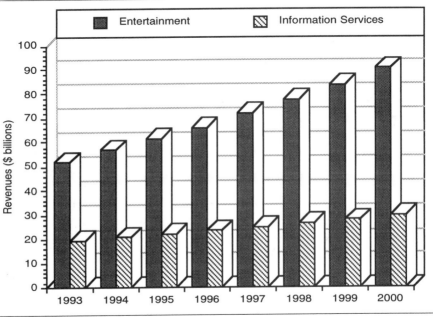

Figure 4-2   US Entertainment/Information Services Revenues
Source: MAST

The entertainment and information services markets are very attractive to the telephone companies. Overall growth is forecast at 8.5 percent compound annual growth rate (CAGR) in the entertainment and 6.6 percent CAGR in the information services and utilities markets over the period 1993 to 2000, as shown in Figure 4-2. Entry into the entertainment market will almost assure the telephone companies of access to advertising revenues. Television advertising pays for half the cost of programs and was more than $30 billion in 1993.

Neither market provides the long-term, double-digit growth that the RBOCs would like to see, but they represent potential new revenue streams. New services will create some growth, but the opportunity for the RBOCs is to provide superior distribution services as carriers, exhibitors, and value-added service providers. As an exhibitor of entertainment services, the RBOCs will need to develop programming skills and acquire programs from Hollywood.

The existing telephone network is not capable of delivering entertainment and information services. The RBOCs and GTE must invest in major network enhancement programs before they can enter these new businesses.

RBOCs Are Upgrading Their Networks

Both the Regional Bell Operating Companies and the larger cable companies are upgrading their networks to support interactive multimedia services. The existing networks are not capable of supporting the enhanced services that both industries plan to offer. Although the starting points are different, the final result will be broadband networks that are capable of supporting point-to-point or pseudo point-to-point services. In the final analysis, the same technologies are available to all parties; the issue is which is capable of planning, deploying, and supporting an array of enhanced services on the information superhighway.

Growth of the telephone industry was based on the fact that shared utilization of network elements allowed telephone companies to build robust networks that were cost effective. Almost every part of the existing public switched network is shared by multiple users. The only exception is the local loop that runs from the central office to the subscriber. Until recently, networking technology did not offer a solution that would transport all traffic types, including video, on a single, shared network.

The RBOCs and the cable companies plan to upgrade their networks to Asynchronous Transfer Mode (ATM) technology. ATM is a switching and multiplexing scheme that supports both continuous and variable bit rate (bursty) services in broadband networks. Thus it is suitable for traditional voice and data traffic and also for image, audio, and video. It is the first technology capable of handling heterogeneous traffic on a single, integrated network.

Originally conceived as the switching technology for the Broadband Integrated Services Digital Network (BISDN) by the telecommunications industry, ATM technology has captured the attention of the data networking, information technology, and cable TV industries. ATM offers the potential to create broadband networks that are independent of services (voice, data, image, and video), rate (1.544, 45, 100, 155, and 622 megabits per second), and transport media (fiber, coaxial cable, twisted pair, satellite, and microwave radio).

ATM DEPLOYMENT COMPANY	SERVICE DATE	LOCATIONS	RATES (MEGABITS PER SECOND)
AT&T	3Q94	300 POPs	1.5 & 45
Ameritech	2Q94	16 cities	45
BellSouth	3Q94	4 cities	45, 155, 622
GTE	1995	CA, HI, NC	45, 100,155
MCI	3Q94	TBD	1.5, 45, 155
NYNEX	3Q94	New York	45, 155
Pacific Bell	1995	4 LATAs	45, 155, 622
Sprint	3Q93	300 POPs	1.5, 45
US West	3Q94	On request	45, 155

Table 4-1   Initial Deployment Plans for ATM Services

ATM will allow the telephone companies to enhance their network to support a full suite of interactive entertainment and consumer information services over existing twisted pair copper plant, fiber to the home, or hybrid fiber/twisted pair or fiber/coax. Further, ATM allows for point-to-point delivery of entertainment, information, and advertising. The initial deployment plans of the RBOCs, GTE, and the major interexchange carriers are shown in Table 4-1. Note that POP stands for point of presence, that is, the demarcation point between local and long-distance service; and LATA is local access transport area, which defines the service boundaries for local telephone companies. Local telephone companies can transport information within a LATA but must rely on long-distance carriers to transport information between LATAs.

The initial deployment plans of several of the carriers are being driven by the data networking requirements of businesses—not by entertainment services. There are no constraints, so the carriers can offer broadband networking capabilities to interconnect Local Area Network (LAN) users on a broad scale. This is important as the investment in the backbone of the ATM network will be justified by both business and consumer revenues.

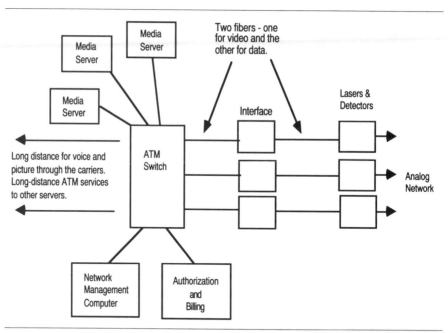

Figure 4-3   Time Warner's Full-Service Network Architecture

In addition, cable operators are planning to use ATM switches to establish full-service networks as shown in Figure 4-3. Existing cable networks cannot support the array of new services that are being planned. Movies and television programs will be stored on media servers that will be local and remote. Servers will store huge amounts of digitized programs as it takes approximately 1 gigabyte to store a full-length feature movie. Some servers will store advertising for insertion at the appropriate point in programs. Others will store videogames, home shopping information, electronic classifieds and yellow pages, and other information. A variety of servers with different capabilities will be needed to store the content that is appropriate to each application.

The telephone companies will use three different cable systems between the central office and the home to deliver entertainment and information services: existing twisted pair copper wire, hybrid fiber/coax, and fiber loops. Since most of the loops from the central office to the homes are twisted pair copper, Bell Atlantic and other telephone companies will use Asymmetric Digital Subscriber Line (ADSL) to upgrade the loops from narrow to wideband capability.

ADSL allows for the simultaneous transmission of compressed video, data, and voice signals over a single copper telephone line. Twisted pair wiring reaches 95 million homes in the United States— 35 million more than are reached by cable TV. When combined with MPEG, the existing plant will allow telephone companies to transmit 6 megabits-per-second video signals to the home with a return path of 384 kilobit per second on the same twisted pair wires. Advances to ADSL will likely allow delivery of 10 megabits per second before the end of the decade.

Given the new regulatory freedoms that are anticipated, the telephone companies expect to be able to justify fiber to the curb and then to the home. As the telephone companies capture a bigger share of the market, they will deploy fiber optics networks. Ultimately, every home will be served by broadband solutions based on fiber or hybrid fiber/coax systems so that bandwidth is no longer limited by copper wiring.

Cable companies intend to deploy hybrid fiber/coax networks with addressable set-top-boxes (STBs), devices that allow them to deliver pseudo point-to-point networks based on ATM, as shown in Figure 4-3. In a point-to-point network, the STBs are addressable by virtue of the network architecture itself. However, in satellite, wireless or cable networks, the boxes must be recognized as unique since the delivery mechanism is fundamentally a broadcast service.

The STB will allow the subscriber to select the desired program from the stream of programs carried on the cable to the subscriber's home. Since the telephone company operates a point-to-point network, only the program selected by the subscriber is delivered from the media server to the home. In the long term, both telephone and cable TV companies have access to the same technology so technology will not determine winners and losers.

The architecture proposed by Time Warner is supported by US West. It allows US West to continue to provide telephone services over the existing telephone network. In those areas where Time Warner has no cable plants, US West could use Fiber-in-the-Loop and copper cable to deliver three or four video signals to the home using ADSL technology.

In its own territory, it is important that US West be able to roll out the service quickly to attract subscribers and hence advertisers. Thus a fiber/copper solution may be very attractive in US West territory.

Pacific Bell plans to deploy the hybrid star/bus technology being used by Time Warner. It plans to replace its existing copper phone lines with a new system that looks exactly like those to be implemented by the cable operators. The projected costs of the hybrid fiber/coax network come to about $900 per household, which is some $200 or more below the costs anticipated for other approaches.

It is likely that telephone companies will use more than one network upgrade scheme to satisfy the requirements of entertainment services. If a telephone company buys a cable company, the hybrid fiber/coax scheme has great merit since much of the existing coaxial cable could be reused. If cable service does not exist in a given area, it may be better to use the existing copper plant and ADSL. In either case, network upgrades are mandatory.

Innovation is key to success, but it has less to do with product design and more to do with managing relationships with customers, suppliers, strategic partners, and even competitors. The winners will be those who assemble the right mix of technology and relationships to successfully manage and operate businesses that deliver enhanced services to the home.

The burgeoning interest in multimedia-based information and entertainment services will create demand for a new type of server—the media server. The market potential has attracted a number of potential media server vendors, as shown in Table 4-2. There will be a variety of servers with different characteristics—features and functions appropriate to the service in question.

For example, a server for Video-on-Demand (VOD) must have large storage capacity and support multiple simultaneous accesses to an individual movie at different points in the movie. This will enable many different subscribers to view the same movie—all of whom requested the movie at a different time. In addition, the media server must work in concert with the STB to provide VCR-like control to the viewer. Viewers will want to be able to pause, rewind, fast forward, and stop the program.

A server for home shopping must be transaction intensive and could be linked to a video server if video clips are used in the selling process. A video mall shopper may browse through several stores and request a closer look at a particular item. A video clip showing the item "in action" could be played for the potential buyer. The services offered must be able to work with a variety of STBs.

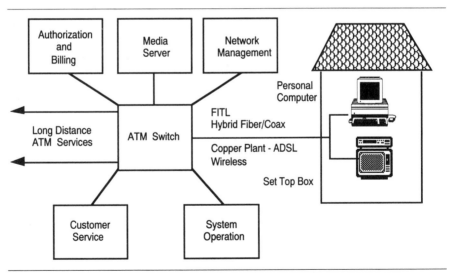

Figure 4-4   Media Server System Components

Each company is developing its own strategy for the video server market. AT&T and DEC are pushing end-to-end solutions, not just one piece of the puzzle. Figure 4-4 shows all of the elements of a media server system. Such systems will allow the exhibitor to deliver local and remote programming to the subscriber, handle all of the network management and control requirements, and provide authorization and billing. The solutions proposed by Microsoft and SGI rely on relatively inexpensive general-purpose computers optimized for the video market.

Hewlett-Packard's system is very different from that of Microsoft or SGI. HP is not trying to scale up the general-purpose computer but is developing an architecture from the ground up that is based on video services. One component—a "smart" disk farm with extremely high-speed interconnect—will be driven by HP's new Video Server. Robert Frankenberg, HP's general manager of the Personal Information Products group, is on record as saying that the interactive TV video server business will be a $20 billion opportunity by the end of the decade.

MEDIA SERVER SUPPLIERS

Amdahl	Kodak	Pyramid
AT&T/NCR	Microsoft	Sequent
Convex	NEC	Sybase
Digital Equipment Corp.	Northern Telecom	Sun Microsystems
Encore	On Command Video	Tamarack
Hewlett-Packard	On Demand Video	Tandem
Hitachi	Oracle	Whittaker

Table 4-2   Potential Media Server Suppliers

The set-top-box has become the subject of intense cross-industry interest as interactive television moves closer to reality. With improved video and graphics capabilities and added intelligence, it is likely to serve as the technology gateway to new entertainment, information, and shopping services delivered to the home. STBs will house graphics chips, digital and analog tuners, compression/ decompression algorithms, and a user interface stored in read-only memory (ROM). Standards are key to widespread implementation and multiple price/performance products.

TCI's (Tele-Communications Inc.) planned purchase of a million new television set-top converters was delayed by nearly a year because of the lack of industry technical standards governing their operation. Earlier this year, Time Warner delayed the start of the Orlando trial and said that additional time was needed for refinements of the underlying system software and the set-top terminal. It is evident that it will take some time to integrate and test enhanced networks, particularly because the standards are not available for any of the elements of the system.

The Video Electronics Standards Association's (VESA) Open Set Top standards special interest group met for the first time on March 18, 1994, in Santa Clara, California. Over 60 companies assembled to address the growing need for standards for digital interactive STBs, including participants from Apple, AT&T, Bell Atlantic, Brooktree, Cirrus Logic, Compaq, Divicom, General Instruments, Goldstar, Hewlett-Packard, IBM, Kaleida, MainStream Control, Media Vision, Microsoft, Motorola, National Semiconductor, Novell, NYNEX Oracle, Philips, Raytheon, SGS-Thomson, Southwestern Bell, 3DO, US West, and Viacom.

The digital interactive STBs represent an ambitious electronics design effort. The standards set by VESA will determine the path for home entertainment capabilities for at least a decade. Personal computers will likely be used for services that are highly interactive. The cost-effectiveness of the PC doubles every 18 months. PC buyers are used to paying $1,500 for the machine and $1,500 for software and peripherals. PCs don't face the restriction of the $200 or $300 price point that has been set for STBs.

3DO	Intel/Microsoft/General Instruments
Apple Computer	Motorola
General Instruments	Scientific-Atlanta
Hewlett-Packard	Silicon Graphics
IBM/Thomson Consumer Electronics	

Table 4-3   Set-Top-Box Suppliers

It may be impossible for the vendors to deliver a set-top-box with appropriate capabilities for less than $500 to $700 unless the network itself contains a good deal of the required intelligence. This has led to the notion of the set-back device, which is a simple device that relies on shared intelligence in the network.

The vendors and consortia shown in Table 4-3 have entered the set-top-box marketplace and there will be more to follow.

The set-top-box has been elevated from its former lowly position to that of the gateway to an array of enhanced services that will be provided by entertainment exhibitors, information service providers, and transactional service providers. There are few of the new breed of STBs in the field at this time.

CABLE TV ACT CHALLENGES

The RBOCs are challenging the Cable TV Act of 1984 to obtain the right to offer multimedia-based services in their operating territories. The RBOCs claim that the Cable Act of 1984 violates their rights under the First and Fifth Amendments to the Constitution. The act prohibits phone companies from competing directly with cable firms.

1984 CABLE ACT COMPANY	FILING DATE	RULING
Bell Atlantic	December 1992	August 1993
Ameritech	November 1993	Pending
Nynex	November 1993	Pending
Pacific Bell	November 1993	Pending
BellSouth	December 1993	Pending
SWBT	February 1994	Pending

Table 4-4   Cable Act Challenges by RBOCs

The ban was passed to prevent phone companies from using profits obtained from their public monopolies to outflank competitors who had no access to such capital. Bell Atlantic and other RBOCs have filed suit in US district courts, claiming that the prohibition violates their rights to free speech and right to control their own property. Refer to Table 4-4 for details.

The Cable Act is being challenged because "video programming is a form of speech protected by the First Amendment of the United States Constitution, and the Cable Act ban on video programming in a telephone company's service area violates the telephone company's right to use its facilities to communicate."

Although such challenges may be successful, they only allow the RBOCs to offer services in the area under the jurisdiction of the specific district court. For example, the United States District Court in Alexandria, Virginia declared unconstitutional a provision of the 1984 Cable Act that blocked Bell Atlantic from providing cable television in the same areas where it provides telephone service. Bell Atlantic Video Services can now offer entertainment services to the 60,000 residents of Alexandria.

It is expected that Congress will pass a bill that allows telephone and cable companies to enter one another's businesses in 1994. Until the new bill is passed, the telephone companies will be forced to challenge the Cable Act in individual district courts so they can compete with cable TV companies in their operating territories. The Cable Act stifles competition and discourages the telephone companies from investing in their own operating territories.

It is likely that the long-favored bans against cross-ownership in the cable and phone businesses will be rescinded. Representative Edward Markey (D-Mass.), who heads the House telecommunications panel, thinks that Congress will pass legislation in 1994 allowing the two industries to enter each other's markets. Markey has already said publicly that such bans are no longer practical, given the new competitive landscape for both industries.

Transport-Only Revenue Is Not Significant

Although the transport of video under the video dialtone ruling from the FCC seems to be consistent with the traditional role of the telephone companies, it does not represent a significant new revenue stream. The much-touted information highway is likely to make bandwidth a commodity compared to the current tariffed services. There are several alternative pathways into the home:

- Telephone network;

- Over the air television;

- Cable television;

- Direct broadcast satellite;

- Cellular/wireless; and

- Radio or Multipoint Microwave Distribution Service (MMDS).

The new services may support multiple delivery mechanisms in a densely populated area such as New York, but how many of these pathways can be justified in a sparsely populated area? Each pathway must be supported by a costly infrastructure.

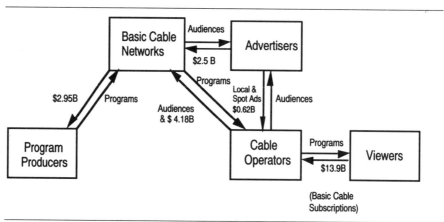

Figure 4-5   Basic Cable TV Value Chain
Source: MAST

At the very best, transport charges for video are only a portion of the cable operator revenues shown in Figure 4-5. The bulk of the revenue would continue to go to the cable operator or programmer. Cable TV, satellite, and telephone companies all have an opportunity to deliver bandwidth to the home. Unless there is some other way to distinguish their service offering, telephone companies would be forced to compete on price alone.

In general, both ends of the value chain are fixed: program producers refuse to accept less for their programs, and viewers will not pay more for entertainment services. Thus all of the "push and pull" occurs in the middle. As exhibitors, the cable operators will select the lowest-cost transport service that is available so they can maximize their earnings.

Attractive New Revenues

As an owner and/or operator of entertainment and information services businesses, the telephone company can hope to generate significant new revenue streams based on direct consumer and advertising revenues. According to Veronis, Suhler & Associates, direct consumer revenues on video entertainment will grow from $33 billion in 1993 to $58 billion in 2000, as shown in Figure 4-6. Over the same period, advertising will grow from $30 billion to $51 billion.

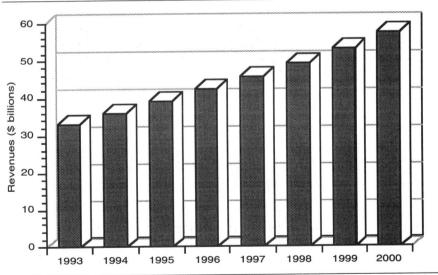

Figure 4-6   Video Entertainment Revenue Forecast

Source: Veronis, Suhler & Associates

Video entertainment includes basic cable, pay TV, pay-per-view, and home video—all of which could be displaced in whole or in part by telephone company services. Even though Video-on-Demand revenues will grow to $7.6 billion by 2000, as shown in Figure 4-7, they only represent 13 percent of the total revenues forecast for video entertainment. Although Video-on-Demand is often referred to as a major new opportunity, it is clear that consumer behavior needs to shift before this becomes true.

Early market research based on focus groups and surveys suggests that the demand for Near-Video-on-Demand will be twice that of pay-per-view, that frequent users will make five buys per month rather than one, and that they will spend $5.45 per month instead of $1.00. VOD is expected to be even more attractive. However, the researchers agree that the results of focus groups and surveys should not be used for business planning purposes.

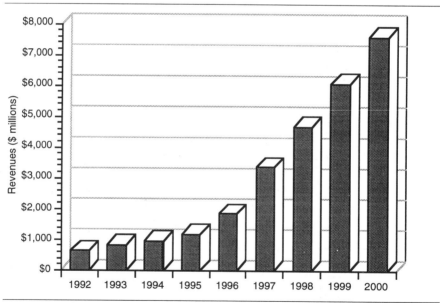

Figure 4-7   Video-on-Demand Revenue Forecast

Source: Wasserstein Perella Securities, Inc. & Granchester Securities

The point-to-point nature of the public network ensures that advertising can be delivered to an individual home in the same way as programming. Point-to-point delivery may prove highly attractive to the advertising industry at a time when audiences are being fragmented by an abundance of programming. Broadcast television cannot guarantee that the target audience is being reached since the measures are not precise. Advertisers could be assured that they are reaching targeted households regardless of the programs that are being watched.

Competition Is Increasing

Telephone companies are already sensitive to the growing competition from competitive access providers, value-added networks and others. Even the last mile (i.e., the telephone cable to the individual homes) is open to competitors. Cable TV companies such as Time Warner have announced their intent to operate full-service networks that would offer POTS, data services, and cellular in addition to entertainment and information services. MCI is working with Jones Intercable on two trials linking phone and cable service on Jones' cable systems. If the trials demonstrate feasibility, MCI will be in a position to bypass the local telephone company's facilities by cooperating with cable TV companies.

Entry Barriers Are Decreasing

The availability of standards-based technologies such as asynchronous transfer mode (ATM) opens the door to new entrants in the services arena. Entry barriers to traditional telephone company services are being lowered, so more competitors can be expected in the future. New entrants can target the high-margin business opportunities and leave the low-margin business to the telephone company.

Current market forces dictate that telephone companies pursue value-added services in addition to traditional service offerings. The technology driver for telephone company service to the home is no longer voice. The new enhanced services will be based on data and video networking, interactive computer service, and interactive entertainment technologies that are the domains of a number of different service providers.

COOPERATION AND COMPETITION

Cable TV and telephone companies are cooperating with each other to develop entertainment-on-demand, interactive TV, and other services. Although the two industries have been positioned as antagonists, they have complementary strengths for building "full-service networks." Both industries have enjoyed de facto and de jure monopolies in the past. The new regulatory freedoms will likely create a competitive landscape for all types of services.

Members of the rough-and-tumble cable TV industry view growth as a company's principal mission, and disdain traditional corporate goals such as reporting earnings and paying dividends as distractions that siphon off money that might otherwise be plowed back into building or acquiring new properties. This is in sharp contrast to the views held by telephone company executives.

Mergers and Alliances

The much-heralded merger between Bell Atlantic and Tele-Communications, Inc. (TCI) collapsed. Although it was noted that "the unsettled regulatory climate made it too difficult for the parties to value the future," the failure was simply because the parties could not come to terms. TCI wanted too much money and Bell Atlantic was not willing to provide it. In spite of all of the fine words about cooperation, it is evident that synergy between the cable companies and the telephone companies is only available for a very high price.

TELCO/CABLE TV ALLIANCES PARTNERS	VALUE	STATUS
Bell Atlantic/TCI	More than $16 billion	Collapsed
SWBT/Cox	$4.9 billion	Collapsed
Jones/BCE Int'l	$400 million	Renegotiated
QVC/BellSouth	$500 million	Being renegotiated
Time Warner/US West	$2.5 billion	Active

Table 4-5   Status of Telco/Cable TV Alliances

Table 4-5 indicates that all of the alliances except for Time Warner/US West are being reexamined or terminated.

Cable TV companies are programmers and not networking technology gurus. Telephone companies have no entertainment programming experience but are steeped in networking technology. Although current regulatory constraints make it difficult to cooperate on a broad scale in the telephone companies' operating territories, telephone companies are working with cable companies and others on a number of fronts, as shown in Table 4-6.

Table 4-6 does not include all of the existing alliances, but it demonstrates the types of services that are being planned. It also indicates that not all of the RBOCs are as enthusiastic about the opportunity as are Bell Atlantic and US West.

Pacific Bell has taken a slightly different tack than other telephone companies. In November 1993, Pacific Bell announced that it will spend $16 billion over the next seven years to accelerate development of the information superhighway in California. It plans to install hybrid fiber/coax networks to serve 5.5 million Californian households by the year 2000. Pacific Telesis Group, the parent of Pacific Bell, explored alliances with cable companies but decided to go ahead on its own.

The announcement represents one of the biggest commitments by any of the regional telecommunications companies to deploying fiber optics and advanced switching equipment to build a network that will deliver television and high-speed data services to consumers.

The broadband network will allow Pacific Bell to compete directly with cable TV operators in their operating territory. Like all of the other Baby Bells, it must get relief from the restrictions of the Cable Act of 1984. Pacific Bell believes that it can become a quality programmer and exhibitor and lure business away from cable TV. Pacific Bell consumer research indicates that approximately 30 percent of existing cable users would sooner buy service from the telephone company than a cable TV company if it were the same price.

PARTNERS	SERVICES/TRIALS
Ameritech / Booth Comm.	Electronic shopping service
Ameritech / IT Network	Electronic yellow pages
AT&T / Paramount	Interactive TV programming
Bell Atlantic/Cellularvision	Wireless cable services
Bell Atlantic/Fourth Comm. Net	Interactive multimedia Yellow pages Directory services
Bell Atlantic / Knight-Ridder	Interactive news, information, and advertising
Bell Atlantic / Oracle Corp.	Entertainment-on-Demand and home shopping
BellSouth / AT&T / Viacom	Video-on-Demand
BellSouth / Dow Jones	Information services and interactive advertising
BellSouth/Prime Management Co.	Interactive TV
GTE / Apollo Cable Vision & Continental Cable & Daniels Cablevision	GTE Main Street— interactive video and services
GTE/ AT&T	Video dialtone
GTE/Philips Interactive Media	Interactive TV
Nynex / Liberty Cable TV	Video dialtone
Southwestern Bell/Cox Enterprises	Electronic information services Classifieds and yellow pages
US West / AT&T / TCI	Interactive TV
US West / Time Warner	Full-Service Networks

Table 4-6   Telco and Cable TV Cooperative Efforts

Entertainment Pilots and Trials

There are a number of cable TV company pilots and trials in the areas of home shopping, consumer information services, data networking services, interactive games, videogames, and POTS.

Pacific Telesis and AT&T

Pacific Telesis Video Services (PTVS) and AT&T announced an advanced interactive television services trial in January 1994 that will let participants influence what will be on California's communications superhighway. Trial customers in Milpitas will be able to choose from a library of movies and TV programs to watch at their convenience.

Milpitas was selected as the market trial site because of its cultural and economic diversity. Approximately 1,000 residents will participate in the first phase of the trial, which will last from 12 to 18 months. PTVS and AT&T expect to learn about consumer preferences for services and the look and feel of interactive TV. They want to understand how entertainment, games, information, and education services are received in the marketplace when choice and control are available to the consumer.

US West, TCI, and AT&T

US West Inc., TCI, and AT&T extended their trial of Video-on-Demand and pay-per-view services until June 30, 1994. The companies began the trial, dubbed Viewer-Controlled Cable Television, in 300 suburban Denver homes in 1992 to measure customer acceptance and use of services expected to be available with the creation of the information superhighway.

The companies are offering pay-per-view services that will allow subscribers to take a break from a movie and to pick it up 15 minutes later on a different channel. They also said that 75 more movie titles will be offered through the Video-on-Demand service. In November 1993, the companies reported that usage of both VOD and pay-per-view services during the first phase of the trial was 12 times greater than the national pay-per-view buy rate.

Viacom and AT&T

Viacom International Inc. and AT&T are conducting a major market test of interactive television in a Northern California suburb. Customers participating in the 18-month test will be able to select a movie from scores of titles and to start watching within one second of placing the order. They will also be able to stop, pause, rewind and fast-forward a program. Customers will also be able to browse through retail catalogues and order products by using remote control devices and play full-motion videogames with household members or other customers.

The test is scheduled to begin by the second quarter of next year in the Castro Valley, located about 20 miles east of San Francisco. It will involve at least 1,000 homes and may be expanded to 4,000 homes.

AT&T has developed a system for dial-up, viewer-controlled video entertainment and information that works on cable television networks, built with a combination of fiber and coaxial cables, and the Baby Bell telephone network, which relies on fiber and copper wire to deliver signals.

Bell Atlantic

In March 1994, Bell Atlantic completed the first year of a technical trial of on-demand video programming in Northern Virginia. The company tested all of the technologies—transmission, switching, video file server and digital compression—that are needed for on-demand delivery of entertainment and information. Trial participants have been able to order movies that are delivered over their telephone line to their TV set in a few moments. The next stage in Bell Atlantic's product development process is to test-market Stargazer on-demand programming. This test will pave the way for the commercial introduction of Stargazer services in the Washington, D.C., area in 1995.

Bell Atlantic plans to serve 1.25 million homes by the end of 1995 and add 1.5 million lines each year up to the year 2000. Services will reach 8.75 million homes. The company will spend $10 billion to $11 billion over the next five years in its home region.

Bell Atlantic will deploy a fully digital system with the capacity, for example, to deliver four digitized movies or television shows and a videoconferencing call to an individual home.

Time Warner

The most significant trial is being conducted by Time Warner in Orlando, Florida, along with multiple partners as shown in Table 4-7. The Full-Service Network will include Video-on-Demand, interactive games, full-motion video shopping, educational programs, and telephone service, to name a few.

ORLANDO	
Time Warner	Video-on-Demand Interactive news Interactive advertising
QUALCOMM	Personal communications service
US Post Office	Postal services
Sega of America	Videogames
CUC International	Home shopping
Spiegel	Video mall
ShopperVision	3-D graphic drugstore
Hewlett-Packard	Literature fulfillment

Table 4-7   Time Warner's Full-Service Network

Silicon Graphics, Inc. (SGI) and Time Warner Cable are developing technology based on the MIPS® microprocessor architecture. The MIPS RISC architecture, developed for the next generation of personal and portable computers, will be used in the home entertainment market. Time Warner is providing research and development funds to enable SGI to apply its digital multimedia and graphics technologies to home markets. SGI's video servers are being used to deliver multimedia programming, and Silicon Graphics will develop a digital set-top device.

It is remarkable that so many companies that are new to the entertainment and consumer information services markets have decided to join the incumbents. Many of the industries face a common, serious problem: rapidly saturating markets for core products and services. They need to create more demand for increasingly full-featured products and services. All of them hope that the market will be large enough to provide new revenue streams.

SUCCESS FOR THE RBOCs

Consumers have demonstrated limited willingness to pay for entertainment so the immediate prospects are for a displacement market with some new growth from new services. Table 4-8 forecasts the growth in consumer spending in relevant areas for the period from 1993 to 1997. History has demonstrated that consumers do not have greater disposable income so new services must be competitive with old services if they are to be successful.

	1993	1997	COMPOUND ANNUAL GROWTH RATE
Cable television	$101	$125	8.2%
Filmed entertainment	$26	$32	6.8%
Home video	$69	$90	7.5%
Recorded music	$41	$48	4.3%
Daily newspapers	$53	$64	4.5%
Consumer books	$77	$94	6.7%
Consumer magazines	$37	$46	5.8%
Total expenditure in dollars	$404	$520	7.1%

Table 4-8   Consumer Expenditures per Person per Year
Source: MAST

From the outset, it will be a displacement market for the telephone companies. New services such as Video-on-Demand must take revenue from cable TV, pay-per-view, home video, and other services if they are going to be successful. Telephone companies will be the second exhibitor in most parts of their territory and the third in others.

Hollywood Meets the Baby Bells

In March 1994, Bell Atlantic announced that it will open a Digital Production Center in Reston, Virginia to support Stargazer interactive video programming. This is the first time that an RBOC has assembled all the elements needed to produce interactive multimedia television services.

Interactive multimedia services will be created and packaged for delivery to consumers. First-generation services will include movies, television programs, documentaries, and video health care information, all delivered on demand.

The Digital Production Center will house a:

- Digital production studio to create the packaging and promotional elements of Stargazer programming and develop new Stargazer interactive products, services, and applications;

- Digital service bureau to digitize and compress analog videotapes and films for storage on and delivery from computers to consumers' homes;

- Operations center to house video servers and databases, with sufficient backup power and communications to support commercial deployment; and

- Demonstration center, where programming can be tested and reviewed by clients and customers.

Quality programming is the most critical element in the success of any exhibitor. Without good programming, a new exhibitor will find it difficult to attract subscribers. The RBOCs must gain access to skilled programming resources by luring individuals away from the entertainment business, partnering with cable TV or other exhibitors or acquiring companies. Other telephone companies may follow the lead of Bell Atlantic to ensure that they have the facilities and human resources needed to acquire, package, and deliver programming as an exhibitor. The telephone companies' programming offerings must be as good as or better than those on cable.

If the telephone company is to be successful in acquiring quality programming, it must demonstrate that it can deliver a large audience to the program producer or rights holder. Exhibitors that cannot deliver large audiences will be in an inferior bargaining position when trying to acquire programming. Thus companies that are able to roll out the required network upgrades rapidly will be more attractive to producers or rights holders.

Advertisers will likely be interested in the point-to-point delivery capability of the public switched network. The winning formula is the same as for programming. The ability to deliver a large audience is very important to the advertiser. As the "new kids on the block," RBOCs will need both advertising and direct consumer revenues. Failure on either count—quality programming or advertising—may put newcomers to the entertainment business in a loss leader position for an extended period. Such a position will be highly unattractive to rate payers.

Bell Atlantic market studies indicate that there is latent consumer demand for an alternative to cable television and that the video services it will provide could capture half the market where it competes with cable. Pacific Bell research indicates similar interest in their video services in the California market. In addition, Bell Atlantic and Pacific Bell feel that there is a tremendous backlog of customers who are looking for competing entertainment services, and the first 15 or 20 percent will move to telephone companies' entertainment services very easy and very quickly.

Although consumer expenditures rise when new services are introduced, overall growth has been remarkably consistent over the past decade. Consumers continue to demonstrate that they are unwilling to pay more. Will addressable households that are spending $40–50 per month really be willing to spend more? Historically, the amount spent on individual services has changed, but the overall amount has been relatively stable.

It is hoped that infotainment in the form of home instruction/education or electronic classifieds or interactive home shopping will create a dislocation that results in a change in consumer behavior. To date, there has been no conclusive evidence gathered to tell us what consumers will be willing to pay for these new services. Undoubtedly, many of the new services will succeed, but will they grow quickly enough to sustain the interest of all of the new entrants in the entertainment and on-line consumer information markets? That is the question!

BIOGRAPHY

Roger L. Fetterman is founder and principal consultant of MAST, a creative marketing practice that provides consulting services to high technology companies. He works with client management teams on the creation and development of markets, the implementation and management of strategic alliances, product positioning to achieve competitive advantage, and business planning activities.

MAST has developed a position in the consulting community based on a strong foundation of knowledge about the multimedia market and its interrelation with the telecommunications industry.

MAST takes advantage of skills and knowledge gained through positions in sales and marketing management in high technology companies over a 25-year period to assist clients in multimedia and networking environments. MAST uses sales, marketing, and product management skills to develop new product concepts, define new markets, and to evaluate cost/value attributes for product applications.

Mr. Fetterman is co-author of a book entitled *Maintstream Multimedia: Applying Multimedia in Business* that was published by Van Nostrand Reinhold in August 1993. The book addresses both the business and technology aspects of this growing field. *Mainstream Multimedia* examines and compares multimedia platforms, applications, and markets. It explains how businesses can uses multimedia systems to improve their efficiency.

He is affiliated with ryan•hankin•kent, inc., a technology research and consulting corporation that focuses on telecommunications, video and cable, and computers and data networks. MAST is located at 2245 Laurelei Avenue, San Jose, CA 95128-1439. ryan•hankin•kent is located at 601 Gateway Blvd., Suite 550, South San Francisco, CA 94080.

Chapter 5

Broadcasting in the Information Age

Robert Yadon
Ball State University

Evolution of Broadcasting

In the rush to the digital altar, many in the broadcasting business are coming to view the convergence of computer technology with audio and video technology as a suitable match. The multimedia movement already affects the generation, storage, and transmission of information internal and external to most stations. However, few remember or recognize broadcasting's historic and economic dependency upon another phenomenon—wired and wireless communication services. It is the growing importance of this mode of delivery that causes the greatest concern in broadcast markets from coast to coast. Ultimately, the question is, what role will broadcasting play in the developing information age?

Broadcasting has come a long way since its formal organization and regulation under the Radio Act of 1927. Under the guidance of the Federal Radio Commission, radio was to experience tremendous growth during the Depression years. The early growth of broadcasting was dependent upon telephone lines to interconnect multiple stations from coast to coast to emerging radio networks.

Wide variations in both quality and cost of telephone service from state to state required a national response if broadcasting was to continue to develop. Thus, it was the wired medium of telephony that forced the government to examine telecommunication policy and, ultimately, adopt a more comprehensive regulation of both wired and wireless communication by passing the Communications Act of 1934.

This dependency on wired and later wireless networks continued with the advent of television in the 1940s. From long line telephone service, microwave links, to eventual satellite and fiber optic transport, the growth and success of television was directly related to the level of technology developed and deployed by AT&T in the transport of network television signals to local affiliates. As television developed, available technology and economies of scale dictated that one-way, over-the-air broadcasting was the most efficient system for local stations to deliver individual television signals to TV households, market by market, from coast to coast.

Where television broadcasting emerged as a predominately local service in the 1950s, today the bulk of each broadcast day is comprised of network feeds, off network and syndicated programming. Reduced to the lowest common denominator, the local station acts as a transport between the program supplier (local, network, syndicator, etc.) and the viewing public.

Another way to envision the process is to consider the broadcaster as a gateway between information providers offering various forms of programming software (news, public affairs, sports, entertainment, etc.) and the television viewer. Success is measured in gaining access to, and being able to attract, more viewers with programming than the competition. The reward for performing this service is the money extracted from advertisers for offering exposure to these viewers through insertion of their commercials within and around that programming. The more popular your program, the greater value it has to potential advertisers.

The success of any delivery system is generally measured against its ability to generate an adequate return on investment. Television is no exception. As indicated, success for television is dependent on the number of viewers it can attract and, in turn, sell to advertisers.

During the early years, economics dictated that only a consortium of stations (network) could afford the expense of producing original, quality programming for one-way, mass distribution. A network affiliate's programming didn't have to be great, only better than the limited alternatives. In this economic environment, with minimal competition, television broadcasting evolved into an efficient, albeit protected, method of mass communication.

The potential for competition always includes a large dose of uncertainty. What is cautiously viewed by broadcasters today as a multimedia "revolution" should more accurately be embraced as a natural "evolution" in the deployment of audio and video news, information, and entertainment programming to the public. How broadcasters strategically plan, protect, implement, and defend their place in the new competitive environment will dictate their level of success. The superhighway road map isn't finished and the waters are still uncharted, yet ignoring the upcoming journey reduces one to the status of bystander, at best.

CRITICAL FACTORS

Cable Television

There are numerous challenges ahead for broadcasters, not the least of which continues to be cable television. Starting in the late 1940s, community antenna television (CATV) has evolved into a highly competitive means of delivering multiple channels of audio and video into American households. As a competitive, multichannel delivery technology that immediately fractionalizes the television audience base, cable has come into its own over the last decade to impact broadcasting in audience share and, in turn, revenues. By

1991, cable television penetration reached 60 percent of all television households, and by 1994 cable passed by 97 percent of all TV households.

This trend has not gone unnoticed by network executives at Capacities/ABC and NBC, who have started to invest in cable programming. In 1993, estimated profits from majority-owned cable networks such as ESPN and CNBC nearly equaled those from their broadcast network counterparts.

Clearly, cable will slowly continue to erode broadcasting's audience share and revenue stream into the next millennium. The math is simple. Broadcast stations deliver a single, local television signal to the household, while cable television can provide 50, 80, 100 or more channels to that same residence.

YEAR (OCT.–SEPT.)	TOTAL TV HOMES (1000s)	CABLE HH PENETRATION (%)	CABLE SUBSCRIBERS (1000s)	HOMES PASSED (1000s)
1992/93	93,192	65.7	61,244	90,375
1991/92	92,183	64.8	59,776	89,025
1990/91	93,017	62.9	58,542	87,425
1989/90	92,183	60.6	55,895	84,575
1988/89	90,542	57.5	52,089	79,425
1987/88	88,750	54.3	48,187	76,325
1986/87	87,500	50.4	44,114	73,175
1985/86	86,025	48.5	41,703	66,875
1984/85	85,993	48.9	41,522	62,725

Table 5-1   Growth of Cable Television

Source: A.C. Nielsen Co. and Paul Kagan Associates, Inc.

While demand for first-run network programming remains high, the oligopoly advantage that served television broadcasters so well throughout the 1950s and 1960s has slowly diminished. No longer are viewers presented with only three choices (ABC, NBC, and CBS). Indeed, cable television presents a varied programming lineup that approximates the multitude of format choices available on radio. There are different programs for different tastes, all available 24 hours a day. From weather to news, from science fiction to sports, the cable lineup provides a smorgasbord of viewing options.

The future impact of cable is more profound when you factor the introduction of digital compression and interactivity into the equation. Broadcasters are already familiar with digital compression. It's not uncommon today for a standard analog broadcast television signal, occupying 6 megahertz of analog channel bandwidth, to be digitized into 90 million bits of data per second (90 megabits per second), compressed at a 2-to-1 ratio, and the resultant 45 megabits per second data stream sent over a DS-3 telephone circuit (i.e., equivalent to 672 separate voice circuits) without any degradation in signal quality.

The most common form of video compression is known as MPEG, named after the Motion Picture Experts Group, a standards-setting body responsible for setting the criteria for compression of moving video and audio. The first standard, MPEG-1, approved in 1992, offers VHS-quality compressed video at 1.5 megabits per second or a compression ratio of 60-to-1.

Another standard from this group, MPEG-2, specifically provides for the compression of broadcast video at 3 megabits per second to 5 megabits per second, with no noticeable loss in signal quality, up to 15 megabits per second for high-definition television. The MPEG-2 standard is scheduled for final approval by summer 1995. Even competing compression technologies, such as General Instrument's proprietary DigiCipher-2 will comply with the MPEG-2 standard. Both compression systems are based on discrete cosine transform technology.

By employing compression, cable television systems now providing 80 channels of service may theoretically be able to carry up to 500 channels of programming to the household. It does little good to argue that there is no demand for such a massive lineup today or that the finite limitations of MPEG-2 compression are substantially less than 500 channels. The fact remains there will be a significant increase in bandwidth within cable to handle future demand for video and new, ancillary services for the foreseeable future.

The primary reason for cable's increased bandwidth capacity is the rapid deployment of fiber optics within the industry. In a two-step process, the cable industry is converting trunk lines from coaxial cable to optical fiber. In the first phase, fiber is run to neighborhood nodes serving between 1,500 to 2,000 subscribers at a cost of about $50 per household. In the second phase, the fiber will be extended to nodes serving 200 to 500 homes, thereby bringing the increased bandwidth capability of fiber much closer to the end user.

It has been estimated that the cost of converting the entire physical coaxial cable television plant in the United States in this manner will run approximately $20 billion. Compare this with estimates running as high as $100 billion to accomplish a similar rebuild of the telephone system.

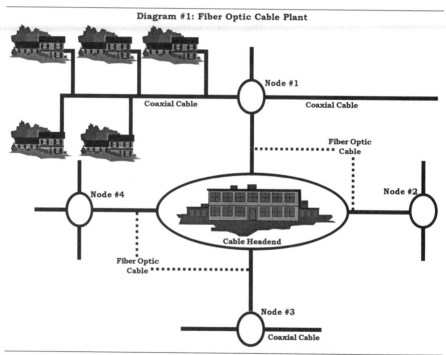

Figure 5-1   Fiber Optic Cable Plant

Local advertisers have also found cable to be an attractive, inexpensive alternative to over-the-air, broadcast television. With numerous advertising availabilities, commercial spots, in most satellite-delivered cable programs, the cable industry is quickly learning how to sell cable television advertising time at near radio rates. And as with radio, advertisers can target their spots to specific demographics on a channel-by-channel basis.

One might argue that cable's impact on broadcast television commercial spot revenues is minimal since the majority of these new cable advertisers aren't being drawn directly from broadcast television's inventory. That may be true in 1994, but the efficiency of cable advertising is just beginning to be universally recognized and tested. Where broadcast revenues are holding their own or at best showing a modest increase, cable advertising is growing annually in revenues and acceptance. National advertisers are finding that satellite cable networks such as ESPN, USA, and Nickelodeon are excellent places to target audiences across varied demographics. There is little doubt that this trend will continue.

YEAR	LOCAL/SPOT CABLE	REGIONAL SPORTS/NEWS	NETWORK CABLE	TOTAL $ MILLIONS
1986	$195	$22	$748	$965
1987	$268	$33	$891	$1,192
1988	$374	$52	$1,135	$1,561
1989	$496	$74	$1,461	$2,031
1990	$634	$103	$2,046	$2,874
1991	$710	$118	$2,046	$2,874
1992	$872	$141	$2,339	$3,352
1993	$1,064	$162	$2,669	$3,895
1994	$1,256	$185	$2,990	$4,431
2000	$2,589	$345	$5,649	$8,583

Table 5-2   Cable Advertising Revenues

Source: Paul Kagan Associates, Inc.

As mentioned, traditional broadcast television has evolved as a one-way, passive service where viewers are generally restricted to watching what is available at the current time. Since 1972, those with a modest technical background have been able to use their VCRs, when properly programmed, to "time shift" viewing. Little did the consumer realize that this represented the first experience in downloading (transfer) of software (video) onto a storage medium (videotape) for later retrieval. The popularity of this singular attachment to the television set spawned the birth of the movie rental industry and provided consumers with the ability to buy or rent prerecorded video programming to be watched, uninterrupted by commercials, in the privacy of the home. No longer was America constrained by the linear offerings of cable and terrestrial broadcasting. Finally, the consumer was gaining a modest level of control over the medium.

Looking forward, we are now introduced to the prospect of interactive television where the viewer calls up a program of interest, on demand, then becomes an active participant for that program. The level of interactivity might be limited to a request for additional information on a product or service displayed within a program or commercial, all the way to full, real-time participation in opinion polls or a televised game show against other remote contestants.

Regardless of the level of interactivity, most proposals, whether coupled with broadcast television or cable television, involve the use of a wired network to handle the return data stream from the subscriber. For example, GTE Main Street is delivered to subscribers via cable, and users respond by keypad through a black box connected between the television set and the telephone line. Viewer Controlled TV is another Video-on-Demand system via cable, jointly developed by US West; TCI, the largest cable operator in the United States; and AT&T.

Two exceptions are TVAnswer and Interactive Network, the first two systems to utilize radio spectrum for interactive television. While Interactive Network relies on unused portions of the FM radio band to communicate with subscribers, TVAnswer takes a different, unique approach. With the TVAnswer system, the subscriber is provided with a black box that contains a transmitter, receiver, and microprocessor that converts a digital bit stream into video text on the screen. The user simply points an infrared device at the screen and selects from choices displayed on a variety of still picture menus. The viewer response is then transmitted back to the source via a network of radio cell sites, similar to cellular telephone, that communicate with an orbiting satellite.

Perhaps the most sophisticated, state-of-the-art, fully interactive system proposed is the Full-Service Network, a $2.5 billion partnership between US West and Time Warner, the second largest cable operator in the United States. Scheduled for introduction in Orlando in 1994, this system employs asynchronous transfer mode (ATM) technology that will deliver a wide variety of voice, data, and video communication services within 25 metropolitan areas over a high-speed, digital, broadband fiber network by the end of the century.

Regardless of the specific technology employed, the interactive applications most often mentioned include Video-on-Demand, home shopping, interactive advertising, videogames, lotteries, education, telemedicine, and information and data services. While some applications are more profitable and are therefore higher on the priority list, none are mutually exclusive. The order of introduction will be based on anticipated profitability, and a number of different interactive applications will eventually co-exist on the system at the same time.

While the introduction of interactive television by the next millennium is virtually guaranteed, of immediate concern is the lack of standards and a common interface at the subscriber household. Will the keypad have full alphanumeric capability or simply four buttons labeled A through D? Will the system deploy an on-screen cursor controlled with a mouse or only predetermined, static screens? What will the interface to the home computer look like, if any? Even if each system developed uses proprietary hardware and software, there must be minimal agreement among the hardware and software vendors on critical human factors issues before video programmers and advertisers fully embrace this developing technology.

Speaking of convergence, if size and standing within the information community have any bearing, then the proposed joint venture between Time Warner, TCI, and Microsoft called Cablesoft should influence the development of standards for interactive television. In 1994, TCI and Time Warner together controlled about one-third of all cable subscribers in the United States. According to Bill Gates, chairman of Microsoft, his firm spends approximately $100 million per year in research and development of new software for interactive television and other leading-edge technologies. On the hardware side, firms such as IBM, Zenith, and Apple have a vested interest in the development of a standard computer interface with the subscriber's set-top-box.

Consumer demand aside, the initial introduction of interactive services will likely embrace two services: Video-on-Demand (VOD) and home shopping. VOD is essentially an electronic movie rental store that allows subscribers to select and watch a video at any time without leaving home. The subscriber will have the ability to start, stop, and pause the program at will. Similar in concept to a merger between cable's premium movie channels and pay-per-view, VOD provides the subscriber with a wider selection and greater flexibility. VOD is contingent on a cable-fiber optic upgrade to the physical plant, video compression, plus the development of the intelligent set-top-box for the household.

While field tests are underway, full deployment may be a few years away. In the interim, cable systems will offer Near-VOD. In this scenario, movies are staggered on multiple, unused channels. A sufficient number of copies of a movie title are playing on different channels at any given time such that subscribers will have to wait no more than a few minutes for their selection to begin.

Home shopping television is already a multibillion-dollar business, with nearly $3 billion in total revenues in 1993. Viewers are exposed to items in a linear fashion, one after the other, and may order any item on display by calling a 1-800 telephone number.

By contrast, consider the interactive home shopping system of tomorrow that allows subscribers electronically to call up to the television screen only those items of interest, browse through them at their convenience, request a 360-degree view of the product, see the item in different colors or sizes, read warning labels on garments and health care products, and order without leaving their easy chairs. This scenario suggests interactive video home shopping at the electronic store of the future. This vision of a "virtual" mall is not that far away.

Interactive advertising has been around for some time. The concept began with direct marketing using coupons, later electronically joining forces with one-way television. When coupled with 1-800 numbers, the result is the infamous "infomercial," boasting product sales in excess of $900 million in 1993. The bottom line is that interactive television is the fastest growth area of the advertising industry, with complex strategies being developed to capture and involve viewers across varied demographic market segments.

Not all cable news is bad. One arena where broadcasters may find comfort is the domain of wireless cable television. Wireless cable uses microwave channels in the 2 GHz band to transmit multiple scrambled cable channels to subscribers.

While not an immense threat to traditional wired cable, compared with DBS, it does present some interesting opportunities for broadcasters. First, FCC rules prohibit local television stations from owning a local cable system, but will allow them to own a wireless cable system. Second, synergy is possible between television broadcasters and local wireless folks via joint marketing agreements and the potential to use wireless bandwidth for the early introduction of high-definition television (HDTV). This would allow broadcasters to delay heavy investment in modification of their entire production and transmission facilities until a significant number of HDTV receivers are sold.

Satellite

Cable television is not immune to competition, and this indirectly affects the commercial broadcast industry. Direct broadcast satellite (DBS) is a one-way communication system that evolved from satellite experiments in the United States and abroad in the 1970s. It was found that by using high-powered transponders or transmitters located on the satellite, receiver dishes at each household need only be 18 inches to 2 feet in diameter in order to receive up to 150 channels of Laserdisc-quality video, coupled with CD-quality audio.

By providing an alternative to traditional wired cable service, direct broadcast satellite simply extends the competitive marketplace to the wireless arena. DBS will immediately target that 40 percent of television households that cable television, for whatever reason, has yet to capture. The impact on terrestrial broadcasting is also cause for some concern. Television networks require hundreds of local television stations linked together to provide national coverage. In contrast, a single DBS satellite can "broadcast" to the entire country.

The DBS system works in the same fashion as the more familiar C-band satellite, except it resides in the K-band (11.7–12.2 GHz), is fully digital, and operates at much higher power. Signals uplinked from a base station are received by the satellite transponder, amplified, digitally retransmitted back to earth, and received on 18-inch parabolic dishes at subscriber households from coast to coast.

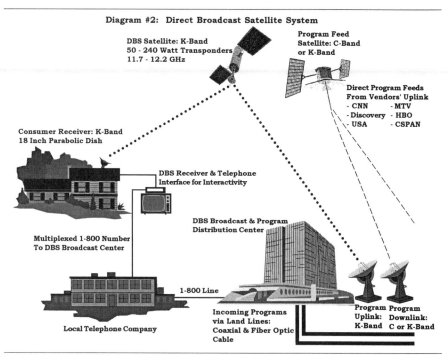

Diagram #2: Direct Broadcast Satellite System

Figure 5-2   Direct Broadcast Satellite

DirecTV, a division of Hughes, launched the first of two DBS satellites, known as DBS-1, on December 17, 1993. Its transponders, rated at 120 watts of power, are capable of being doubled to 240 watts for future applications, such as high-definition television. The marketing plan called for service to begin in summer of 1994, with at least 50 channels digitally compressed, using only 11 of the 16 transponders. The balance of five transponders are used by the competing firm, United States Satellite Broadcasting (USSB), a subsidiary of Hubbard Broadcasting. USSB plans call for 20 channels of programming, predominately premium services such as HBO and Showtime.

From a competitive standpoint, a DBS system might be at a disadvantage when compared with a cable or telephone system boasting full interactive capability. To address this issue, RCA has designed a set-top-box that decompresses the digital signal and converts it to analog for display on the television screen. The box also includes a standard telephone interface. Subscribers can order premium movies, shop interactively or request information when the box automatically dials a 1-800 telephone number. Unlike the "standards" quandary facing the interactive television industry, the RCA-designed set-top device will work with either of the competing DirecTV or USSB services or off-air broadcasting.

The impact of DBS may not be felt with the launch of a single satellite. However, the United States was awarded eight orbital slots for DBS at the 1983 Region II Administrative Radio Conference. Each orbital slot can carry 32 channels. The first Hughes satellite, DBS-1, used 16 of the available 32 channels in the 101 degrees west longitude orbit. All 16 transponders on a second Hughes satellite will be reserved for DirecTV. This leaves a balance of seven orbital slots for additional DBS competition with cable and, indirectly, terrestrial broadcasters.

While there are numerous technological advances that may compete with terrestrial broadcasting, it's another satellite technology that promises to have a dramatic impact on radio— digital audio broadcasting (DAB). The benefits of DAB are beyond question. It provides compact-disc quality audio that is noise-free and immune to interference. The problem has always been how to introduce a clearly superior technology without the wholesale bankruptcy of the current radio broadcasting system. DAB technology offers the potential for an economically viable national radio service to be delivered by satellite. This means one could receive the same station, on a single frequency, anywhere in the country.

Originally developed in Europe by a consortium named Eureka, DAB technology was introduced in the United States at a National Association of Broadcasters convention in 1990. Immediately a controversy arose concerning the allocation of space on the radio spectrum to deliver DAB and priority access to the bandwidth. In other words, where will the service be located, and will current radio broadcasters have a preference over newcomers to DAB frequencies?

Broadcasters would prefer that any movement to digital radio be confined to existing stations and within the existing AM and FM bands. They claim that anything less than an in-band, on-channel digital system would not serve the public interest. Unfortunately, significant questions concerning multipath interference for FM, coupled with performance problems associated with the limited channel bandwidth of AM radio, have caused delays in the development of an in-band, on-channel digital solution. Given both the technical questions and financial interests involved, this quandary will likely be with us into the next millennium.

Video Dialtone

Clearly the greatest threat to cable and, in turn, broadcasters is the pending introduction of video competition from the telephone company. For years, the phone company has been prohibited from entering the cable television business. These restrictions came from the Cable Communications Policy Act of 1984 and the Modification of Final Judgment (MFJ) of 1982, also known as the AT&T Consent Decree. The 1984 Cable Act applies to all local exchange carriers (LECs), while the MFJ deals directly with the 22 LECs owned by the seven Regional Bell Operating Companies (RBOCs). Within the industry, these rules are collectively known as cross-ownership restrictions. That was then, and as we enter the new millennium, the competitive landscape is changing.

Since divestiture in 1982, the telephone industry has had a keen interest in moving into the video arena. Few of the RBOCs view themselves as simply a telephone company anymore, and the promise of direct competition with cable television systems on a market-by-market basis was in sync with the wishes of Congress and the White House. As history demonstrated, allowing the cable industry to exist as an unbridled monopoly was not serving the public interest. The only question was how to open up the entertainment industry to local telephone competition without creating another antitrust problem.

The movement toward video competition came in tandem with a desire by Washington to encourage the convergence of voice, data, and video through the formation of hybrid information providers capable of providing or carrying a wide variety of services. That strategy has been called the National Information Infrastructure (NII). The role of government in this development is to ensure that this infrastructure is available to all Americans at reasonable cost. For the telephone industry, the first step to full participation in the digital migration of images along the superhighway is video dialtone.

The initial question concerning video dialtone is one of perspective. Allowing the telephone industry to "carry" video information is one view. Another is allowing phone companies to participate actively in the programming of that information.

As envisioned by the FCC in 1987, video dialtone simply extends the "carrier/user" relationship that we now enjoy with voice service to the video arena. This means that telephone companies would transmit a wide variety of video to their subscribers, but not own that information. As a common carrier, the telephone company would be required to provide access to this network for outside video programmers, without discrimination in terms of conditions and rates.

The FCC model involved two levels. First, the video dialtone regulations would provide for a "basic" platform that allows fundamental transmission of video services between programmers and subscribers. The second phase would allow for the development of the LEC's own advanced gateway for enhanced nonregulated services, other than video programming and other nonregulated enhanced services related to video programming. Regardless of FCC support and vision, the cross-ownership restrictions contained in the 1984 Cable Act prohibited full, unencumbered participation in the cable arena. The FCC cannot independently change provisions codified by Congress.

In 1991, Federal Judge Harold Green lifted some of the restrictions against RBOCs providing information services such as video dialtone. And in July 1992, the FCC adopted the video dialtone ruling providing for common carriage of a single channel of video in competition with local cable firms.

One RBOC, Bell Atlantic, wasted little time in forging strategic alliances with firms such as Oracle Corp., IBM, Compression Labs, and others to develop VOD and other interactive TV hardware and software for introduction in suburban Washington, D.C. The proposed service would ride on the existing telephone network utilizing a technology called asymmetrical digital subscriber line (ADSL). An ADSL network is capable of supplying VHS-quality video or data at 1.5 megabits per second to the household along with standard telephone service. Control signals returning from each home run at 16 kilobits per second.

Recognized as an interim step to the eventual deployment of a hybrid fiber-coax network, Bell Atlantic believes these initial trials will serve as an excellent test bed as it moves to bring VOD services to nearly nine million households throughout its region by the end of the decade. To comply with FCC regulations, Bell Atlantic will permit nonaffiliated programmers to offer services over the new network. Since 1992, over 20 applications have been filed with the FCC by local telephone companies to offer video dialtone services.

In December of 1992, C&P Telephone, a LEC subsidiary of Bell Atlantic, filed suit in the U.S. Court of Appeals against the FCC, claiming that the government had denied them their First Amendment right to offer video programming over their telephone network. In ruling on this case, Judge T. S. Ellis found that the 1984 Cable Act regulates substantially more speech than is necessary to further the government's legitimate interests and declared that portion of the act to be unconstitutional.

While this ruling only applies to the Bell Atlantic region, it does allow this one RBOC to offer cable television in the same areas where they currently provide telephone service. For the cable industry, the ruling represents the camel's nose under the tent; soon you end up with the whole camel.

With telephone company interest at a peak, BroadBand Technologies (BBT) announced in August of 1993 a partnership with Compression Labs (CLI) and Phillips Consumer Electronics to develop the necessary technology to introduce video dialtone service. The consortium seeks to develop encoding and decoding technology that will permit subscribers to access a wide variety of interactive services offered by the local phone company. The firms indicated that they will develop the system to be compatible with the MPEG-2 compression algorithm, suitable for transmission over the BBT Fiber Loop Access (FLXTM) platform. This will preserve the integrity of the system when high-definition television arrives. The proposed fiber-to-the-curb system will offer interactive switched video service in concert with plain old telephone service (POTS).

Regulation

As a regulated industry, broadcasting has been protected for 60 years as a vital resource serving in the public interest, convenience, and necessity. While that role remains, the script has changed. In 1972, for example, the FCC enacted the financial syndication rules that prohibited networks from acquiring a financial interest in the programs that they air, as well as any rerun of those programs. The purpose of the rule was to protect Hollywood programmers from the market power of the networks.

When the television industry was an oligopoly, the financial syndication rules were prudent. However, as Hollywood began to find other, competing outlets for their programs, the rules made less sense. In 1991, the rules were relaxed to allow the networks into foreign markets. In 1994, the financial syndication rules were partially lifted. The new rules allow networks to own a financial interest in the programs they air, but still prohibits them from syndication until November 1995.

The importance of these events should be obvious. The success of the broadcast networks, and in turn the local affiliates, is directly related to the quality of programming. In order for the networks to be competitive, they must strive to attract the best that Hollywood has to offer, each and every season. With increasing numbers of new video delivery technologies, the competition for that quality programming increases. The virtual elimination of the financial syndication rules allows broadcast networks to compete on an even playing field with cable, DBS, and others who are not financially restricted in program production and distribution.

It is impossible for broadcasters to deny the intrusion of cable television into society while insisting on mandatory carriage of their signals. With over half of all television households wired, absent competition, the cable systems of America hold most of the cards. From 1972 on, the FCC has attempted to level the playing field by instituting "must carry" rules that require the carriage of local television stations. On two successive attempts, rules jointly crafted by representatives of the cable and broadcast industries, and mandated by the FCC, have been successfully challenged in federal court and dismissed as the unconstitutional regulation of free speech.

In 1992, however, Congress adopted a new cable act with a new must-carry provision. This time the new rules survived the initial constitutional challenge in U.S. District Court.

While no one is prepared to nominate cable television as the winner in the race to construct the information superhighway of tomorrow, it is an industry with significant economic and technical standing. Over half of American households have elected cable television to be their multichannel video gateway to news, entertainment, sports, and public affairs. As a monopoly in most markets, unbridled by common carrier requirements, cable television has significant market power.

Every three years, broadcasters must elect whether they wish must-carry status or would prefer retransmission consent. By selecting the former, must-carry, the local broadcaster forces the local cable system to carry their station. If they elect the latter, retransmission consent, then the two parties must negotiate the terms of carriage, if any, and what form of compensation is warranted. If there is no agreement, then the cable system is prohibited from carrying the local station, or bringing in a distant signal from the same network to replace it.

It is interesting to note that, in 1993, when the first must-carry election was made under the 1992 Cable Act, the majority of commercial television broadcasters selected retransmission consent. Believing that cable subscribers would demand that local stations be included on their cable system, the broadcasters demanded monetary compensation from cable for carriage.

The cable industry held fast, however, reasoning that "free" over-the-air broadcasters represented only marginal value when compared with the magnitude of other channels provided. In the end, most stations and cable systems settled for the broadcaster's right to program an additional channel on the cable system if immediately available or upon rebuild of the cable system.

As the information industry moves into the digital environment, the broadcasters are not exempt. The FCC is requiring television stations to move to a digital transmission scheme that will not only dramatically improve picture quality and increase the physical dimensions of the television picture, called the aspect ratio, from 4:3 to 16:9, but also provide a compatible digital signal for the rest of the communications industry. This scheme is known as high-definition television, and the industry is being told to be HDTV-compliant by the year 2015.

As with the introduction of any new technology, the industry is trying to be proactive in the process of selecting an acceptable HDTV transmission standard. Broadcasters learned long ago not to leave important technical decisions, with major economic consequences, to the FCC alone. The prolonged introduction of an AM stereo standard in the 1980s under an FCC-mandated "marketplace philosophy" still haunts the broadcast industry today.

While the selection of a complete HDTV standard won't occur until 1995 at the earliest, a few things are already known. First, the Grand Alliance, a consortium of formerly competing HDTV developers, proposed a 1,920 pixel by 1,080 line, interlaced scanned picture with Dolby AC-3, six channel, CD-quality audio, and MPEG-2 compression. Eventually, the service will migrate to progressive scanning at 720 lines. While this smorgasbord seems to include something for everyone, one major obstacle is the type of modulation employed.

The Grand Alliance has proposed a vestigial sideband (VSB) transmission scheme that is similar to the technology employed with our current television broadcast system. The Broadcaster's Caucus, composed of the NAB, the Association for Maximum Service Television, the three networks, Fox, and PBS, would like the FCC's Advisory Committee on Advanced Television (ACATS) to withhold any recommendation until a new transmission system, called coded orthogonal frequency division multiplexing (COFDM), is tested. Unlike conventional over-the-air transmission systems, with a single, high-powered transmitter, COFDM involves the use of multiple, low-powered transmitters, which greatly reduces ghosting and co-channel interference problems common to major markets.

Although the move to HDTV will involve a large investment, the technology should open up many opportunities for broadcasters. Because the standard will be for a digital transmission system, HDTV will allow broadcasters to investigate new markets. The role that broadcasters will eventually play in the information superhighway is sketchy; however, a liaison between broadcasters and groups working on the National Information Infrastructure (NII) issue is paramount.

THE DECADE AHEAD—THE NEW MULTIMEDIA ENVIRONMENT

For a single-channel provider to succeed in a multichannel environment, it must be allowed to compete, unencumbered by regulations adopted during the vacuum tube era. The destination for broadcasters in the next millennium is clear; it's the superhighway route to that destination that needs some clarification.

At the January 1994 board meeting, the NAB outlined its immediate plans for the journey ahead. First, broadcasters seek marketplace parity with other service providers. They also want a relaxation in ownership rules, plus the freedom to offer auxiliary digital services on both existing and future HDTV channels. Yet, all of this comes in the fourth quarter as both Congress and the White House move forward a national infrastructure agenda that initially excludes broadcasters from the mix.

Suggestions of troubled waters ahead have come at successive NAB conventions where keynote speakers such as John Sculley and Ray Smith have essentially hinted to broadcasters that they were no longer in control of their own destiny, but under the proper circumstances would enjoy the ride. Indeed, broadcasters have become a minority at their own convention, where telephone company, cable MSO, programmer, production house, and multimedia personnel lifted attendance figures above a record 70,000 in 1994.

By all accounts, the future of the information industry will be based on the digitalization of content, interactivity, and the movement of that information in an efficient manner. If true, this favors the computer manufacturers and the transport providers, both cable and telephone. Without some significant change, broadcasters will remain a single-channel provider in a multichannel world. Fortunately, there are a number of things the industry can do and must do to capitalize on the current frenzy.

Strategic Planning

Sufficient warning has been provided to the broadcast industry concerning the advent of the information age and the superhighway bandwagon. Individual stations and group owners should be planning on how to become a competitive player in this digital, interactive environment. Clearly, the active participation of two major television networks in ancillary arenas such as cable programming, multimedia news services, and CD-ROM interactive suggest a level of readiness that should be duplicated at stations from coast to coast.

Whether a broadcast station is viewed as an information provider or simply a transport for information providers, the movement to digital and high definition is FCC-mandated by the year 2015. To that end, many broadcasters have already invested in digital cameras, high-end digital editing stations complete with D-2 and D-3 digital videotape machines, digital still store machines, digital audiotape (DAT) and compact disc (CD) audio, etc. The investment is significant, and the trick is to utilize these resources in innovative ways.

On Ramp

One way that broadcasters can begin the multimedia journey is by thinking of themselves as information gatekeepers and the stations as vehicles ready to enter the "on ramp" of the electronic superhighway. The more channels of voice, data, or video that you control, the more access points you have to the superhighway. For those who successfully negotiate a separate channel under retransmission consent, this is a cable access point of entry. For those stations that market unused studio time and production equipment for video conferences, this is a telephone access point of entry.

With the availability of Integrated Services Digital Network (ISDN) service from your local telephone company, videoconference access can be available digitally, end-to-end, even on the desktop, and in turn suggests the potential of establishing a multimedia hub offering various production-level services to organizations and firms in each market. Finally, if television stations are provided the opportunity to multiplex auxiliary digital services within their channel bandwidth, this would provide another point of entry.

Information comes in various forms and formats: voice, data, still images, and real-time video. To be competitive means that you have the capability to generate, manipulate, store, and forward information across a number of formats and standards. To be successful means that you also have the ability to market the end product both internal and external to the station.

Broadcasting is a business and, like any commercial enterprise, it has requirements that are well suited to the multimedia world. From local area networks, electronic mail, and wire services to numerous databases, the broadcast station has typical day-to-day functions that are easily classified and are common to most businesses.

Yet the end product of the broadcaster is unique. As an information provider, the broadcaster seeks to address numerous markets with quality programming that has value. Today, that value is realized by the over-the-air transmission of this information to viewers on a single channel. More often than not, it's also a time-specific, single transmission, suggesting little residual value for this information. In reality, other markets might exist or be created as opportunities for the broadcast entrepreneur.

Success down the road might be measured by the creativity that a broadcaster employs in identifying these residual markets. Whether these markets can be tapped alone or through some strategic partnership is specific to the individual application.

Multimedia

As we approach the millennium, the vehicle to success at most television broadcast stations is multimedia. A term coined in the 1980s to signify the convergence of voice, data, and image on a single, user-friendly platform, it also summarizes the transition that stations have made to the digital domain over the past decade.

From a consumer standpoint, the term "multimedia" describes a personal computer that complies with the Multimedia PC (MPC) standard. Introduced in 1990 by Microsoft, and licensed by the Multimedia Market Council, the standard prescribes the foundation computer platform. It consists of an Intel 80386SX computer, operating at 16 megahertz (MHz), with a minimum 30-megabyte (MB) hard drive, and 2 MB of random-access memory (RAM), running disk operating system (DOS) software. To this is added a CD-ROM drive, an 8-bit audio card, and a VGA monitor, video graphics adapter card, and perhaps a separate multimedia graphics card for the input and scan conversion of images and video. The entire package is held together using Microsoft's *Windows* software with multimedia extensions and *Video for Windows*, a software package that allows the incorporation of compressed "real-time" video applications.

While this configuration is sufficient for general business and nominal multimedia applications at most stations, it is hardly robust enough for the broadcast studio. Each still graphics video frame on a VGA display of 640 x 480 pixels (picture elements) represents 7.4 million bits of data. This is compounded when you add real-time full-motion to the mix. For example, at an NTSC rate of 30 frames per second, one second of motion video would require 27.65 MB of disk storage. Thus, a 30-second commercial would consume over 800 megabytes of video memory, assuming that your computer system and peripherals are fast enough to handle the processing, transport, and display.

At a minimum, multimedia platforms utilized in broadcast video production require up to a 50-MHz system (80386DX/50) motherboard, up to 64 MB of RAM, with 1.2 GB or more of hard disk storage, and a 16-bit (CD-quality) audio card. The import of NTSC video images requires a separate discussion.

It's clear that the standard AT-class computer alone is not robust enough for NTSC motion video applications without some form of digital signal processing and compression. The ideal multimedia graphics card, also known as a multimedia engine, has the ability to convert NTSC, interlaced scanned, analog pictures into digital signals that can be interpreted by the computer, stored, and displayed on a computer monitor at VGA or higher resolution, using progressive scanning. Further, the graphics board must contain enough dynamic video RAM, up to 2 MB, to handle the efficient transfer of digital picture information to the screen, plus graphical overlay capability. The overlay feature is important when combining images or video with other multimedia applications.

Regardless of platform or vendor (IBM, Apple, Silicon Graphics, etc.), the necessity to handle NTSC full-motion video at 30 frames per second in a digital environment requires some form of signal compression. This can be accomplished at the low end by software alone or at the high end in combination with digital compression boards. Regardless of that route one takes, there is an inverse relationship between the amount of compression employed and picture quality.

The qualities of different compression schemes (algorithms) make them more or less applicable to the broadcast industry. Software-only compression programs, such as Apple's *QuickTime* and Microsoft's *Video for Windows,* are an inexpensive way to allow the user to input, compress, decompress, and display different levels of motion video and images on a Multimedia PC in a windows environment. At any television station, these applications allow for the quick storage and display of stills, cataloging of video clips, generation of moving storyboards, a new way for salespeople to promote upcoming programs, all the way to desktop video e-mail over a local area network (LAN). Unfortunately, neither of these systems, nor any other available software-only compression scheme, is robust enough to handle the real-time compression and decompression of full-screen, full-motion, NTSC video at 30 frames per second at an acceptable resolution level. Enter the compression engine.

The compression engine is a hardware board added to the computer that accelerates the digital coding and decoding of the video signal. For broadcasters, video images are classified as "stills" or "moving," and compression can be viewed from two perspectives—production and transport.

For the production side, the industry standard employed most often is known as JPEG, named after the Joint Photographic Experts Group, a standards body charged with developing a uniform approach to handling digital still images. With JPEG compression, a form of discrete cosine transform (DCT) is employed to reduce image file sizes, without noticeable artifacts, at ratios of 15:1 up to 20:1. A hybrid "moving-JPEG" compression scheme is also employed with most off-line editing stations, allowing for the capture of 30 frames per minute, full-screen, full-motion, at near-VHS quality. Motion-JPEG effectively overcomes interframe or frame-to-frame editing problems inherent with other compression schemes.

A second compression standard referenced earlier, MPEG, is actually a series of standards that deal with full-motion video, named for the Motion Picture Experts Group. While not suitable for off-line editing, the MPEG series is recognized as the leader and the most common form of motion compression. The first standard, MPEG-1, was approved in 1992 to handle the storage of motion video on various magnetic and optical media (e.g., CD-ROM, CDi, and hard disks). Using MPEG-1, it is possible to obtain VHS-quality video images, compressed at 200:1, in a digital bit stream of 1.5 MB per second.

The potential for application of MPEG-1 compression within any television station is significant. From repackaging file footage in interactive form (sports, special events, convention and tourism, maps, etc.) to the creation of special advertiser promotions using interactive media, the opportunities are endless. Multimedia workstations at the television studio would be used to author various multimedia packages using available resources. The end result, on removable hard drive, would be sent off for compression and pressing into the appropriate format, CD-ROM or CDi.

The third form of compression is an extension of the same series and is called MPEG-2. Where MPEG-1 was designed to address the storage of moving video information, MPEG-2 is designed exclusively for the transport of video. Scheduled for adoption in 1995, the MPEG-2 standard deals with the compression of NTSC video in a digital bit stream at rates between 3 and 5 MB per second, up to HDTV signal compression in a bit stream of 15 MB per second.

Recognized as the compression algorithm of choice by the Grand Alliance, it will allow for the transport of digital HDTV screens that are approximately four times the resolution of a VGA computer screen. With the FCC-mandated migration to HDTV by 2015, the adoption of MPEG-2 compression is more reality than risk. However, as with all other compression schemes, it's also a tool for exploring interactive, residual markets in an environment where television broadcasters are comfortable—the world of video.

SUMMARY AND CONCLUSIONS

The information infrastructure movement is beyond the control of any individual broadcaster. The superhighway will be constructed, creating opportunities for many new service providers. Some, like broadcasters, have an edge simply because they already deal in a video world and are migrating to digital anyway. By recognizing that the broadcast industry is already at the multimedia threshold, the journey and risks are minimized. As with any journey, it all begins with that first step.

The levels of competition in the information industry will become more intense as we approach the next millennium. To assume that any one industry will maintain a singular strategic advantage in this competitive environment without aggressive and creative measures is sheer folly. There are no sacred cows left in the information age.

National policy is moving us closer to a total digital environment. Thousands of miles of fiber optics are being deployed by telephone and cable firms to bring the information highway to each neighborhood. New advances in compression technology and computer process speeds suggest that future interactive applications and services are limited only by imagination. In the end, from a public policy perspective, the best we can do is provide as level a playing field as technology allows. Success under this scenario is based purely on individual initiative.

BIOGRAPHY

Dr. Robert Yadon is a professor in the Center for Information and Communication Sciences at Ball State University in Muncie, Indiana. He came to Ball State in 1987 from the National Association of Broadcasters (NAB) in Washington, D.C., where he was Vice President of Television Operations for that trade organization. During this three years at NAB, Dr. Yadon was responsible for ongoing communication with member television stations, the development of a one-hour monthly satellite news magazine, public service projects, and various regulatory issues.

Prior to joining NAB, he spent a number of years on the graduate faculty at both Michigan State University and the University of Oklahoma. While at MSU, he was named Director of System Development for the NSF-funded Rockford Two-Way Cable Project, one of the premier interactive broadband cable systems in the country. In addition to research on interactive cable, he was co-founder of East Lansing Research Associates (ELRA Group), one of the leading cable television consulting firms in the industry. Over the years, he has worked with a number of major cable systems, including Teleprompter, United Cable, Continental Cablevision, TCI, and others, conducting marketing and feasibility studies and assisting in the development of franchise applications.

He graduated in 1973 from Northwestern Oklahoma State University with a bachelor's degree in speech and journalism, and in 1975 was awarded a Master of Science degree from Oklahoma State University where he majored in mass communication. He was awarded a Ph.D. from Michigan State University in mass media in 1983. Over the past 15 years, he has authored a number of articles and manuscripts on interactive media and telecommunication technology and has appeared as a guest speaker before telecommunication industry groups in the United States and Canada.

Since his arrival at Ball State, Dr. Yadon has been involved with the early development of the Center for Information and Communication Sciences, to include primary responsibility for development of the Applied Research Institute. He has personally brought in over $2 million in equipment and research grants. His research work includes the development of a networked, interactive video kiosk system in concert with AT&T, and he regularly consults with Bell Labs, GTE Labs, and US West on applied research problems.

Chapter 6

LEGAL ISSUES IN NEW MEDIA

MARK RADCLIFFE, ESQ.
GRAY CARY WARE & FREIDENRICH

An understanding of the legal issues in the development, production, and distribution of multimedia works is critical to the success of the multimedia developer. The failure to understand these issues can cost the developer thousands of dollars in legal fees defending a lawsuit and could result in a court order preventing further distribution of the product.

Even though the multimedia industry is young, it already has had a number of lawsuits. In the fall of 1993, Delrina Corporation introduced a screen saver that, out of twenty potential screen savers, included the Opus cartoon character shooting down "flying toasters" very similar to those that Berkeley Systems had made famous. Berkeley Systems sued Delrina and won an order requiring a recall of the product, preventing its further distribution and making Delrina pay damages. Delrina admitted that they lost hundreds of thousands of dollars in the recall and destruction of the existing products.

In another case filed in the fall, Joe Sparks, the well-known developer, is suing his former friend Mike Saenz over the ownership of the copyright in their well-known *Spaceship Warlock* product. Joe claims that he and Mike worked on the product together as partners and that they are co-owners of the copyright. They would share equally in the profits. Mike claims that Joe was an employee of his company, Reactor, Inc. As an employee, Joe is only due his salary without any share of the profits.

Copyright is the primary form of protection for multimedia works. Copyright law permits the owner to prevent the reproduction, distribution, modification, and public performance of a work. Under copyright law, the difference between an employee and an independent contractor is critical. The copyrights in works (such as videogames) prepared by an employee as part of his job are automatically owned by the employer. However, copyrights in a work prepared both by an employee and independent contractor are "jointly owned." This joint ownership gives both parties the right to nonexclusively license the work and to share equally in all profits from its sale or license.

Another crucial issue for multimedia publishers is the "trademark" they use to identify their product. The failure to properly select and clear a trademark can be very expensive. If a developer starts using "Mickey Mouse" or other famous trademarks, it will be sued by the trademark owner. All of its products using the mark will be seized and destroyed and it will have to stop using all letterhead, marketing literature, and business cards using the infringing mark. The cost of replacing all of these materials can be significant. It can also be very embarrassing to be forced to change the name of a company or a product because someone else owns it.

The exploitation of multimedia opportunities is complicated because the works that are combined into a multimedia work—books, computer software, photographs, film, and music—arise in separate industries. These industries have developed their own legal customs and traditional license terms.

The book publishing industry, for example, has a tradition of long and comprehensive contracts. The movie industry, on the other hand, frequently works from brief deal memos. In addition, multimedia works generally require a developer to obtain rights beyond those traditionally granted in these industries.

The situation is similar to that faced by the movie industry with the introduction of the home video market. This new method of distribution quickly became the subject of disputes over who had the right to exploit it. For example, in 1993 a court awarded damages of $2.2 million against Time Warner for distributing "Yellow Submarine" on videocassette when it did not have the rights to do so. The issue for multimedia works will be even more complex due to the fundamental differences between multimedia works and traditional ones. For example, unlike videocassette versions of films, multimedia works change the nature of the underlying work.

OVERVIEW OF COPYRIGHT PRINCIPLES

These principles outlined here will provide an overview of the critical intellectual property issues that arise in the creation and distribution of multimedia works. Intellectual property rights in the United States are created by either federal or state law. Federal intellectual property rights include patent, copyright, and federally registered trademarks. State intellectual property rights include unfair competition, certain sound recordings, nonfederally registered trademarks, and trade secrets.

Legal issues outside of intellectual property that may be relevant to the creation and exploitation of multimedia works include defamation, slander, privacy, and rights of publicity. Although several of these intellectual property regimes may apply to multimedia works, the most important regime is federal copyright law, and I will focus primarily on that.

Copyright Law

Copyrights are protected almost entirely by federal law in the United States. Copyright law is national, and copyright laws in other countries differ from those in the United States. This discussion will be limited to United States copyright law. This discussion provides an overview of the law, but it is not comprehensive. To answer specific questions, multimedia developers should contact their attorney.

Copyright law protects a wide variety of works: photographs, films, plays, databases, musical recordings, computer software, and toys. Copyright law also protects "compilations" of public domain works, such as a collection of the plays of Shakespeare, and collections of information, such as parts catalogs.

In the United States, federal copyright law protects "original works of authorship fixed in a tangible medium of expression." Each one of these words has important legal significance. For example, "original" does not mean "novel" or "unique," such as is required for protection under patent law. Rather, it means a minimal level of creativity.

The phrase "fixed in a tangible medium" is also very important. For example, a football game that is not recorded in a "tangible medium" such as film or videotape is not protected under federal copyright law.

The term "expression" is also very important in copyright law. Copyright law is based upon an economic balancing. Copyright law grants sufficient protection for new works to encourage an author to distribute them to the public, but the scope is limited to avoid discouraging the creation of future works. This policy is embodied in the "idea–expression dichotomy." This dichotomy is a fundamental principle of copyright law and is stated as the limitation of copyright protection to the "expression," not the "idea," of a work.

Separating the "expression" from the "idea" of a work is one of the most difficult tasks in copyright law. For example, George Lucas's copyright in the *Star Wars* films cannot prevent the creation of another film that includes a dashing hero who saves a princess in the midst of numerous space battles set in the future. Nonetheless,

George Lucas sued the developers of the television program *Battlestar Galactica* on the basis that the creators were "too close" to the *Star Wars* films. He was not ultimately successful.

Quantum of Copyrightability

The search for the lowest common denominator, "the quantum," of copyright protection continues in recent court decisions. Copyright law, for example, will protect business forms that have sufficient "information" on them but not "blank" forms. This doctrine has existed for decades, but disputes continue to arise under it. Copyright law will not protect short phrases or purely functional objects such as the shape of a simple hoop belt buckle. One court protected the "command structure" of the Lotus 1-2-3 software program. More recently, a Supreme Court decision stated that copyright law would not protect the "compilation" in the white pages of a telephone book, since the selection, ordering, and arrangement of the names in the white pages is not sufficiently "original."

This question may also arise in the context of modifying a preexisting work. How much change is necessary to create a new work, protected by a separate copyright? Court decisions make clear that this standard is very low. Many decisions state that a "distinguishable" variation from an underlying work is all that is necessary to create a new copyright. However, mere correction of typographical or grammatical errors does not create a new copyright. These issues arise in a slightly different context in determining whether or not modifications are "derivative" works, i.e., works that have been created based on existing ones.

Rights Under Copyright Law

The owner of a copyright has five exclusive rights:

- Right to reproduce the work;

- Right to adapt the work (to create "derivative" works);

- Right to distribute the work;

- Right to perform the work publicly; and

• Right to display the work publicly.

Some of these rights overlap. For example, the reproduction of a work may be essential to make a derivative work.

All of these rights are subject to exceptions. Most of them have specific exceptions for educational and religious uses and for libraries. The scope of these exceptions varies among the rights. Some exceptions are peculiar to a particular type of work. For example, copyright law grants a "compulsory license" to reproduce musical works for nondramatic uses but requires the payment of fixed royalties to the owners of the copyright. Other exceptions apply to specific rights. The public performance right is subject to exceptions that include "face-to-face" classroom instruction in a nonprofit institution and a "compulsory license" for noncommercial broadcasting.

One of the most important exceptions to the rights of a copyright owner is the "first sale" doctrine. This exception to the distribution right provides that once an object (i.e., a book) embodying a copyrightable work is sold either by the owner of the copyright or under his authority, that particular copy may be resold without the copyright owner's permission. This exception permits a buyer to resell a book that he has purchased from a bookstore. However, the buyer is not allowed to reproduce the book or create a screenplay based on the book, since neither the reproduction nor the adaption right are subject to the first-sale doctrine.

When considering what rights are needed to create a work, the multimedia developer should keep clearly in mind that each right under the copyright law is independent. The developer may need one or more of them to create and distribute its multimedia work.

Another important exception to the rights of a copyright owner is the "fair use" privilege. This privilege merits a separate section.

Fair Use

Fair use is an exception to all five of the rights of a copyright owner. The fair-use privilege permits the use of a work for limited purposes, whose economic value outweighs the reduction in the scope of the copyright owner's rights. For example, the use of quotations from a book in a review of that book is a classic example of the "fair use" privilege. The application of the fair-use privilege is judged by a four-part test:

- The purpose and character of the use. In particular, is the use commercial or noncommercial?

- The nature of the work. Is it a work of fiction or a description of an historical event?

- The amount and substantiality of the portion used. Is it a brief quote from a long book or is it the "last five minutes" of a mystery film in which the mystery is solved?

- The effect of the use on the economic value of the work. Will the use substantially reduce the value of the work?

Although decisions under the fair-use privilege have not been entirely consistent, the assertion of the fair-use privilege for a purely commercial work (except in very limited circumstances) entails substantial risk of liability of copyright infringement.

Scope of Protection

Copyright law protects against "copying." Since direct copying is rarely discovered, copyright law depends on a two-part test: access to the allegedly copied work, and "substantial similarity" between the expression of the two works. The "access" portion of the test is rarely an issue. For example, access can be satisfied by showing that the work is "available" in stores that are geographically near the alleged infringer.

The critical issue is, generally, substantial similarity. Substantial similarity means different degrees of similarity for different works. The amount of similarity necessary to find infringement for very creative works, such as novels or screenplays, is much less than the amount of similarity necessary for fact-intensive works such as historical descriptions. This difference is based on the commonsense principle that the facts of historical events are fixed and can only be described in a limited number of ways. The comparison to determine "substantial similarity" is limited to the "expression" of the two works, not their ideas.

Courts have found infringement even when the amount of copying is quite moderate. For example, the courts found copyright infringement when a television network used a thirteen-minute selection out of six Charlie Chaplin films for a television retrospective on his career. The court determined that those thirteen minutes were the most critical parts of the films. Thus, by copying them, the television station was potentially depriving the films' copyright owner of substantial revenues.

A HYPOTHETICAL MULTIMEDIA WORK

This section will analyze how these legal principles apply to the creation and distribution of a hypothetical new multimedia work. The work is being created by a new company, Hollywood Productions, as a history of the Vietnam War and the role of the United States' military in the war. It will be distributed on a CD-ROM to the home market and projected onto screens at conventions of Vietnam veterans. The work will consist of the following elements:

- New text;

- Excepts from various books about the era, including *Fire in the Lake* and *The Best and the Brightest*;

- Software to permit the viewer to search the work for particular issues;

- Newspaper articles from the period;

- Still photographs;

- Film clips of news programs and excerpts from relevant motion pictures such as *The Deer Hunter*;

- New video works created by Hollywood Productions to explain the progress of the war; and

- Music, including some of the hit songs of the era, such as *Purple Haze*.

Text Works and Computer Software

The new text, the excerpts from the preexisting books, the computer software, and the newspaper articles may all be treated differently from a legal point of view. Hollywood Productions is creating the new text and the computer software. As the creator, it will probably own the copyright in those elements, either through the work-for-hire doctrine or assignments. On the other hand, Hollywood Productions must go to the owners of the copyrights, or licensees of the copyrights, in the books and newspapers to obtain the rights to use them in its work. Many of these rights may no longer be held by the "author" since publishing houses increasingly demand very broad rights to exploit books in other media.

Photographs

Copyrights in photographs are initially owned by the photographer, although they may either be assigned to another party or transferred to his employer under the work-for-hire doctrine. The determination of who owns the appropriate rights in the photograph can be very difficult and time consuming because of fragmentation in this industry.

For example, the fact that a photograph appeared in the *New York Times* does not necessarily mean that the *New York Times* owns the copyright in the photograph. The *New York Times* may only have a license to use it in a newspaper. Common limitations in the licensing of photographs include the color of reproduction, the medium (i.e., newspapers, magazines, etc.), and attribution, as well as those relating to numbers of copies.

The rights required for an interactive multimedia work would be quite different from those that are normally granted for photographs. For example, the photograph may appear several times throughout the work, and the number of its appearances could be controlled by the viewer. Such flexibility is quite different from the traditional agreements in the photography industry.

Film Clips and Video

Once again, Hollywood Productions must distinguish between videotapes that it has created for which, if properly structured, it will own the copyrights and those for which it needs to obtain rights. The rights holders who need to be "cleared" of a videotape may include the actors, directors, scriptwriters, music composers, and cameramen. To avoid the problems of joint ownership, Hollywood Productions should obtain the appropriate agreements from the individuals who are creating its videotapes.

News Programs and Other Stock Film

Stock footage is available from stock houses in many cities. Materials available from stock houses range from still photographs, historical footage of various locations, to commercials. Many stock houses are now prepared to serve the multimedia market, but Hollywood Productions must be careful. The licenses obtained by many stock houses do not permit public performances, which will be needed to show the work at conventions. Such rights need to be negotiated separately.

Other institutions, such as television stations, may also license their newscasts. These institutions generally base their royalty on the type of use of the film. For example, different royalties are due for use on national television or regional television. Since the multimedia work would not fit easily into any of these categories, Hollywood Productions would probably have to negotiate a special license with these institutions.

Recorded Music

The right to use music in the new work may require obtaining rights from several different parties. The necessary rights depend on whether or not Hollywood Productions produces the music itself or wishes to use the performance or recordings of a third party.

Mechanical Rights

Mechanical rights are the basic right to use a musical composition. They do not include the right to publicly perform the music (see below). A mechanical license also does not permit the use of the music with still or moving images. Such use requires a "synchronization" license (see below). Although copyright law provides a compulsory license for mechanical rights, most licensees prefer to obtain these rights commercially through the Harry Fox Agency or other professional clearance agencies. This preference is based on the very onerous payment and accounting requirements imposed on the "compulsory" license in the Copyright Act. The compulsory mechanical license probably does not apply to the CD-ROMs that include video because such a CD-ROM is not a "phonorecord" as defined within the copyright statute.

Synchronization License

If the music is to be synchronized with still or moving images on a screen, the licensee must obtain a "synchronization" license. Although these rights may also be handled by the Harry Fox Agency, in some cases Hollywood Productions may need to contact the musical publisher directly.

Public Performance Rights

Hollywood Productions will need a license for public performance if its work is shown at conventions. A performance is considered public if it is "open to the public" or takes place where a substantial number of persons outside of the "normal circle of family and social acquaintances" gather. Most music publishers permit either ASCAP or BMI to license their public performance rights. These rights do not apply to use of a particular performance by a particular individual or group. Thus, obtaining a mechanical license to *Purple Haze* would not permit Hollywood Productions to use Jimi Hendrix's performance of the song.

Right to a Particular Performance or Recording

As described above, if Hollywood Productions desires the musical composition to be performed by a particular group or individual, it must also obtain the right of the copyright holder for that particular performance. The licenses described above are limited solely to the right to use the musical composition. Thus, unless Hollywood Productions is prepared to have new artists record the music, it must negotiate with the holder of the rights to the particular performance that it desires to use. These rights are generally held by record companies.

In certain limited instances, the creator might need a special type of performance right known as "grand performance" rights. These rights are required for public performances of music that is an integral part of a dramatic work, such as a musical review.

Feature Films

The use of feature films can be particularly complex and expensive. Feature films are frequently based on a novel that is licensed to the film and may use music developed by a third party. For example, *Jurassic Park* was based on a book of the same name by Michael Crichton. Consequently, the owner of the copyright in the film may not have the necessary rights to the music or the underlying work to permit their use in the multimedia work. This situation is further complicated by provisions of the various motion picture industry guild agreements (such as the Screen Actors' Guild and the Directors' Guild of America) that require payment of fees upon incorporation of parts or portions of the film into another work. The developer may need to go to the music publishers for the rights to use the song and to the record company to get rights to use the particular recording of the song.

OTHER COPYRIGHT ISSUES

Ownership

Except in the limited circumstances described below, the individual "author" of a work in the United States is the owner of its copyright. The choice of the "author," however, may not be obvious. For example, in the case of sound recordings, the sound engineer, the performing artists, and even the record producer may all be "authors" under copyright law. On the other hand, a photographer is considered to be the author of his photograph.

The exception to this rule in the United States is called the "work-for-hire" doctrine. Although similar rules exist in some other countries, each country's approach to this issue is different. The work-for-hire doctrine in the United States has two branches: employee and "specially commissioned works."

The employee branch of this doctrine states that the employer is the author of a work created by an employee "within the scope of his employment." Thus, an employee working for a company creating a multimedia work would not be the "author" of the work he has created; the company would automatically be the author. Many companies, however, do not rely solely on the work-for-hire doctrine. They obtain express assignments of copyright from their employees of any works that the employee develops on company time or using company materials. Such assignments avoid uncertainty about the scope of the "work-for-hire" doctrine. Some states, such as California, impose limits on the scope of the assignment of rights that an employer may demand of its employees.

The second branch of the work-for-hire doctrine is for "specially commissioned works." This provision was included in United States copyright law because of lobbying by businesses interested in such works. The rationale was that some types of works are rarely created by a single author, but rather by a team of individuals working together. In order to avoid disputes over the ownership of such works, Congress was asked to create special rules to govern their ownership. Nine types of works are eligible for this treatment:

- Contributions to collective works;
- Parts of a motion picture or other audiovisual work (most multimedia works would qualify for this category);
- Translations;
- Supplementary works (such as forewords, afterwords, maps, tables, charts, etc.);
- Compilations;

- Instructional texts;

- Tests;

- Answer materials for tests; and

- Atlases.

If the work being created fits into one of these categories, and the contracting party has obtained a written agreement including the words "work-for-hire" with the individual creator, then the contracting party (not the individual creator) will be the initial author of the work. This "commissioned work" rule is limited to United States copyright law.

If the work is created by more than one individual and it does not fall within the scope of the work-for-hire doctrine, the copyright in the work may be "jointly" owned. A jointly owned work is one where all the creators of the work have an "intention" that their contribution should be merged or the independent parts made part of a unitary whole. The lack of such intention means that the copyright in the work is not jointly owned. A classic example is a song where the tune is created by the composer and the lyrics by a lyricist. Moreover, the contribution of each "joint" author must be copyrightable, it cannot be merely an "idea."

Joint ownership permits each owner to nonexclusively license and otherwise exploit the work without the permission of any other author. However, under United States law, each author has the "duty to account" and share profits for his exploitation of the work with his other joint owners in proportion to their ownership of the copyright. Joint owners also have the obligation not to "waste," or destroy, the commercial value of the work.

Derivative Work

A derivative work is one that recasts, transforms, or adapts one or more preexisting works. An example of a derivative work is a translation of a book into a foreign language, which requires the modification of the grammar and syntax to fit the new language. Another classic example of a "derivative work" is a film based on a book, such as the film *Bonfire of the Vanities* based on the book of the same name. A "compilation" is another important type of copyrightable work in the multimedia field (see below).

The rules of originality apply to the creation of derivative works. Modifications to an existing work that do not meet the originality standard under copyright law will not give rise to a derivative work. For example, 40,000 editorial changes, including the elimination and addition of punctuation, addition of quotation marks, and correction of typographical errors, is insufficient "originality" to create a derivative work in the "edited work." On the other hand, the condensation of a 200-page book into a 100-page book would qualify for copyright protection as a derivative work.

The new copyright in the "derivative work" will extend only to the new material. Copyright in the underlying material will remain the property of the existing owner. Thus, the copyright in the authorized French translation of a book originally written in English may be owned by the translator. The owner of the copyright of the original English book will not change.

However, to be a creator of the derivative work, the developer must have appropriate rights from the copyright owner in the underlying work in order to create its derivative work. For example, if the developer creates a film based on a book, the developer will own a copyright for the film only to the extent the "expression" differs from the expression in the underlying book. The developer needs to have the right to use the book in its film.

This need was starkly illustrated when the license to use the short story underlying Hitchcock's film *Rear Window* expired due to the "termination of transfer" provisions in the Copyright Act of 1909. The Supreme Court found that the filmmaker could no longer exhibit the film without infringing the copyright in the book. (This rule has been modified for certain works by a change in the copyright law in 1992.)

If the developer creates a derivative work beyond the scope of its license rights, the developer will infringe the copyright in the original work. For example, the developer could not legally create a multimedia project from a book when it is only licensed to create a stage play.

Compilations

A compilation is a copyrightable work consisting of preexisting elements, which may or may not be copyrightable in and of themselves. The selection, ordering, or arrangement is the protectable element of the compilation under copyright law. It must meet the originality standards described above. For example, an alphabetical list of names of all persons having telephone numbers in a particular geographic area is not sufficiently original to qualify for copyright protection.

A compilation can be of elements that are not copyrightable. These elements may not be protected under copyright law because the term of copyright on them has expired, such as Shakespeare's plays, or because the elements are not sufficiently original to be copyrightable, such as part numbers.

The copyright in the compilation protects only the selection, order or arrangement of the elements. For example, if a publisher selected five Shakespearean plays, and annotated and arranged them in a particular order, such a compilation would be protected under copyright law. On the other hand, if a second publisher were to select another five Shakespearean plays (even including some of those selected by the first publisher) and order them in a different way and annotate them differently, that work would also be protected by copyright law as a compilation. However, the second work would probably not violate the copyright in the first compilation unless the selection, order, or arrangement of the second work was "substantially similar" to the first compilation.

LEGAL PROBLEMS IN THE MULTIMEDIA MARKET

A significant legal problem in exploiting new opportunities in the multimedia market is that many traditional license arrangements in the film and book publishing industries may not be broad enough to permit exploitation in multimedia markets. The difficulty of obtaining the necessary legal rights is increased because the copyrightable works that are combined into a multimedia work—

books, computer software, photographs, film, and music—arise in separate industries with their own legal customs and expectations.

Multimedia works generally require the developer to obtain rights beyond those traditionally granted in these industries. The developer of a multimedia work must carefully determine what rights it and its customers will need and ensure that the developer negotiates appropriate licenses with the holders of those rights. In fact, the differences in these legal customs mean that the transaction costs (including determining who owns the rights and negotiating to obtain them) of obtaining some of these rights could be prohibitive.

For example, the creator of a multimedia work may find that it is less expensive to have music specifically written and recorded for the project than to try to determine what rights are needed for existing musical works and then to negotiate obtaining such rights from different parties.

The developer of a multimedia work should be aware of these issues as he or she plans which works to create. In fact, he or she should consider including an experienced attorney as part of the team at an early stage in the planning process to ensure that these issues are understood. By obtaining such advice at an early stage in the development process, the developer can avoid becoming committed to obtaining rights that would be too expensive or require too long to obtain.

The failure to foresee successfully what rights the developer will need in creating and distributing the multimedia work could result in the significant impairment of its ability to create the work or exploit it. For example, many film companies were surprised by the advent of the videocassette rental market. Many licenses for the rights in such films were drafted prior to the introduction of the videocassette and the videocassette recorder (VCR). Consequently, even sophisticated film companies did not have the right to distribute videocassette versions of the films that they had distributed for performance at movie theaters.

The copyright law has a long history of dealing with new technologies. In this century, it has dealt with the advent of talking pictures, broadcast television, and videocassette. Yet disputes over rights in new technologies can still arise even between sophisticated companies. The publishing house of Simon & Schuster and the film maker Quintex Entertainment, Inc. sued one another over certain rights to the book *Lonesome Dove*. Simon & Schuster, one of the largest publishing houses in the United States, obtained the exclusive right to publish *Lonesome Dove* from the author, Larry McMurtry. However, Larry McMurtry had retained the motion picture, educational picture, and television picture rights. He then licensed the motion picture rights to Quintex, which produced a well-known miniseries based on the book.

The Simon & Schuster contract included an "electronic rights" clause that was very broadly drafted to cover exploitation of *Lonesome Dove* in all types of media. A dispute then arose over Quintex's attempt to distribute an audiocassette of the sound track of the miniseries. Simon & Schuster objected to this distribution as being beyond the scope of Quintex's license to the "movie rights." Despite the planning by a sophisticated major publisher such as Simon & Schuster, they did not foresee all of the potential "spinoff" products arising from the novel *Lonesome Dove*.

Disputes regarding videocassette rights are still continuing. Walt Disney Co. has just been sued by the music publisher of Stravinsky's *Rite of Spring* over the performance of the ballet music in the videotape of *Fantasia* released by Disney. The music publisher, Boosey & Hawkes Music Publishers, Ltd. (B&H), claims that the use of the ballet music in the video version of *Fantasia* exceeds the scope of the license granted to Disney. B&H claims that the license is limited to "one motion picture to be exhibited solely in theaters."

The National Writers Union has recently sued several large publishers over the inclusion of articles written by their members in computer on-line databases. The National Writers Union alleges that the publishers were permitted to use articles only once in printed form and were not permitted to include the articles in on-line computer databases. The Harry Fox Agency and several other music publishers have sued the CompuServe on-line information service. They claim that CompuServe is illegally permitting the distribution of their music in digital form through its forums.

These examples demonstrate the importance of understanding the legal principles involved in multimedia works and carefully considering what rights will be necessary to create and exploit the work.

Some of the most important legal problems for multimedia developers and publishers can be summarized as follows:

- *Limited media rights.* The "owner" (such as a film company) of copyright in the work may not have the rights to exploit the existing work in a new media or format. This problem will be particularly acute with adaptations of third-party works, such as books or plays, where the author may have retained significant rights. For example, the Hitchcock film *Rear Window* was based on a short story. The movie *Oklahoma* was based on the musical of the same name.

- *Limited scope of rights.* This problem is similar to the one described above. However, it is sufficiently important to warrant special attention. The development of multimedia works will generally require significant modifications of the original work. These rights may require contacting several different entities to obtain rights, such as the owner of the underlying work. In certain cases, actors may have individual contracts with a studio that would require permission to use their name and likeness.

- *Music rights.* The licensing of music presents special problems for multimedia works because of the nontraditional manner for which it is used. Most of the standard performance and synchronization licenses for television programs and movies do not include the rights necessary to create multimedia works. The Harry Fox Agency has developed a "Multimedia License" for new productions, but it does not solve the problem of dealing with music in films or other "preexisting" works.

- *Special treatment of news.* The use of news reports requires a reexamination of the conditions under which the material was acquired. The broadcast of news has significant legal protection. The use of such material in a different context might not be permitted. For example, the Rodney King video was broadcast as news with no payment or a minimal payment to the cameraman. But when Spike Lee used the news segment in his Malcolm X film, the cameraman sued him for copyright infringement. The parties later settled.

- *Treatment of residuals.* The entertainment unions such as SAG and AFTRA are just beginning to develop contracts for new media productions. Other unions, such as the Writers Guild and the Directors Guild, are just beginning to consider the problem.

- *Interaction with common industry provisions.* The creation of multimedia works may result in unanticipated consequences under common provisions in industry agreements. For example, if Video-on-Demand is introduced, how will it be treated under the current syndication structure, which assumes that the broadcaster will control the time at which the program is viewed? Similarly, existing agreements with networks or other distributors may hurt the ability of a producer to exploit the rights in certain areas of multimedia.

- *Different traditions of the computer industry.* Multimedia products depend on computer software and hardware to operate. The computer industry has developed its own expectations and licensing traditions, which are very different from those of the broadcast industry. For example, the performance right is rarely addressed in licenses for computer programs because, until recently, computer programs had little or no graphic content. The computer industry also is not familiar with the requirements of the various Hollywood union contracts, which are quite well known in the entertainment industry.

- *Pricing.* Multimedia works may require very small parts of the existing work. For example, how much should be charged for a 30-second video clip of a television program in a CD-ROM?

- *Scope of rights to obtain for future works.* The potential multimedia publisher should ensure that it obtains rights to all of the potential multimedia markets, both those currently in existence and those that may come into existence. The failure to do so may result in problems similar to those of the Disney and Quintex Entertainment audiocassette dispute.

OTHER LEGAL ISSUES

While copyright law is the most important intellectual property law for protecting rights in multimedia works, the developer and publisher need to know enough about patent, trademark, and trade secret law to avoid infringing intellectual property rights owned by others and to protect their multimedia works.

Patent Law

Patent law in the United States is based on a federal statute, the Patent Act. States are prohibited from granting protection similar to that provided by the Patent Act.

Types of Works Protected

Patent law protects inventions and processes ("utility" patents) and ornamental designs ("design" patents).

Inventions and processes protected by utility patents can be electrical, mechanical, or chemical in nature. Examples of works protected by utility patents are a microwave oven, genetically engineered bacteria for cleaning up oil spills, a computerized method of running cash management accounts, and a method for curing rubber. The Compton's patent, which caused such concern before it was reviewed and rejected, was a utility patent.

Examples of works protected by design patents are designs for the sole of running shoes, sterling silver tableware, and a water fountain. They have also been used to protect "icons" in computer software.

Exclusive Rights

A patent owner has the right to exclude others from making, using or selling the patented invention or design in the United States during the term of the patent. Anyone who makes, uses, or sells a patented invention or design within the United States during the term of the patent without permission from the patent owner is an infringer even if he or she did not copy the patented invention or design or even know about it.

Standards

There are strict requirements for the grant of utility patents and design patents.

Utility Patents

To qualify for a utility patent, an invention must be new, useful, and "nonobvious." To meet the novelty requirement, the invention must not have been known or used by others in this country before the applicant invented it, and it also must not have been patented or described in a printed publication in the United States or a foreign country before the applicant invented it. The policy behind the novelty requirement is that a patent is issued in exchange for the inventor's disclosure to the public of the details of the invention. If the inventor's work is not novel, the inventor is not adding to the public knowledge, so the inventor should not be granted a patent.

Meeting the usefulness requirement is easy for most inventions. An invention is useful if it can be applied to some beneficial use in society.

To meet the nonobvious requirement, the invention must be sufficiently different from existing technology and knowledge so that, at the time the invention was made, the invention as a whole would not have been obvious to a person having ordinary skill for that field. The policy behind this requirement is that patents should only be granted for real advances, not for mere technical tinkering or modifications of existing inventions.

It is difficult to obtain a utility patent. Even if the invention or process meets the requirements of novelty, utility, and nonobviousness, a patent will not be granted if the invention was patented or described in a printed publication in the United States or a foreign country more than one year before the application date or if the invention was in public use or on sale in the United States for more than one year before the application date.

If a developer believes that his or her multimedia work involves technology that might be patentable, he or she should contact a patent attorney before distribution of the product, preferably in the design stage. Once a patentable invention is used in a "distributed" product, certain limits to protection arise. In the multimedia field, an example of an invention that might be patentable is a software engine for multimedia works. An example of a process that might be patentable is an instructional method for using interactive video technology in classrooms. (Optical Data Corporation was recently granted two patents covering such a process.)

Some ideas are not patentable. Methods of transacting business and printed matter without physical structure are not patentable. Discoveries of scientific principles, laws of nature, and natural phenomena are not patentable (although applications of such discoveries are). The discovery of a new use for an old product is not patentable.

Design Patents

To qualify for a design patent, a design must be new, original, and ornamental. Design patents may be an option for protecting some elements of multimedia works (user interfaces, for example, which can also be protected through copyright law). However, design patents are considered rather weak intellectual property protection, and owners of design patents rarely sue to enforce their patents against infringers.

Procedure for Getting Protection

Patent protection is obtained by demonstrating in an application filed with the U.S. Patent and Trademark Office that the invention meets the stringent standards for grant of a patent. The patent application process is an expensive, time-consuming process (for utility patents, it generally takes at least two years). Although a company can file a patent application on its own, the application process is very complex. Generally, a company should use an experienced patent attorney or patent agent (a nonlawyer who has passed the special patent bar exam given by the U.S. Patent and Trademark Office).

Duration

Utility patents are granted for a period of 17 years. Design patents are granted for a period of 14 years. Once the patent on an invention or design has expired, anyone is free to make, use, or sell the invention or design.

Trademark Law

Trademarks and service marks are words, names, symbols, or devices used by manufacturers of goods and providers of services to identify their goods and services, and to distinguish their goods and services from goods manufactured and sold by others. For ease of expression, "trademark" is used in this chapter to refer to both trademarks (used on goods) and service marks (used for services).

For trademarks used in commerce, federal trademark protection is available under the federal trademark statute, the Lanham Act. Many states have trademark registration statutes that resemble the Lanham Act, and all states protect unregistered trademarks under the common law (nonstatutory law) of trademarks.

Types of Works Protected

Examples of words used as trademarks are MGM and United Artists for film distribution services. Examples of slogans used as trademarks are "Fly the Friendly Skies of United" for airline services and "Get a Piece of the Rock" for insurance services. Examples of characters used as trademarks are Mickey Mouse for movies and Sonic the Hedgehog for games.

Sounds can be used as trademarks, such as the tune used by National Public Radio. Product shapes and configurations—for example, the distinctively shaped bottle used for Coca Cola—can also serve as trademarks.

Standards

Trademark protection is available for words, names, symbols, or devices that are capable of distinguishing the owner's goods or services from the goods or services of others. A trademark that merely describes a class of goods rather than distinguishing the trademark owner's goods from goods provided by others is not protectable. For example, "Apple" is protectable as a trademark for computers, but not for apples.

Exclusive Rights

Trademark law in general, whether federal or state, protects a trademark owner's commercial identity (goodwill, reputation, and investment in advertising) by giving the trademark owner the exclusive right to use the trademark on the type of goods or services for which the owner is using the trademark. Any person who uses a trademark in connection with goods or services in a way that is likely to cause confusion is an infringer. Trademark owners can obtain injunctions against the confusing use of their trademarks by others, and they can collect damages for infringement.

Duration

A certificate of federal trademark registration remains in effect for ten years, provided that an affidavit of continued use is filed in the sixth year. A federal registration may be renewed for any number of successive ten-year terms so long as the mark is still in use in commerce. The duration of state registrations varies from state to state. Common-law rights endure so long as use of the trademark continues.

Trade Secret Law

A trade secret is information of any sort that is valuable to its owner, is not generally known, and has been kept secret by the owner. Trade secrets are protected only under state law. The Uniform Trade Secrets Act, in effect in a number of states, defines trade secrets as "information, including a formula, pattern, compilation, program, device, method, technique or process that derives independent economic value from not being generally known and not being readily ascertainable and is subject to reasonable efforts to maintain secrecy."

Types of Works Protected

The following types of technical and business information are examples of material that can be protected by trade secret law:

- Customer lists;
- Designs;

- Instructional methods;

- Manufacturing processes;

- Document tracking processes; and

- Formulas for producing products.

Inventions and processes that are not patentable can be protected under trade secret law. Patent applicants generally rely on trade secret law to protect their inventions while the patent applications are pending.

Standards

Six factors are generally used to determine whether material is a trade secret:

- The extent to which the information is known outside the claimant's business;

- The extent to which the information is known by the claimant's employees;

- The extent of measures taken by the claimant to guard the secrecy of the information;

- The value of the information to the claimant and the claimant's competitors;

- The amount of effort or money expended by the claimant in developing the information; and

- The ease with which the information could be acquired by others.

Information has value if it gives rise to actual or potential commercial advantage for the owner of the information. Although a trade secret need not be unique in the patent law sense, information that is generally known is not protected under trade secrets law. The traditional methods that companies use to protect their trade secrets are nondisclosure agreements, marking documents with stamps, and locked storage cabinets.

Exclusive Rights

A trade secret owner has the right to keep others from misappropriating and using the trade secret. Sometimes the misappropriation is a result of industrial espionage. Many trade secret cases involve people who have taken their former employers' trade secrets for use in new businesses or for new employers.

Duration

Trade secret protection endures so long as the requirements for protection—generally, value to the owner and secrecy—continue to be met. The protection is lost if the owner fails to take reasonable steps to keep the information secret.

Publicity/Privacy

The creation and exploitation of multimedia work may raise other legal issues. For example, a publisher and developer should be concerned about potential defamation or violation of publicity or privacy rights. Defamation is a doctrine that prevents the dissemination of false or wrongful statements about a person that expose him or her to hate, ridicule, or contempt or that injure or have a tendency to injure his or her reputation.

On the other end of the spectrum are the restrictions on the invasion of a person's privacy or the unauthorized exploitation of his or her name or image. For example, a person generally has the right to avoid intrusion into his or her private affairs. This right may be waived if the affairs are no longer private. The use of the image or voice of a famous person in a way that adversely affects his or her reputation or that falsely implies that he or she sponsors or approves the project can result in liability. Recently, a court awarded significant damages to Bette Midler for a commercial that used a singer specifically hired to imitate her style.

To avoid this type of liability, the film and television industry commonly obtains releases from those who appear in an identifiable manner in a film. To the extent that the developer is incorporating a preexisting film or other work into its new work, he or she may wish to examine the releases obtained by the author of that work. The developer may also wish to obtain a release from governments in key locations if the locations are presented in a negative light. For example, the makers of the film *Bonfire of the Vanities* obtained a release from the government of the Bronx because of the negative portrayal of the town in the movie.

Moral Rights

Moral rights are another legal doctrine that may affect the creation and distribution of the work. Moral rights generally protect authors by providing control over their work after they have completed it. Moral rights are distinct from the economic rights of copyright discussed earlier. Moral rights are much more common in Continental Europe than in the United States. However, since joining the Berne Convention in 1988, the United States has been required to provide moral rights protection for works created in the United States. To date, this protection has been limited to certain works of visual art or "fine" arts.

However, in foreign jurisdictions, such as France and Germany, moral rights exist in a much wider range of copyrightable works. These rights are very important for works that will be distributed in foreign countries. The two most important of these rights are "attribution" (the right to require acknowledgment of the author's role in the creation of the work) and "integrity" (the right to prevent the distortion or modification of the work). For example, when Ted Turner colorized a number of black and white films he was sued in France by the directors of the movies not for copyright infringement (he owned the copyright), but for violation of the directors' "integrity" rights. In some countries, such moral rights may be waived by contract. However, other countries provide that they may not be waived by contract as a matter of public policy.

The developer must be careful to ensure that an appropriate waiver of these moral rights is obtained for the multimedia work that he or she creates and that the creation of the work will not violate the moral rights in one of the preexisting works included in the work.

LEGAL CONTRACTS

Multimedia developers enter into business relationships with both individuals and businesses to help them create and distribute multimedia works. Most of these relationships result in "contracts" that have legal consequences. Most contracts don't have to be in writing to be enforceable. However, the developer should try to get all of these agreements in writing for the reasons discussed below. An understanding of contracts is critical for multimedia developers.

What Is a Contract?

A contract is a legally enforceable agreement between two or more parties. The core of most contracts is a set of mutual promises (in legal terminology, "consideration"). The promises made by the parties define the rights and obligations of the parties.

Contracts are enforceable in the courts. If one party meets its contractual obligations and the other party doesn't ("breaches the contract"), the nonbreaching party is entitled to receive relief through the courts.

Example 1: Breach of Contract for Nonpayment of Acceptable Work

A developer promised to pay a graphic designer $5,000 for creating spaceship animation for his videogame. The graphic designer created the materials and delivered them to the developer, as required in the contract. The developer admits that the materials meet the contract specifications. If the developer does not pay the graphic designer, the graphic designer can go to court and get a judgment against the developer for breach of contract.

Generally, the nonbreaching party's remedy for breach of contract is money damages that will put the nonbreaching party in the position it would have enjoyed if the contract had been performed. Under special circumstances, a court will order the breaching party to perform its contractual obligations. Because contracts are enforceable, parties who enter into contracts can rely on contracts in structuring their business relationships.

Example 2: Breach of Contract for Work Not Done

A developer entered into a contract with a composer, promising to pay the composer $4,000 for composing a brief composition for the developer's multimedia work. Shortly after the composer started work on the piece for the developer—before the developer paid the composer any money—the composer got an offer from a movie studio to compose all the music for a movie and abandoned the developer's project. The developer had to pay another composer $6,000 to do the work that the composer had contracted to do. The developer can sue the composer and obtain a judgment against the composer for $2,000 (the amount that will result in the developer's obtaining the music for a net cost of $4,000, the contract price).

In this country and most others, businesses have significant flexibility in setting the terms of their contracts. Contracts are, in a sense, private law created by the agreement of the parties. The rights and obligations of the parties are determined by the contract's terms, subject to limits imposed by relevant statutes.

Example 3: Breach of Contract for Failure to Pay Agreed Cost

A developer promised to pay a composer $5,000 to create music for the developer's multimedia training work. The composer created the music and delivered it to the developer, as required in the contract. The developer did not pay the composer, so the composer sued the developer for breach of contract. The developer's defense was that the composer did what was promised, but the developer never should have agreed to pay more than $2,000 for that work, a fair price. The court will enforce the developer's promise to pay the composer $5,000.

Written Contracts

A deal done on a handshake—"You adapt your book into a screen play and I'll pay you $10,000"—is a contract, because it is a legally enforceable agreement involving an exchange of promises. Most contracts are enforceable, whether they are oral or written. Nonetheless, a developer should always have written contracts for all of its business relationships.

A developer should always use a written contract for the following reasons:

- The process of writing down the contract's terms and signing the contract forces both parties to think about and be precise about the obligations they are undertaking. With an oral contract, it is too easy for both parties to say "yes" and then have second thoughts.

- When the terms of a contract are written down, the parties are likely to create a more complete and thorough agreement than they would by oral agreement. A hastily made oral agreement is likely to have gaps that will have to be resolved later when the relationship may have deteriorated.

- With an oral contract, the parties may have different recollections of what they agreed on (just as two witnesses to a car accident will disagree over what happened). A written agreement eliminates disputes over who promised what.

- Some types of contracts must be in writing to be enforced. The Copyright Act requires a copyright assignment or exclusive license to be in writing. State law requirements vary from state to state, but, in most states, a contract for the sale of goods for $500 or more must be in writing.

- If a developer has to go to court to enforce a contract or get damages, a written contract will mean less dispute about the contract's terms.

Who Can Enter into a Contract

Minors and the mentally incompetent lack the legal capacity to enter into contracts. All others are generally assumed to have full power to bind themselves by entering into contracts. They can also give other people the right to "bind" them. For example, many Hollywood agents have the right to bind the actors and directors whom they represent. In most states, the legal age for entering into contracts is eighteen. The test for mental capacity is whether the party understood the nature and consequences of the transaction in question.

Corporations have the power to enter into contracts. They make contracts through the acts of their agents, officers, and employees. Whether a particular employee has the power to bind the corporation to a contract is determined by an area of law called agency law or corporate law.

A corporation has a separate legal existence from its founders, officers, and employees. Generally, the individuals associated with a corporation are not themselves responsible for the corporation's debts or liabilities, including liability for breach of contract.

Offer and Acceptance

A contract is formed when one party (the "offeror") makes an offer that is accepted by the other party (the "offeree"). An offer—a proposal to form a contract—can be as simple as the words, "I'll create the music composition for $2500." An acceptance—the offeree's assent to the terms of the offer—can be as simple as "You've got a deal." Sometimes acceptance can be shown by conduct rather than by words.

When an offer has been made, no contract is formed until the offeree accepts the offer. Never assume that the offeree will accept the offer. Contractual liability is based on consent.

Example 1: Infringement Due to Indefinite Acceptance

A developer offered to pay a photographer $500 to use photographs in the developer's multimedia work. The photographer said, "Let me think about it." The developer, assuming that the photographer would accept the offer, went ahead and used the photo. The photographer then rejected the developer's offer. The developer has infringed the photographer's copyright by reproducing the photograph for use in the multimedia work. The developer must now either remove the photographs from the multimedia work before distributing the work (or showing the work to others) or reach an agreement with the photographer. Once the photographer files suit or sends a demand letter, the developer will have difficulty financing the product and the photographer may be able to get an injunction to stop its distribution.

The offeree should not assume that an offer will remain open indefinitely. In general, an offeror is free to revoke the offer at any time before acceptance by the offeree. Once the offeror terminates the offer, the offeree no longer has the legal power to accept the offer and form a contract.

Example 2: Work Interrupted Due to Indefinite Acceptance

An animator offered his services to a developer, who said, "I'll get back to you." The developer then contracted with the client to quickly produce a multimedia work involving animation (making the assumption that the animator was still available to do the animation work). Before the developer could tell the animator that he accepted the animator's offer, the animator sent the developer a fax that said, "Leaving for Mexico. I'll call when I get back." The developer and the animator did not have a contract. The developer should not have assumed, in entering into the contract with the client, that the animator was still available.

If a developer is the offeree, he or she should not start contract performance before notifying the offeror of his or her acceptance. Prior to acceptance, there is no contract. An offer can be accepted by starting performance only if the offer itself invites such acceptance, but this type of offer is rare.

Example 3: Withdrawn Work Offer

Big Co. offered to pay a developer $5,000 to create a corporate presentation multimedia work for Big Co. Before the developer's president notified Big Co. that the developer accepted the offer, Big Co. sent the developer a fax that said, "We've changed our minds. Due to budget cuts at Big Co., we can't afford to do the multimedia project." In the meantime, the developer's staff had begun preliminary work on the project. The developer and Big Co. did not have a contract, so the developer has no legal recourse against Big Co. for loss of the deal or for the costs of the preliminary work.

Until an offer is accepted, the offeror is free to revoke the offer, unless it has promised to hold the offer open.

Example 4: Work Offer Made to Competitors

On June 1, Big Co. offered to hire a developer to create an interactive training work for Big Co. On June 4 (before acceptance by the developer), Big Co. notified the developer that it was giving the contract to the developer's competitor. Big Co. terminated the offer to the developer. The developer has no legal recourse against Big Co.

The offeree may need time to make up his or her mind before accepting an offer. He or she should get the offeror to give a written promise to hold the offer open for a few days. That will give the offeree time to decide whether to accept.

Don't reject an offer and then try to accept it. Once an offeree rejects an offer, the offer dies and the offeree's legal power to accept the offer and form a contract terminates.

Example 5: Reopening an Offer

A publisher offered to buy all rights in the developer's multimedia work for $100,000. The developer, hoping for a better offer, said no. Then the developer realized that the publisher's offer was the best the developer could do. The developer called the publisher and said, "I accept your offer." Because the offer was no longer open, the developer cannot form a contract by trying to accept the offer.

Except for the simplest deals, it is wise for the developer to have his attorney involved as soon as possible. Generally, it takes more than one round of negotiations to form a contract. Often, the offeree responds to the initial offer with a counter offer. A counter offer is an offer made by an offeree on the same subject matter as the original offer, but proposing a different bargain than the original offer. A counter offer, like an outright rejection, terminates the offeree's legal power of acceptance.

Example 6: Counter Offer

A publisher offered to buy all rights in the developer's multimedia work for $100,000. The developer responded by saying, "I'll give you the right to distribute the work in the United States for $100,000." The developer's response to the offer was a counter offer. The developer no longer has the legal power to form a contract based on the publisher's offer to purchase all rights in the work.

Consideration

Consideration, in legal terminology, is what one party to a contract will get from the other party in return for performing contract obligations.

Example 1: Consideration for Developer and Artist

A developer promised to pay an artist $500 if the artist would let the developer use one of the artist's drawings in the developer's multimedia work. The consideration for the developer's promise to pay the artist $500 is the artist's promise to let the developer use the drawing. The consideration for the artist's promise to let the developer use the drawing is the developer's promise to pay the artist $500.

According to traditional legal doctrine, if one party makes a promise and the other party offers nothing in exchange for that promise, the promise is unenforceable. Such a promise is known as a "gratuitous promise." Gratuitous promises are said to be "unenforceable for lack of consideration."

Example 2: Gratuitous Promise

John told Sam, "When I buy a new Silicon Graphics computer for my animation work, I'll give you my Sun computer." John bought a new Silicon Graphics computer but did not give Sam the Sun computer. According to traditional legal doctrine, John's promise to give Sam the Sun computer is an unenforceable gratuitous promise. Sam gave nothing to John in exchange for John's promise to give Sam the Sun computer.

In some states, a gratuitous promise can be enforced if the party to whom the promise was made relied on the promise. Other states no longer require consideration for certain types of promises.

Lack of consideration is rarely a problem for promises made in the context of business relationships. In most business contracts, there is consideration for both parties ("mutual consideration," in legal terminology).

The lack of consideration problem can arise in the context of amendments to contracts, however. Also, in some states, a promise to hold an offer open (see "Offer and Acceptance" earlier in this chapter) is unenforceable unless the offeree gives the offeror consideration (pays the offeror money) to keep the offer open.

Typical Contract Provisions

Many contracts include special types of provisions. This section discusses the common types of provisions.

Duties and Obligations

The duties and obligations section of a contract is a detailed description of the duties and obligations of the parties and the deadlines for performance. If one party's obligation is to create a multimedia work, software, or content for a multimedia work, detailed specifications should be stated.

Representations and Warranties

A warranty is a legal promise that certain facts are true. Typical representations or warranties in contracts concern such matters as ownership of the contract's subject matter (for example, the software) and the right to sell or assign the subject matter. In multimedia industry contracts, warranties of ownership of intellectual property rights and noninfringement of third parties' intellectual property rights are common. For contracts involving the sale of goods, certain warranties are implied under state law unless specifically disclaimed by the parties.

Termination Clauses

These clauses ensure that either or both parties have the right to terminate the contract under certain circumstances. Generally, termination clauses describe breach of contract events that trigger the right to terminate the contract (for example, nonpayment of royalties). Termination clauses also describe the methods of giving notice of exercise of the termination right, and whether the breaching party must be given an opportunity to cure the breach before the other party can terminate the contract.

Remedy Clauses

These clauses state what rights the nonbreaching party has if the other party breaches the contract. In contracts for the sale of goods, remedy clauses are usually designed to limit the seller's liability for damages.

Arbitration Clauses

An arbitration clause states that disputes arising under the contract must be settled through arbitration rather than through court litigation. Such clauses generally include the name of the organization that will conduct the arbitration (the American Arbitration Association, for example), the city in which the arbitration will be held, and the method for selecting arbitrators. For some transactions, the arbitration will be handled through the special arbitration arrangements of Hollywood unions.

Merger Clauses

Merger clauses state that the written document contains the entire understanding of the parties. The purpose of merger clauses is to ensure that evidence outside the written document will not be admissible in court to contradict or supplement the terms of the written agreement.

Tips for Contracts

The contract formation process varies widely, from contracts formed quickly in face-to-face meetings to contracts formed after teams of attorneys have spent months in negotiations.

Here are some general tips for all types of contracts:

- *Be comfortable with the obligations undertaken.* If a term—for example, a deadline—makes the developer uneasy, he or she should make a counter offer that substitutes a term with which he or she is more comfortable. Do not assume that the publisher or other party will excuse the developer from strict compliance and do not rely on the other party's oral assurances that it will not insist on strict compliance.

- *Remember Murphy's Law.* Before signing a contract, consider what could go wrong or what could make performance of obligations difficult or expensive. If the actual performance is more difficult or expensive than the developer anticipated, that is not a valid excuse for not performing.

- *Don't leave anything out.* Cover all aspects of the understanding accurately with the other party. If the other party wrote the agreement based on an oral understanding reached earlier, make certain that the written terms match the terms of the oral agreement. Don't leave points out of the written document, even if the other party says, "We don't need to put that in writing."

- *Cover all options, consequences, and possibilities.* Do not avoid an issue because it is "sensitive." Deal with the sensitive issue during the negotiations. Make sure that the contract includes a merger clause to avoid disputes about whether proposals made during negotiations but not included in the final written agreement are part of the contract.

Use an experienced lawyer to draft or at least check the agreement. Multimedia products involve the application of a wide variety of legal principles. A mistake can cost the developer thousands of dollars in legal fees to solve. It's cheaper and easier to solve such problems before signing an agreement. The developer should use an experienced lawyer either to draft the agreement or to review it.

FUTURE ISSUES

The law is still evolving in many of the areas that will be important to multimedia developers. For example, the application of the law to on-line computer services is just beginning. A recent case established for the first time that a bulletin board operator is responsible for "infringing materials" (in this case, scanned photos from Playboy) that are posted on his bulletin board even though he didn't know that it was there. Other issues such as the liability of the on-line computer service (and the sysop) for libel and slander are still open.

The Hollywood unions are very interested in being active in this area, but they have a long history of dealing with a very centralized film industry. Consequently they may not be ready for the large number of multimedia developers. They do not yet have a method to deal quickly and cheaply with clearing rights to existing film clips. Even the identification of the actors and other guild members in such performances can be very difficult.

The protection of virtual reality experiences is a completely open issue. Copyright law will protect the software and graphics that help create the virtual reality environment. The protection of the "interactive" experience itself under present copyright law would be difficult because it is not "fixed," just as a live television program that is not recorded or videotaped is not protected by copyright.

CONCLUSION

The multimedia developer must recognize that basic knowledge about these legal issues is essential for success in this industry. He or she should also secure the assistance of an experienced attorney and should get the attorney involved early in the project, for example, in deciding what content to use for his project. The failure to do so can lead to spending thousands of dollars in legal fees to defend a lawsuit or obtain the necessary clearances.

BIOGRAPHY

Mark Radcliffe is a partner with Gray Cary Ware & Freidenrich, Palo Alto, California, who focuses his practice on representing high technology and multimedia clients in their licensing and financing transactions. He is a member of the Board of Directors of the Computer Law Association. He was chairman of the Licensing Executives Society's Computer Industry Committee. He is on the editorial board of the *Computer Lawyer* and is a country correspondent for the *European Intellectual Property Review*. He was the reporter of the Task Force on the United Kingdom Trademark Law for the United States Trademark Association.

Mr. Radcliffe speaks frequently on multimedia issues such as at the following: Seybold San Francisco Conference, Practicing Law Institute, Prentice Hall Law and Business, Multimedia Law and Business, National Association of Broadcasters' Multimedia World, Game Developers' Workshop, and Multimedia Communications '93. He publishes widely on multimedia topics and is the co-author of *Multimedia Law Handbook*, which was published in January, 1994.

Chapter 7

VIRTUAL REALITY
THE FORWARD EDGE OF MULTIMEDIA

DR. FRANK BIOCCA
UNIVERSITY OF NORTH CAROLINA

KENNETH MEYER
CYBEREDGE JOURNAL

Virtual reality (VR) rides the forward edge of multimedia. Put on a head-mounted computer display that resembles a visor and suddenly you are plunged into another world, a world that exists only in a computer. You turn to the left and a panorama of new surroundings sweeps past your view. You look down and see your hand floating in front of you. You point your finger and you fly over the computer landscape (see Figure 7-1).

Without analysis, without a crystal ball, you know in your gut that this will change the way we communicate. It's as if you are a TV viewer in the 1930s. You can see the snow-spotted image of the first television broadcasts: crude, blurry, but the outline of something more is clear. Despite the primitive technology, clumsy devices, and cartoonish pictures, the force of the idea of virtual reality is plain. VR pushes the logic of multimedia technology over a boundary that separates this radically new medium from the media that preceded it.

The Kaiser Electro-Optics VIM personal viewer is one of the more advanced virtual reality display systems. The VIM has a wide field of view and includes high fidelity sound. The VIM immerses the user in the sights and sounds of the virtual world. (Photo courtesy of Kaiser Electro-Optics)

Figure 7-1   The Kaiser Electro-Optics VIM

Multimedia technologies merge computer and video technologies and enhances both. On one hand, multimedia extends traditional text-based computing by adding the vividness of full-motion video and stereo sound. On the other, multimedia extends traditional audiovisual technologies, adding the interactivity and "intelligence" of the computer. But VR, unlike other forms of multimedia, extends the domain beyond the realm of traditional communication technologies. In VR, viewers enter a computer-generated world; they are no longer on the outside looking in.

VR pushes the representational power of multimedia along three forward edges:

- VR evokes a world that the user can enter;

- VR provides computer-generated images to more senses than traditional media;[1] and

- VR extends and intensifies interactivity.

On the first edge, VR evokes a world with dimension and depth: a world of 3D objects with properties that resemble the physical world. In VR, a viewer may travel around a virtual house or admire a virtual sculpture from any angle.

The simulations of virtual worlds need not be limited to the visual sense. VR presents a 3D sound space instead of the static audio imaging of consumer stereo. The sounds of VR appear to emanate from their point of origin. For example, as you walk through the middle of a virtual string quartet, the sounds of the cello and viola pass to the right while the violins pass to the left. And like the physical world, VR sounds change in timbre and volume as the viewer moves around virtual sound sources. As you leave the virtual music hall, the sounds of the quartet diminish and give way to the sounds of the virtual lobby.

On the second forward edge, virtual reality extends multimedia by generating information for the other senses, not just sight and sound. VR systems equipped with tactile feedback can provide the illusion of touching a virtual object or moving physically through a virtual space. For example, as you climb virtual stairs, a banister slides through your hand and stairs rise to meet your step.

On the third forward edge, VR extends the interactivity of multimedia. Instead of using a computer mouse to click on a canned video tour of a building, viewers can move freely around a virtual building. They can walk the halls, climb the stairs, or peer out the windows. Moreover, since viewers can interact with the virtual objects, they can do more than merely walk around; they can move the tables, the chairs, or even the walls. When the technology matures, a viewer might have convincing haptic experiences,[2] like picking up a baseball, sensing its texture, heft, and solidity, and then pitching from a full windup. The baseball may or may not obey the rules of gravity.

Interactivity is not restricted to inanimate objects. Users may see, hear, feel or, perhaps, smell and taste representations of other users "inside" the virtual world. The experience of others in virtual worlds may give rise to new virtual communities that parallel established communities. With VR, the audience finally has climbed inside the TV set.

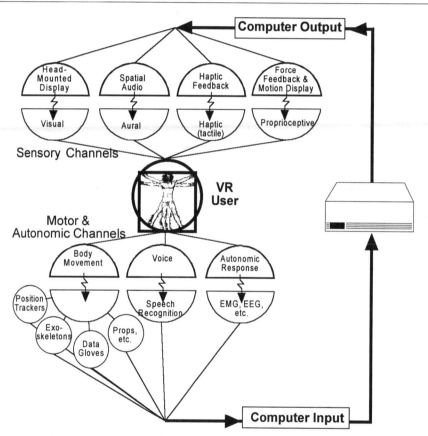

Virtual reality hardware can be thought of as an array of possible input and output devices. These input and output devices transmit information to and from a user. Each device is coupled to one of the user's senses or motor channels: Output devices serve a sensory channel; input devices are linked to a user's motor or autonomic channels. No single VR system incorporates all of these input and output devices, but most have been used in one or another system. (From Biocca & Delaney, in press)

Figure 7-2　　　　Types of VR Input and Output Devices

Marshall McLuhan pointed out that media are environments. With VR, this is literally true. In the long-term, VR devices may mediate our every sense of the physical world and interweave computer-generated images of another world—one that is created in a database. At that point, the body enters into the illusion, and the user can touch and interact with the media images. This prospect sets VR radically apart from other media.

For the foreseeable near term, no VR system will be able to capture all the senses. As yet, the technology is in its infancy. But we need not wait for the ultimate implementation. Today's VR systems can generate a very compelling sense of place. Contemporary flight simulators create an experience that is so engaging that pilots react to training exercises as if they are actually flying. With VR, it is easy to suspend disbelief in the 3D illusion. Consequently, it is best not to think of VR just as technology, but rather as a conceptual model for creating experiences with vividness and interactivity that were never before possible.

A Peek Inside the Box

On the nuts-and-bolts level, there is nothing radical about VR technology. At core, it's just a way of assembling available technologies in a novel arrangement. The first rudimentary system was demonstrated 25 years ago.[3] Since then, improvements in the enabling technologies have been driven by basic computer-graphics research and high-end military flight simulators. In the last five years, technology has reached a plateau where it is practical to build VR systems outside the rarefied lab environment.

A prototypical VR system has three types of components (see Figure 7-2):

- *Output devices (displays)*. Information is provided to the user's senses. An example is a head-mounted display with earphones;

- *Computer*. The computer keeps track of the virtual objects and renders pictures of the world that match the viewer's perspective; and

- *Input devices (sensors)*. Input devices sense the actions of the user. For example, a position tracker tells the computer the viewer's location and direction, and a Dataglove tells the computer the position of the hand.

In operation, a VR system senses the activity of the viewer through input devices. For example, when the viewer looks left, the tracker[4] reports the head movement to the computer. The computer maintains a database of objects and can determine which objects are part of the changing view and what part of those objects are visible. The objects are actually computer models that incorporate descriptions of sensory qualities such as sight, sound, and touch. The result is rendered by the computer and sent to the display devices. So when the viewer turns, the sights and sounds follow. This is how the computer creates the illusion of a virtual world.

There are a variety of both input and display devices. Each device is suited to a particular kind of input or display. These separate system components will be discussed in the section on VR paraphernalia.

Fundamentally, a VR system is an integration of these three kinds of system components. Unlike Artificial Intelligence (AI), no basic technological breakthroughs are required. Although VR is crude, the basic technology exists.

VR Is Not Just a Medium— It's a Destination

VR is not just a technology; it's a destination or at least the illusion of one. Current research has focused on the psychological components that contribute to the VR illusion. The terms in Table 7-1 describe some elements that are key to creating the impression of being in a virtual place.

TERMS	DESCRIPTIONS
Immersion	The degree to which a virtual environment immerses the perceptual system of the user. The more the system blocks out stimuli from the physical world and captures the senses, the greater the immersion.
Presence	The perceptual illusion of being actively present in another place, sometimes called "being there." The sensation of presence is influenced by three factors: 1) The intensity, sensory range, and sensory resolution of the mediated experience; 2) The amount of interactive control; for example, the ability to move in the virtual environment to better "see" details, to hear and place sounds, or to move your virtual hand and "touch" virtual objects; 3) The ability to modify the environment with your actions. Presence is understood to be a continuum; the viewer is more or less present. At the extreme end of the continuum is a hypothetical point called "perfect presence." With perfect presence, the illusion of presence is so strong that the user's experience of the virtual world is indistinguishable from direct experience of the physical world.[5]
Telepresence	Telepresence refers to the feeling of being in some distant physical location. In a typical telepresence application, virtual reality devices are connected to a robotic system located in a remote location. The user sees, hears, touches, and moves through the distant physical location through links to the robot's sensors (e.g., cameras, microphones, touch sensors, etc.).

Table 7-1   Key Virtual Reality Terms

VR is also a destination for the evolution of communication technology. It is the logical next step. The progress in technology from naturalistic painting to photography, film, high-definition TV (HDTV), and large-screen projection systems such as IMAX has been a steady march toward greater sensory vividness. The same trend is apparent in the development of aural media from the Edison phonograph to digital surround-sound. Figure 7-3 shows how the vividness of VR compares to other media.

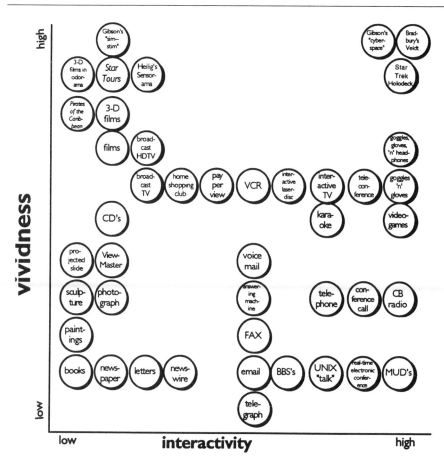

This graph charts communication media according to their level of interactivity and vividness. For example, books have a low level of interactivity and sensory vividness. Present-day VR systems sit close to the top of this array but fall short of the visions of future media imagined in the pages of science fiction. (From Steuer, in press)

Figure 7-3   Types of Communication Media

THE VR INDUSTRY

The VR market is beginning to emerge. Estimates from Machover Associates (White Plains, NY) predict that VR sales and services will gross $250 million in 1994. Projections from 4th Wave Inc.

(Alexandria, VA) predict a $2.5 billion potential market with about $500 million in sales by 1997. Machover's projections of potential market size are even more optimistic. They forecast an annual growth of 60 percent with revenues of $1 billion by 1997. If Machover's predictions bear out, VR business will expand at twice the pace that computer graphics grew in the 1970s.

Where will the growth come from? 4th Wave divides the market into three segments: research and development, entertainment, and general applications. To date, R&D sales represent the bulk of market activity; 90 percent of current VR sales are to university, government, and industry labs. But the research and development opportunity is limited and will not be able to keep pace with the entertainment segment.

In the next five years, entertainment will outstrip all comers, realizing nearly half of its market potential by 1997. Entertainment sales will come from two principal sources: so-called location-based entertainment (LBEs) and consumer electronics. Several LBE vendors, including Virtual World Entertainment (Chicago, IL), IWERKS (Burbank, CA), Visions of Reality (Irvine, CA), Magic Edge (Mountain View, CA), FighterTown (Lake Forest, CA), and Virtuality Group (London), have announced aggressive plans. Visions of Reality announced that it will place 150 sites nationwide by the summer of 1995. Since installations are estimated to cost $1–2 million each, LBEs will be a strong market driver.

The consumer electronics market will be more significant. The first VR consumer product was the Mattel Powerglove,[6] which sold nearly 2 million units. The next products to be marketed in the retail stores will be $200 VR helmets that can be hooked to videogames. One manufacturer, VictorMaxx, sold a crude VR head-mounted display (HMD) during the 1993 Christmas season. SEGA announced a product for Christmas 1994, and Nintendo has long been rumored to have something in the works.

Additionally, the convergence of phone and cable companies will broaden the VR consumer market. Most of the telecommunication companies have strategic alliances with videogame companies. With the aid of devices such as AT&T's EDGE, VR viewers will be able to occupy the same virtual world while playing from home. Add a respectable market potential for virtual sports equipment, and gross sales for VR entertainment goods should approach $400 million in 1997.

The largest potential market may be in the general applications segment where VR will become an integral part of ordinary work, integration will be slow. VR developers must first bring added value to existing tools. While theories on the benefits of VR are abundant, but there are as yet no clear examples of added value. Consequently, general applications will lag far behind both entertainment and research.

If these predictions prove true, companies building VR components will enjoy the benefits of catching the wave early.

THE MANY FACES OF VR

VR systems come in a variety of forms. The five most common forms are immersive systems, augmented systems, vehicle systems, through-the-window systems, and mirror systems. All these configurations use input devices, computers, and display devices. The differences stem from the type of input and display devices used.

These different configurations have evolved to fill the needs of various applications. The following section describes the qualities of each VR form and the approach used in its implementation.

Immersive Systems

The most familiar VR system is immersive. This configuration is typically featured in popular press articles about VR. In immersive VR, the viewer dons a HMD and Dataglove. The HMD blocks the sights and sounds of physical surroundings—only the virtual world is experienced. The telepresence system pictured in Figure 7-4 (see "telepresence" definition in Table 7-1) illustrates how elaborate the equipment may become when full interactivity is the key design criterion. The ultimate goal is more powerful perceptual illusions and an undiminished sense of presence.

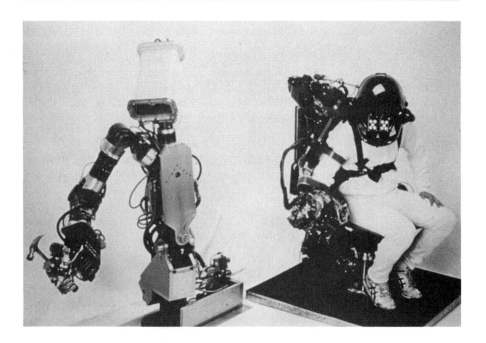

Example of a virtual reality system designed to give the user the sensation of being present in some distant location (telepresence). The unit on the right controls the actions of the robot on the left. The user sees the 3D world of the robot and experiences some of the sensations of touching the objects the robot touches. This particular system is used to control the actions of a robot in remote-sensing, underwater applications. A version of the unit on the left can also be used to see and touch purely virtual objects created by a computer. (Courtesy Naval Ocean Systems Center)

Figure 7-4   Telepresence VR System

When the immersed viewer moves, the images of the virtual world change just as if the viewer were looking at a physical scene. These changes include visual properties that our vision system normally interprets as cues for depth perception. These depth cues include stereopsis, motion parallax, texture gradients, spatial localization, and object interposition. These scientific terms break down the different ways that retinal images of the physical world change when viewers or objects move. The VR system mimics these changes so that the viewer's experience of the computer graphic world resembles the 3D experience of the physical world.

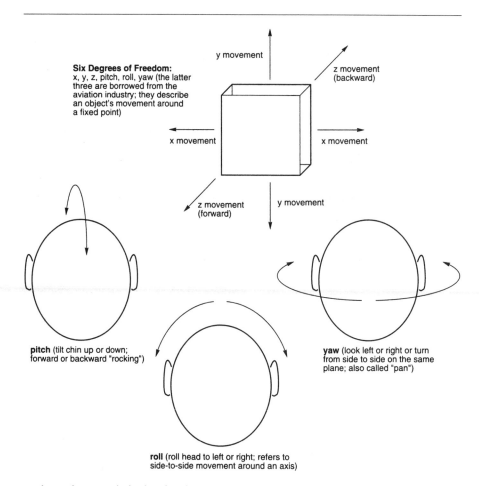

Six Degrees of Freedom:
x, y, z, pitch, roll, yaw (the latter three are borrowed from the aviation industry; they describe an object's movement around a fixed point)

y movement

z movement (backward)

x movement   x movement

z movement (forward)   y movement

pitch (tilt chin up or down; forward or backward "rocking")

yaw (look left or right or turn from side to side on the same plane; also called "pan")

roll (roll head to left or right; refers to side-to-side movement around an axis)

Six degrees characterize the freedom of an object to move in space (6 degrees of freedom [DOF]). Three degrees define the motion of the object in 3D space: horizontal motion, vertical motion, and motion in depth. Three degrees of freedom characterize the orientation of an object: pitch, yaw, and roll. The importance of this kind of information for VR systems is most apparent in immersive systems where the user's head position and motion must be carefully monitored by the computer. (From *Garage Virtual Reality*, written by Linda Jacobson and published by SAMS Publishing. Diagram provided courtesy of Linda Jacobson.)

Figure 7-5   Six Degrees of Freedom (DOF)

This deft coordination is triggered by movement-sensing devices called *position trackers*. The tracker measures up to six different directions of movement. Three of the directions describe position and correspond to the familiar three dimensions of space. The remaining three dimensions refer to orientation and describe the direction in which the object is pointed (see Figure 7-5). The computer's world management system records this position data and uses them to determine what parts of the virtual world the viewer should see. The result is the illusion of a stable 3D world.

Immersive systems are far from perfected. They suffer from two principal shortcomings: They are slow to respond, and they generate worlds that lack detail. Not even state-of-the-art systems found at key research labs like NASA Ames (Alameda, CA), University of North Carolina at Chapel Hill, the University of Washington, and IBM Watson Institute (Yorktown Heights, NY) are highly vivid or responsive. The results from these systems are more like a hazy dream than a nerve-jarring hallucination.

However, the 3D illusion is strong and the effect can be powerful. Viewers feel as if they are inside the computer-generated world and not merely peering at a flat image of it. The effect is good enough so that several VR companies are making immersive systems for entertainment. Systems from Virtuality Entertainment (a.k.a. W-Industries), Alternate World Technologies (Prospect, KY), Straylight (Warren, NJ), and Visions of Reality are either currently or soon to be on the market.

Augmented Reality Systems

In an augmented reality (AR) system the virtual world is superimposed on the physical world; it does not replace it. The augmented reality viewer wears a "see-through" display so the physical world is not blocked. The augmented display superimposes computer graphic images over the physical surroundings.[7]

Except for the see-through HMD, an AR system closely resembles an immersive system. Despite similarity of hardware, the utility of the approach is quite different. AR systems offer a unique advantage. Data or instructions can be superimposed on physical objects. Steve Feiner and his team at Columbia University have been exploring this idea. They have built an AR system that shows users how to maintain a laser printer. Arrows point out the steps needed to add paper, change a toner cartridge, or open the printer lid (see Figure 7-6).

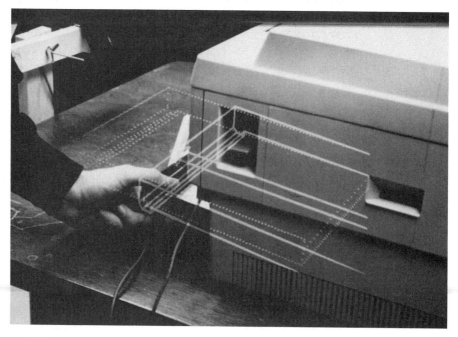

In this demonstration of an augmented reality system, the user perceives a computer-generated maintenance diagram of a laser printer. The head-mounted display superimposes virtual objects on real-world scenes, but the technology still has many limitations (see text). (Photo courtesy of Steven Feiner, Blair MacIntyre, and Dore Seligmann, Columbia University and copyrighted © 1993 Steven Feiner, Blair MacIntyre, and Dore Seligmann)

Figure 7-6   Augmented Reality System

Boeing Aircraft has discussed building a more ambitious system. Maintenance engineers will don a "see-through" display to follow the wiring and hydraulic tubing inside the walls of an aircraft fuselage. One day similar techniques could be used to help researchers find their way through a library or an archive.

However, the effective implementation of an augmented system faces several obstacles. Apart from the limitations associated with immersive VR systems, the see-through displays have several additional shortcomings: They do not create images that are bright enough to be merged with the real world. They cannot display objects at different focal depths, and they cannot produce opaque objects that occlude the real world instead of merely overlaying it. Similarly, position tracking is inadequate; existing tracers cover only a small area and tend to be inaccurate and slow. As a result of poor position tracking, AR systems cannot maintain registration with the real world, and their virtual images will not properly align to physical objects. Improvements in both see-through displays and position trackers are essential before a commercially viable AR system can be built.

Vehicle Systems

Vehicle systems have been around longer than the other forms of VR. Also known as simulators, they were initially developed by the military to train pilots. Much of the simulator technology was developed for military training.

Instead of wearing a HMD, the viewer sits in a vehicle and looks out windows onto the virtual world. In a typical vehicle system, high-resolution displays are mounted outside the windows. But since the viewer is focusing on the surface of the display, the effect is much like looking at surround TV. Better systems use collimated displays that place the optical image at infinity. The visual effect is quite convincing, although some significant visual cues of depth are absent.

Vehicle systems can be mounted on motion platforms that provide a compelling illusion of motion through the virtual space. The motion platform simulates such physical sensations as acceleration, deceleration, or other physical forces acting on the vehicle. The users are usually seated, though they may, in some cases, lie or stand. By moving the platform in conjunction with the visual and audio images, the user may have the illusion of moving a greater distance than the actual short movements of the platform.

Motion platforms have been used for years in high-volume, location-based entertainment (LBE) systems at Disneyland, Universal Studios, and, more recently, the Luxor Hotel in Las Vegas. In the next couple of years, LBEs mounted on motion platforms will become more common. A number of LBE companies including Sega, Magic Edge, Xatrix, and Ride & Show have shown systems designed for use in shopping malls.

However, a vehicle system can create a compelling illusion without a motion platform. Virtual World Entertainment has become one of the more successful VR companies with their BattleTech game. Battletech players sit in an instrumented Mech capsule that has a view of a hundred-square-mile battlefield. (A Mech is a tank on two legs.) The players drive the Mechs around the battlefield trying to vanquish competing players. Other companies such as IWERKS (Virtual Adventures) and FighterTown are also creating vehicle simulations without motion platforms.

Through-the-Window Systems

Before we see the widespread adoption of highly immersive systems, we are likely to see a proliferation of through-the-window systems. A through-the-window system gives the viewer a porthole onto the virtual world by using a standard monitor, HDTV screens or video-projection systems. The view through the window can be 3D. There is no HMD.

Several companies sell devices that provide a different view to each eye. If the views are offset, like they are in a HMD, the images are combined by the viewer's vision system into a 3D illusion.

These through-the-window systems can produce very convincing 3D effects when equipped with a position tracker. The effect is similar to looking at a hologram. As the viewer moves right or left, a different perspective of the world comes into view. However, the view into the world is restricted, just as it is when looking out a window. Consequently, through-the-window systems have a less compelling sense of presence, but, because of their reasonable cost, they are proving to be popular among VR developers.

Mirror Worlds

In a mirror world, unlike other VR systems, viewers do not directly experience being inside the virtual world. Instead, viewers stand before a video camera, and their image is matted into a virtual environment. The composite is viewed on an ordinary monitor. Viewers do not wear a HMD.

Myron Krueger, who coined the expression "artificial reality" to describe his mirror worlds, has developed a well-known and widely respected system called Videoplace (Vernon, CT). In Videoplace, a silhouette of the viewer's image is projected onto a large screen. The system recognizes the shape of fingers so the user can interact with objects in the world without using an input device such as a Dataglove. The effect is highly interactive. In one application called *Critter*, a virtual entity follows the user around. Krueger called the critter a "playful sprite with an artificial personality." Much of Krueger's work shows a sense of whimsy.

Vivid Effects (Toronto) makes an artificial reality system called Mandala. The Vivid Effects system has been successfully marketed to museums and entertainment complexes around the world.

VR Paraphernalia

At the beginning of this chapter, we mentioned that a prototypical VR system has three kinds of system components: output devices, computers, and input devices. Output or display devices present the images that allow the viewer to experience the virtual world. Computers maintain the database of the virtual world and calculate its appearance. Input devices report the user's activity to the computer. In this section, we will discuss each of these components in detail.

Output Devices

VR experiences must come through output devices. This section discusses some of them in detail. (See Table 7-2 at the end of this section for an overview.)

Seeing 3D All Around You: Head-Mounted Visual Displays

Head-mounted displays borrow an old stereo imaging trick that goes back to the 19th-century Brewster stereoscope and the familiar ViewMaster. Since our eyes are set apart (interpupilary distance), each sees a slightly different view of any scene (binocular disparity)— the key to seeing 3D. The Brewster stereoscope captures these different views in paired images, each slightly different, matching the separation of the eyes. This image pair is called a *stereo pair*. When a viewer looks in a stereoscope, each eye sees a different image; the effect is 3D.

Similarly, the HMD puts a slightly different video image in front of each eye. Two small cathode ray tubes (CRTs) or liquid crystal displays (LCDs) are used to present the stereo pair. A series of lenses increase the size of each image in order to fill more of the user's visual field. The assembly of monitors and lenses is mounted inside the HMD. Currently more than thirty VR developers manufacture HMDs.

The current generation of wide-view HMDs shows only low-resolution, cartoonlike images. In the near future, however, we will see improvements in new high-resolution LCDs. But better resolution is no panacea. To better understand this state of affairs, it necessary to discuss the basic challenges that face a HMD developer.

The acuity of our vision places extreme demands on HMD resolution since the eye can resolve an arcminute of detail. Roughly speaking, this means that we can see a detail of one-third of an inch at a distance of 100 feet, which is like seeing a shirt button across the length of a basketball court.

This has an important implication for video displays. Video displays build images from picture elements called *pixels*. These pixels are just solid squares or dots. Typically, we do not see pixels because they are smaller than the acuity of our vision; they just blend together to create an image. However, if the pixels are larger than the acuity of vision, the pixels become visible, and this limits the detail we can see. On low-resolution displays, the detail is limited because the pixels do not dissolve into the image. Generally speaking, the more pixels in a display, the more detail it can show, and vice versa.

To put this in perspective, let's consider a 35mm movie screen. A typical movie screen covers a 40-degree field of view. Since 35mm film has the equivalent of 3,600 pixels across its width, there are 90 pixels spread across each degree of the screen's viewing area. This equals 1.5 pixels per arcminute, which is slightly better than we can see. The pixels per arcminute are called the display's *pixel size*. The smaller the pixel size, the better the detail of the image. This means that if we move closer to the movie screen, the pixel size increases with the field of view since the same number of pixels must cover a greater area. If we move back in the auditorium, the field of view and pixel size both decrease since the same number of pixels are available to cover a smaller viewing angle.

HMD developers must try to cover a wider field of view with fewer pixels. Our visual field is approximately 200 degrees wide and 120 degrees high. Some evidence suggests that as the images cover more of our visual field, we feel a greater sense of presence. Covering a wide field of view with a small pixel size requires a lot of pixels, many more than are currently available. Many HMD developers use LCDs that are 512 pixels wide, a far cry from the effective resolution of 35mm film. In fact, if 512 pixels are used to cover a 40-degree field of view, the pixel size is 4.7 arcminutes, about one-seventh as sharp as human vision. However, if the same display is used to cover a 90-degree view, the pixel size swells to over 10 arcminutes.[8] This is why a viewer is legally blind in most HMDs.

There is good news on the horizon. Several manufacturers have announced new high-resolution technologies that could decrease the pixel size of HMDs in half. But even at these resolutions, HMD developers will have to reduce the field of view in order to keep the pixel size small enough so the virtual world can be seen in acceptable detail.

One exciting prospect, which is still in the research stage, is retinal scanner displays. Instead of assembling the image line by line on a display surface, the image is assembled on the retina itself. The light from the display is directed into the eye, creating a virtual image that is suspended in space. Anyone who ever twirled a sparkler to make a circle has created a "virtual" image. At the University of Washington Human Interface Technology (HIT) Lab, researchers are developing a laser-based retinal scanner. The device promises to be a forerunner of lightweight, affordable displays that offer small pixel size over a wide field of view. Some VR insiders are betting that the ultimate HMD will be laser based.

Seeing Through-the-Window: 3D on a Monitor

Through-the-window systems provide a 3D image from a single picture on a standard monitor, HDTV screen, or video-projection system. Like HMDs, through-the-window systems must present each eye with a different image. Unlike HMDs, the images must be presented from a single monitor.

The CrystalEyes system is used in through-the-window VR systems. The glasses are composed of two liquid-crystal shutters, one each for the left and right eyes. The shutters alternately open and close rapidly in sync with the visual display. Separate images are shown to each eye. When the left eye's image is on the screen, the right eye's shutter is closed, and vice versa. The mind fuses the two images to perceive a 3D object floating above the screen or receding in depth. (Photo courtesy of Stereographics Corporation.)

Figure 7-7　　　CrystalEyes System

There are several methods for presenting separate images from a single monitor: separated-image systems, LCD shutter systems, polarized lens systems, anaglyph systems, and lenticular lens systems. Separated-image systems, such as Simsalabim's Cyberscope (Berkeley, CA), work like old-fashioned stereoscopes. They use mirrors or lenses to present a different image to each eye. LCD shutter systems such as StereoGraphics's CrystalEyes (San Rafael, CA) and polarized lens systems such as Reveo's VRex (Hawthorne, NY) combine the two images into a single picture; the viewer sees in 3D with the aid of glasses (see Figure 7-7). The lenses of the glasses block light to each eye in a rapid sequence so that the right eye lens passes only right-eye images and the left eye lens passes only left-eye images. LCD shutter systems block light with LCDs; polarized lens systems block light with polarizing filters.

Anaglyph systems work in a similar fashion except that they use red and green filters to block light. These anaglyph systems are inexpensive and have been used in 3D cinema. Lenticular lens systems, such as Dimension Technology's Autostereoscope (Rochester, NY), combine the two images in narrow vertical slices. Each slice is covered by a half-cylindrical lens that directs the image's slices to the proper eye. Lenticular lens systems produce a stereo picture without glasses, but the viewer must sit in a "sweet spot" to get the effect.

Through-the-window systems offer several advantages over HMDs. Because of the high resolution of desktop monitors and their small viewing angle, through-the-window displays have a pixel size that is smaller than the acuity of vision. The high-resolution images are especially useful for viewing 3D scientific data. Also, when it comes to ordinary work, the through-the-window systems are more comfortable and convenient than HMDs. Users can see the surrounding physical environment without the inconvenience of putting on or taking off a HMD.

Hearing All Around You: Spatially Dynamic 3D Sound

Fully experiencing a virtual environment means hearing it as a space. Hearing is three dimensional; it is one of the ways that we create a mental concept of the space around us. Audio "objects" have a spatial location just as visual objects do. Think of how we rely on our hearing to track the sound of a mosquito buzzing around our heads. The aural realism of virtual spaces requires replicating the spatial characteristics of sounds: for example, the changing intensity of a race car engine as it approaches a listener and screeches past or the diminishing tap of footsteps as they echo down a dark, empty corridor or the chatter of a conversation in the far corner of a room. Like changing 3D visual images, aural images must also change as users move between virtual voices, musical instruments, clanging metal objects, and roaring virtual engines.

For a virtual sound object to appear to originate from a location, the generated sounds must change to preserve the spatial relationship between the listener's ears and the sound source. If spatially distinct audio "objects" are to be a convincing part of the illusion, they should ideally do the following:

- Match the stereophonic properties of the user's two ears, including the spectral mix of frequencies, delays, and distortions;

- Change in relation to a space's acoustics, which are determined by its size, shape, and absorption properties; and

- Change in relation to the user's position and orientation in the space.

Although current systems such as Crystal River Engineering's Convolvotron (Groveland, CA) can produce some impressive audio spaces, they have problems. The acoustic imaging system needs to be designed for an "average" set of ears. Knowing exactly what constitutes average ears is a technical challenge since human ears have different acoustic properties. As a result not all listeners get a good 3D sound effect. Sometimes a sound that originates in front appears to come from behind or the height (azimuth) of the sound's origin is uncertain. In some cases, the sound is no different from traditional stereo: The 3D effect completely fails, and the sounds appear to originate inside the user's head. Research projects at NASA Ames and the University of Wisconsin-Madison are focusing on these problems.

There is little doubt that audio imaging is an essential part of generating the full illusion of being there. Powerful audio imaging also can provide spatial information about objects. Spatial audio can alert a user to objects or virtual beings that are visually occluded. Spatial audio can also enhance the verisimilitude of visual and tactile illusions.

Feeling All Around You: Haptic (Tactile) Displays

When you view a film, you experience the look and sound of objects, but you cannot feel them. VR can go the extra step. With haptic feedback, you are able to feel a wall, a hammer, or a pen. Future haptic displays might even be able to create subtle and complex illusions like holding a virtual violin and sensing its heft, shape, and solidity. And, of course, many have talked about using tactile displays for computer-generated sexual pleasure (sometimes referred to as "cybersex" or "teledildonics"). Before any of this is possible, research is needed to better understand how to direct images to the muscles and organs that give us a sense of texture, force, balance, and spatial coordination (tactile, haptic, and proprioceptive sensors).[9]

Simulating the feel of things is not easy. Let's take the example of picking up a hammer. The presence of a sturdy, top-heavy object in your hands is communicated by the surface skin sensations and pressures. Signals from the tactile receptors communicate the solidity of the handle. Signals from the muscles communicate gravity's pull on the hammer and the impulse of the hammer striking a board.

Though haptic display is still in its infancy, a number of strategies are under development.[10] Some devices produce an illusion of an object's surface with a device that presses rounded pins against the fingertips. Other devices inflate small bladders to create a pattern of touch. Some apply small electrical charges to the skin or directly to the nerves. None of these devices can simulate complex surfaces like sandpaper or powder; at best, the effect could be interpreted as touching an edge.

Another variety of haptic display produces force-feedback so that when you push on an object, it pushes back at you. The physical sensation comes not only from the surface of the skin but also from various other sensors attached to our muscles and joints. These sensations from forces on the muscles and positions of the joints are part of the proprioceptive system that informs us of the location and movement of our body and limbs in space.

These force-feedback displays combine both display and input functions through a mediating object that transmits the "feel" of an object. Just as a blind person uses a cane, a user may hold a joystick, steering wheel, or mechanical hand grip to feel the virtual world. Using characteristics assigned to the virtual object, the system calculates the amount and direction of force to display. Varying the force to the device creates illusions that might be described as springiness, bumpiness, hardness, or viscosity. For example, at MIT's Media Lab, Margaret Minsky has demonstrated how a user might experience stirring a stick in a virtual bucket of ice. Users feel the sensation of the stick pressing and sliding past the virtual ice cubes.

However, creating a satisfying force-feedback experience has proven difficult. For example, Louis Rosenberg at Stanford University has been working to create an effective experience of a virtual wall. Walls prove to be a tough problem because creating the effect of a dead stop places impossible demands on the haptic display mechanism. Consequently, virtual walls can never be as rigid as real walls. However, Rosenberg has decomposed the experience of a wall into its component parts and is working to develop models for creating a credible illusion of hardness.

Another way of obtaining haptic illusions is to encase the hand or, more radically, the body in an external brace-like device known as an exoskeleton (see Figure 7-8). As the name suggests, an exoskeleton is like an external skeleton having joints positioned at the same locations as the body. When fully anchored and connected to motors, an exoskeleton applies forces that simulate sensations such as grasping, pushing, or lifting. The development of exoskeletons for force-feedback has been fueled by military and aerospace telepresence applications. The Navy Ocean Systems Center's advanced teleoperator system manufactured by Sarcos is a good, but expensive, example.

Developments in haptic display are still in the very early stages. Tactile-haptic illusions are still crude and expensive. Force-feedback devices are furthest along and are already finding their way into game systems and to a lesser degree in some professional engineering and medical telepresence applications.

Why the need for haptic imagery? It facilitates communication and enhances the sense of presence. We are equipped with over 17 million tactile receptors so tactile imagery and force-feedback can be

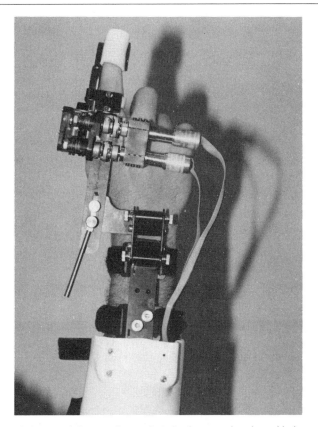

This device is an exoskeleton. Exoskeletons conform to the limbs of a user and can be used both as input and output devices. Operating as an output device, this exoskeleton can simulate the feel of moving or touching objects by transmitting forces to the hand and forearm. For example, the exoskeleton can simulate the resistance of a drinking glass when it is grasped. As input devices, some exoskeletons can also register the location, flexion, and motion of a limb. (Photo of EXOS SaFire, courtesy of EXOS Inc.)

Figure 7-8   Exoskeleton Device

major sources of information. We learn very subtle information about the environment through our sense of touch. Haptic images have proven to be particularly important to telepresence applications. Without it, manipulating distant objects can be like playing the children's game Pin the Tail on the Donkey, but reversed: Teleoperators can see the objects to manipulate, but they do not know exactly where they are reaching. Haptic feedback can improve performance dramatically. One study found it reduced completion times by 50 percent on difficult manual tasks.

Haptic images can even provide new insights in more abstract displays such as 3D tactile graphs. For example, a team headed by Dr. Fred Brooks of the University of North Carolina has demonstrated that haptic information can significantly enhance a chemist's understanding of the docking properties of a molecule. This is only the beginning. Haptic displays promise to lead communication media onto new ground, but only after significant technical challenges are solved.

Smelling and Tasting: Epicurean Pleasures of the Virtual World?

The olfactory and flavor senses are usually ignored by contemporary VR systems. The reason is that both sensations require the application of chemicals to the sense organs. Presently, no display device can effectively control odors and tastes.

Despite this fact, olfactory illusions have been part of simulations in the past. Morton Heilig's Sensorama, built in 1960, included smells. Recently rediscovered, Sensorama has become one of the best-known precursors to present entertainment virtual reality systems. The Sensorama viewer is taken on a high-speed motorcycle ride through the streets of Manhattan. Along the way, they are treated to the smell of vehicle exhaust, pizza, and flowers. Heilig used a vacuum over the user's head to evacuate the smells so they would not linger. (Lingering smell was a chronic problem in the "Smell-o-rama" cinema experiment in the 1950s.) Smells have also been used at Disney's Epcot Center to increase the illusion of displays such as an orange grove, a smoke-filled prehistoric scene, and a humid underwater simulation.

To date, no VR developer has announced either an olfactory or a flavor display, and no well-known research effort has incorporated smell and taste in a virtual world. Savory television is not likely to exist any time soon.

DISPLAY DEVICES	COMMENTS
HMDs and See-Through Displays	As of this writing there are nearly thirty developers of HMDs. Only one commercial "see-through" display is produced.
Boom Displays	The Boom is a stereo display mounted in a box on the end of a balanced-and-jointed linkage. When the user moves the "boom," the movement of the boom's linkages is reported to the computer as position changes.
Through-the-Window Displays	Desktop monitors, HDTV, Vvdeo projection,and collimated displays. Through-the-window display systems are the least expensive approach to 3D visual images. Several approaches are available for producing 3D images from a single display.
Haptic Displays	Haptic displays let the user feel the virtual world. Force-feedback displays have been built into remote manipulators and hand controllers. Tactile feedback displays have been built into gloves and joysticks.
3D Sound Systems	Unlike standard stereo, the sound effects of 3D sound appear to originate from a point of origin outside the listener's head.

Table 7-2   A Sampling of VR Display Devices

Computer Systems

The computer is the "guts" and "brains" of a VR system. Because VR takes a lot of processing power, powerful computers are required. Without low-cost, high-powered processors, VR would be too expensive for all but the most rarefied research lab. But the current state of the technology is only just adequate. Alvy Ray Smith claims that a 50-fold improvement in performance is needed before VR will look real. These improvements will arrive gradually over the next 5 to 15 years.

When we speak of the computer, we are referring to both hardware and software. The VR functions managed by the computer can be implemented in either. For our purposes, we will ignore how a particular function is implemented and focus on what the computer must do to generate a virtual world.

The VR computer performs four principal functions: database management, object–task processing, image rendering, and world management.

The database contains the objects that make up the virtual world. Every virtual structure and every virtual being resides in the database. These database objects contain a description of all the object's attributes. Some attributes like structure and physical property are static, whereas others like position and status are dynamic. The computer updates the database to record changes and, in this way, maintains the virtual world.

Each object may have a program that produces behavior. A ball may bounce. A clock may keep time. A ceiling fan may spin. More complex tasks may determine the effect of gravity, grow a new branch on a virtual plant, or dissipate the steam from a boiling virtual teapot. For virtual creatures and other synthetic beings, the object tasks may involve the coordinated behavior of several object systems like arms, legs, and torso. Each of these object tasks must be computed.

For database objects to become perceptible, their images must be rendered. The rendered images are typically visual, aural, and haptic. The imaging process works roughly like this: The computer knows the user's viewpoint and takes a snapshot of the world from that perspective. Hidden surfaces are excluded, visible surfaces are illuminated or shaded to match light sources, and sounds are attenuated and filtered to match sound sources. The results are drawn element by element and made available to the display devices.

The world manager coordinates all these activities and the data from the input devices. The world management process may take many forms, but a simple case may operate like this: Read the database to determine the state of the world; poll the input devices for user input, update the database to reflect changes, perform the object tasks to determine the actual state of the objects, and render the images (see Figure 7-9).

All of these processes take time, but they must run at a rapid clip in order to create the illusion of smooth motion. Each cycle of the world manager produces one image. VR systems need to produce 18 frames per second to generate an image that does not flicker.

The result is a heavy computational load, and the systems often fall behind. This causes users to experience a perceptual lag. For example, when the user looks left to identify a sound, the view of the virtual world lags behind the movement. The effect is unpleasant and can contribute to motion sickness.

As the complexity of the virtual worlds increases so does the computational overhead and the system lag. The ultimate solution to lag is faster systems. Meanwhile, VR developers must reduce the complexity of their worlds to make the VR experience more responsive.

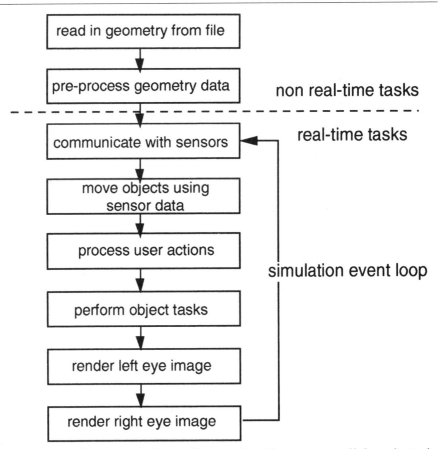

This diagram shows the basic operation of the world manager. The world manager is responsible for coordinating the processes needed to maintain the virtual world. (Diagram from *Virtual Reality, Through the New Looking Glass* by Ken Pimentel and Kevin Teixeira , published by Windcrest Books. Diagram provided courtesy of Ken Pimentel.)

Figure 7-9   World Manager

Input Devices

To create a convincing illusion, immersive VR systems must keep track of the user's body. Input devices track the user's body so the computer can adjust the output in order to maintain the 3D illusion. A full range of input devices maps the movement to changes in the virtual world. Table 7-3 lists several types of VR input devices.

INPUT DEVICES	COMMENTS
Position trackers	Position trackers tell the computer the position of an object in the physical world. The object may be a HMD, a Dataglove, or anything else the system needs to track. Trackers work in a variety of ways. Some trackers are mechanical linkages that attach objects to a fixed position. Other trackers work by measuring light, sound, or magnetic flux. Each system has its advantages and disadvantages.
Gloves, body suits, eye-trackers, and exoskeletons	Input devices can fit the body like clothing. These devices allow the viewer to control the system with the body's natural dexterity. No learning is required. The Dataglove was one of the first VR devices to capture public attention.
Mice, joysticks, and spaceballs	These devices are traditional input devices that have been modified to work in three dimensions. The devices are widely used by VR developers because of their low cost and widespread support.
Speech recognition	In some systems, a user can control virtual objects with voice commands. Speech recognition will eventually become a standard feature of VR systems.

Table 7-3   A Sampling of VR Input Devices

Since the keyboard will be replaced as the primary input device in VR systems, the development of novel input devices is being closely watched by VR researchers and developers. Developments in position-tracking technology are of particular interest. Currently, position trackers are a bottleneck in system performance. Tracker systems with reduced lag, improved accuracy, greater working volume, and better support for multiple users will prove to be a boon to the field.

There's more to body movement than just position information. When people interact with one another, they make inferences about the actions, intentions, and emotional states of others by observing facial expressions, body posture, and movements. Some researchers are trying to develop systems that can sense the intentions of users by "reading" their body postures, movements, and autonomic responses. For example, eye movement especially fixations tell the computer what aspect of the visual world has caught the attention of the user.

VR ALMOST WORKS

During a recent keynote address at Visualization '93, one of VR's leading researchers, Dr. Fred Brooks, told a group of colleagues that VR "almost works." What he meant was that it doesn't work as well as the popular media contends, but it is starting to work.

In his address, Brooks pointed out several shortcomings of current VR technology:

- The biggest problem in VR is system lag. It takes too long for the image to catch up to the viewer's movement. The effect, often called swimming, is like moving in a viscous liquid. Swimming interferes with interactivity and can cause motion sickness. The lag comes from two sources: underpowered computers and slow position tracking.

- The second biggest problem is display resolution. The images are not currently good enough to print readable text.

- The third problem is the narrow field of view. It is difficult to navigate with a narrow field of view.

- The fourth problem is that virtual worlds lack detail. This is due in part to the fact that building a virtual world is an expensive process.

- Finally, position tracking is not accurate enough and does not cover a large enough area.

None of the researchers were surprised by Brooks' statements and many of them are actively working on solutions to these problems. The prospects are good for a rapid and steady progress in the coming years. Here's what we can expect:

- System delays will be reduced by improvements in computer systems. The cost of high-end hardware will drop dramatically. Improvements in system software will allow developers to distribute computations across computer processors.

- New displays that are capable of improved resolution are just around the corner. The displays will improve field of view as well as resolution. But these additional pixels require more computational power. In early implementations, improved displays may cause system delays.

- The virtual worlds will become more detailed because there will be VR customers who will pay to have them built. Also, libraries of 3D images will come on-line, and "world designers" will be able to purchase the furnishings for their worlds. Synthesis Corporation (Jefferson, WI) presently sells libraries of 3D objects.

Also the technology for capturing 3D images is improving. Physical objects can be directly digitized. Technologies exist for mapping a 3D surface using methods based on photogrammetry (construction of 3D features from matched stereo images), ultrasound imaging, and magnetic resonance imaging. The shapes of objects, and even people, can be imported into the virtual environment. For example, students in computer graphics at the University of North Carolina (UNC) can travel inside the head of a digital model of one of their professors, Henry Fuchs, an award-winning computer designer. A white, ghostly, hollow bust of the professor floats in one of the virtual rooms at UNC.

Position tracking, however, will remain a problem. There are no good solutions on the horizon. A new generation of trackers will have to be developed. This next generation will have to combine data gathered from multiple sources, but figuring out when to believe the various sources of tracking information is a difficult technical challenge. Good solutions are a ways off, but we should see incremental improvements in the next 15 years.

BUYING VR RETAIL

We have seen that VR is not a single system but a family of devices and a set of principles for generating the illusion of a virtual place. Improvements will not spring fully formed from VR developers, but they will arrive piecemeal. This will suit the market. The VR industry will most likely expand through the sale of add-in devices such as HMDs and Datagloves for use in existing computer systems rather than the sale of turnkey systems. In this respect, VR will resemble the general market of computer products.

No doubt, the term "virtual reality" will be attached to a number of products that may not deserve the name. Some companies already use the term "virtual reality" to hype low-end interactive games and systems that have no provision for creating a world or invoking a sense of presence.

But enabling technologies alone will not drive the VR business. There must be applications that add value to the way we work or play. Useful applications are the key to industry growth.

THREE VR COMMUNICATION APPLICATIONS

Vice President Al Gore looks at the proposed national fiber-optic communications network and sees a "data superhighway." Fiber-optic-based telecommunication gives us enough transmission capacity to support full-interactive communication with VR. In effect, viewers will go on-line to be in a place that only exists in the network. This place has been dubbed "Cyberspace." Like 15th-century Europeans eager to carve up the Americas, companies all over the globe are eager to colonize new virtual territory. Virtual reality interfaces promise to be the ships that will ultimately carry individuals along fiber-optic rivers to the vast data seas of Cyberspace.

Teleconferencing and Virtual Communities

The most compelling experience in a virtual world will be other people. As you read this, primitive virtual communities are forming on computer networks such as Internet, CompuServe, and Prodigy, where users interact by sending notes and posting notices. Over 3.3 million people use commercial services, 4 million use the government-supported Internet system, and as many as 11 million plug into over 45,000 public access on-line systems. They cluster around topics: arguing, role playing, telling jokes, seeking companionship or just peering in. On Prodigy alone, this chatter leads to 22,000 messages a day.

There is apparently no limit to the types of service that will be built around the growth of virtual communities. A number of companies are watching. For example, Apple recently explored the anthropology of virtual communities with an eye toward the development of future products.

Teleconferencing and virtual communities represent the virtual frontier. Communications by telephone and keyboard provide only a low sense of presence. However, as VR technologies become affordable, the quality of personal telecommunication could radically change.

Consider the following scenario. Three engineers in different cities need to discuss a new prototype of a hydraulic valve. Each enters a specially equipped conference room with projection walls that butt against a conference table. The table appears to extend into the projection walls where each engineer sees his or her colleagues seated across the virtual table. After a short discussion, they put on see-through HMDs for viewing the prototype valve. They examine it from all sides and watch simulations of fluid flowing through it. They decide that a change is needed and call up virtual tools that help them make precise changes to the valve.

Preposterous? Not really. Although the technology for this level of interaction is not yet available, distributed multiuser VR spaces have been demonstrated. VPL gave the world a glimpse with its Reality-Built-for-2 demo where two people interacted with VR representations of each other. More impressive is the military's Simnet system, which allows tank crews located around the globe to climb into simulators and meet on a virtual battlefield. There are more than 200 connected simulator units around the world, but the battlefield exists only in Cyberspace.

Investigators at Japan's Advanced Telecommunication Research Institute International (ARTII) are exploring the possible shape of Cyberspace. Armed with a significant budget from Japan's leading communications companies, ARTII is doing research that explores VR telecommunication interfaces. Their "Communication with Realistic Sensations" project purportedly has a $5.3 million-a-year budget and a ten-year time line.

On the American side, Pacific Bell, US West, NYNEX, and other telecommunication companies are considering the possibility of what some call "televirtuality." US West, the University of Washington, and Fujitsu are working on a televirtuality system for cooperative work that they've dubbed "Greenspaces." Additionally, several VR companies have announced on-line VR systems that take advantage of available telecommunication resources. In fact, one researcher from Carnegie Mellon University has demonstrated a virtual museum where viewers can see the exhibits from a remote location. When the telephone system fully supports virtual reality, the nature of communication will be drastically altered.

Virtual News Environments

The broadcast journalist Edward R. Murrow and his colleague Walter Cronkite sometimes used the phrase "You are there." The phrase captures something essential about news. A news service doesn't really bring the world into the viewer's living room; it brings the viewer out to a location in the world. The names of Murrow's news shows, "Hear it Now" and "See it Now," suggested the direct sensory nature of the broadcast news experience. For example, CNN's continuous reporting during the Persian Gulf war brought the audience to the front line. Audiences watched anxiously as a reporter waited for the arrival of deadly Scud missiles. Such reporting provides the viewer with a sense of being present at a battlefront, summit, or raging fire.

VR forces us to reconsider the two essential dimensions of news presentations: Witnessing events (i.e., "You are there" or "On the scene") and analyzing of the meaning of an event. Both can be radically transformed by 3D news presentation systems.

One idea under consideration is the presentation of news as a 3D interactive simulation. For example, viewers might dial up graphic simulation of the local air pollution forecast. The information would be presented as darkening clouds hovering over a 3D model of their city. Users could "fly" around the model and see it from all sides. Animations of weather and smog data are already available but only as video recordings that require days of calculations on a supercomputer. The simulations cannot as yet be presented in real-time in response to changing weather conditions. Three-dimensional interactive weather models are not ready for news.

However, other types of data, such as stock and commodity data, have been successfully modeled in real-time. Avatar Partners (Boulder Creek, CA) in conjunction with Data Broadcasting Corporation (San Mateo, CA), is selling a product called vrTrader that displays 3D financial data in real-time. Maxus Systems' (New York, NY) Metaphor Mixer also displays financial information with an emphasis on data analysis.

Models such as these allow the user to experience the news in a visceral fashion. Proposals for legislative action could be demonstrated and visualized with user-driven models. Similar concepts can be applied to simulations of economic issues or war tactics. Reporting is now verbal or filmic storytelling. In VR, reporting can become theatrical storytelling in a large, interactive theater—a news room in Cyberspace.

Entertainment: Interactive Narrative Environments

Storytelling has changed dramatically in the last 3,000 years. There is a tremendous experiential difference between a story told around a night fire in the forest and an IMAX film drama crashing around you in Dolby, multi-channel sound. VR storytelling can become participatory. The audience does not just listen and watch; it questions and acts.

Interactive fiction is still in its infancy. In the early days of film, techniques such as montage needed to be developed to discover how to tell stories in this medium. In VR, theatrical devices are still being invented to place the user in the center of an interesting and experientially enriching story. Projects at computer science labs such as Carnegie Mellon's OZ project attempt to create a new form of interactive fiction using artificially intelligent (AI) actors and directors. (For a detailed description of related projects in the filed, see Meyer's article in Biocca and Levy.) Successful interactive fiction systems are likely to be implemented in multimedia environments before they can be transferred to the more complex world of VR.

THE ULTIMATE COMMUNICATION INTERFACE

To understand the strategic role of virtual reality in the future of communication media, we need only appreciate two basic functions of communication media:

- The collapse of space and time; and

- The modeling of ordinary experience in entertainment, role playing, and training.

The telegraph, telephone, and all modern telecommunications attempt to collapse space. The written word, the photograph, and the video camera collapse time. They store vivid information of past events. All media are used to capture experience that is distant in both time and space or is constructed from the imagination.

The most advanced applications of virtual reality stretch the envelope of these basic communication functions. At the Naval Ocean Systems Center, virtual reality interfaces are used as a means of transporting an operator to deep-sea environments for military action, exploration, and rescue missions. At NASA, projects under the direction of Stephen Ellis and Mike McGreevy explore the application of virtual reality interfaces for remotely transporting geologists and other scientists to 3D models of planetary landscapes where they can remotely control a robotic planetary explorer. In some cases, robot surrogates have intelligence enabling them to assist the operator with the task at hand. As Fred Brooks of UNC is fond of pointing out, VR is not AI but IA—not artificial intelligence, but intelligence augmentation, where computers are used to help humans work more effectively.

The use of VR for simulations is the other basic function. Better simulations are needed for military, architectural, medical, engineering, educational, and entertainment applications. For example, the military knows that simulating dangerous or difficult situations will be a great benefit in training their personnel to cope with hazards in the physical world. Similarly, architectural applications of VR interfaces give users a direct experience of buildings before they are constructed. Finally, entertainment VR prototypes and applications seek to simulate all kinds of human experience in the virtual worlds of art and games for the sheer pleasure of experience. But one thing is suggested by all these various applications—the real product of VR may not be experience but insight.

For researchers who are active in the development of VR, the ultimate goal is nothing short of the amplification of human perception and cognition. According to Warren Robinett, a key designer of NASA's first VR prototype, "The electronic expansion of human perception has, as its manifest destiny, to cover the entire human sensorium." And for Fred Brooks, the long-term developmental goal of the technology is nothing short of an attempt to have our perceptual systems accept the reality of a computer-generated illusion, "to fool eye and mind into seeing . . . worlds that are not and never can be."

The technology will improve significantly with these advances. VR gear will become less intrusive and more compelling. It will become part of our everyday attire like a watch, a beeper, or a pen. HMDs with integrated audio and tracking will be carried comfortably in a pocket or purse until needed. They will be equally well suited for either immersive or augmented applications. Our living spaces will be equipped to support the parallel virtual spaces that will become part of our daily work or play. A new breed of input device with haptic display will be developed to facilitate interaction with virtual objects. But before these advances are part of daily life, extensive support will have to be built into the infrastructure. Changes of this order take decades, and we may not see VR integrated into the daily routine for 50 years or more.

As mentioned earlier, VR is not just a technology; it is a destination. What we see now is just part of a long road ahead. Looking back on this road, we can see that today's versions of VR are just the latest step in a millennial march toward the ultimate communication interface, one that gives the user a phenomenal sensation of presence in some distant location or time, the experience of another human's thoughts or inner reality or of the thinker's fantasies about places, people, things, and actions. Books already do this. But print is a crude interface that must be augmented by a lot of imagination. VR tries to print the images directly on the senses. In some ways film does this with the visual sense. VR may eventually render our senses raw, but our imaginations will still actively shape our experience.

Notes

1. "Images" refers not just to visual images, but to aural or tactile images as well. We will use "image" to describe any computer output that appeals directly to the senses. Different kins of images will be discussed in the Output Devices section.

2. "Haptic" refers to the several senses of touch such as tactile and force feedback. Haptic display devices are discussed later in the chapter.

3. Specifying the date of the first VR system depends on how one defines virtual reality. Some stretch it back to the first Link flight stimulator patented in 1929. Others suggest that virtual reality might be a continuum of illusionist technologies stretching back hundreds of years. We think that Ivan Sutherland's experiments with head-mounted, computer-graphic displays are a milestone that marks a significant transition to a different kind of mediated experience. But we are well aware that historical dating is somewhat indeterminate when the definition of virtual reality is still unsettled. In fact, Sutherland can be credited with founding the field because his work in the mid-1960s inspired much, if not most, of the current VR research and development.

4. A tracker is an electronic system that measures the position and orientation of a head, arm, or object in space.

5. Possibly, in some future VR system, the sensation of presence may be more intense than physical reality itself. VR may create a sense of place that not only feels "real" but "hyper-real."

6. The Powerglove is a gauntlet-like input device for Nintendo games. Players pull the glove over their hands and control the game with gestures and finger movements. The Powerglove has become a popular component of garage VR systems.

7. Ivan Sutherland is credited with building the first see-through display. This is one of many contributions Sutherland made in computer graphics during his long and remarkable career.

8. In a HMD, the field of view is increased by wide-angle optics, not by moving the LCD screens closer to the eyes. In addition, the optics place the image at a comfortable focal distance so that images can be viewed without discomfort.

9. Proprioception refers to sense of space through limbs and body.

10. Research in haptic displays dates back to Mike Noll's experiments in the early 1970s. Noll built a force-feedback device using electric motors to exert force on a knob at the end

of a shaft. The knob was moved to explore the surface of simulated objects.

Recommended Reading

Benedikt, M. (Ed). (1991). *Cyberspace: First Steps*. Cambridge, MA: MIT Press.

Biocca, F. & Delaney, B. (Fall, 1994). Immersive virtual reality technology. In Biocca, F. & Levy, M. (Eds.), *Communication in the Age of Virtual Reality*. Hillsdale, NJ: Lawrence Erlbaum Associates.

Biocca, F. & Levy, M. (Eds.) (Fall, 1994). *Communication in the Age of Virtual Reality*. Hillsdale, NJ: Lawrence Erlbaum Associates.

Brooks, F. (1988). Grasping reality through illusion: Interactive graphics serving science (TR88-007) . Chapel Hill: Dept. of Computer Science, University of North Carolina at Chapel Hill.

Durlach, N. (1992). Virtual environment technology for training (BBN Systems and Technologies, Report No. 7661). Cambridge: Virtual Environment and Teleoperator Research Consortium, MIT.

Earnshaw, R., Gigante, M., & Jones, H. (1993). Virtual Reality Systems. New York: Academic Press.

Ellis, S. R., Kaiser, M., & Grunwald, A. (1991). *Pictorial Communication in Virtual and Real Environments*. London: Taylor & Francis.

Feiner, S., MacIntyre, B., Seligmann, D. (1993). Knowledge-based augmented reality. *Communications*, **36**, 7, 53–62.

Furness, T. A. (1988). Harnessing virtual space. *Society for Information Display Digest*, 4–7.

Hamit, F. (1993). *Virtual Reality and the Exploration of Cyberspace*. Carmel, IN: SAMS Publishing.

Jacobson, L. (1994. *Garage Virtual Reality*. Indianapolis, IN: SAMS Publishing.

Krueger, M. (1991). *Artificial Reality*. New York: Addison-Wesley.

Laurel, B. (1991). *Computers as Theater*. Menlo Park, CA: Addison-Wesley.

Meyer, K. (Fall, 1994). Dramatic narrative in virtual reality. In Biocca, F. & Levy, M. (Eds.), *Communication in the Age of Virtual Reality*. Hillsdale, NJ: Lawrence Erlbaum Associates.

Proceedings of the 1993 IEEE Virtual Reality International Symposium (pp. 263-271). Piscataway, NJ: Washington.

Rheingold, H. (1991). *Virtual Reality*. New York: Summit Books.

Steuer, J. (Fall, 1994). Defining virtual reality: Dimensions determining telepresence. In Biocca, F. & Levy, M. (Eds.), *Communication in the Age of Virtual Reality*. Hillsdale, NJ: Lawrence Erlbaum Associates.

Sutherland, I. (1968). A head-mounted three dimensional display. FJCC, **33**, 757–764.

Wexelblat, A. (1993). *Virtual Reality: Applications and Explorations*. Boston: AP PROFESSIONAL.

BIOGRAPHY

Dr. Biocca is Director of the Center for Research in Journalism and Mass Communication and head of the Communication Technology Group at the University of North Carolina. Dr. Biocca's research explores how media interfaces affect the cognitive processing of users. He is particularly interested in how new communication interfaces like virtual reality can be adapted to better communicate information to the senses and the mind.

Dr. Biocca has examined the communication applications and social implications of virtual reality technology. Among Dr. Biocca's books is *Communication in the Age of Virtual Reality* (Fall, 1994), which he co-edited with Dr. Mark Levy. He recently gathered a team of communication researchers for a special issue of the *Journal of Communication* on virutal reality technologies, and prepared a review of virtual reality for the National Association of Broadcasters. Dr. Biocca has also been awarded two grants to study the implications of the diffusion of virtual reality technology into the communication environment. He is presently working on several experiments on perceptual adaptation to virtual environments and augmented reality displays.

Dr. Biocca, a Canadian citizen, was a student of Marshall McLuhan in the early 1970s. Prior to returning to the university, Dr. Biocca worked in the communication and computer industries of Silicon Valley, Calfiornia, where he participated in the introduction of the first portable computer. Dr. Biocca's research team has conducted computer-based public opinion studies for several Fortune 500 companies. Dr. Biocca has commented on media, cognition, and communication for ABC Nightline, NBC News, the *Washington Post*, *USA TODAY*, CSPAN, Voice of Ameria, the USA Radio Network, and other broadcast and print organizations.

Dr. Biocca has lectured at the University of California-Berkeley, University of Wisconsin-Madison, and the University of North Carolina at Chapel Hill. He is on the editorial board of the *Journal of Communication, Computers & Communication*, and other scholarly journals. Dr. Biocca's articles on communication, technology, and cognition have appeared in the *Journal of Communication, Presence, Media Culture & Society, Communication Yearbook, Mass Communication Review, Journal of Popular Culture, Semiotic Web, Journalism Quarterly*, and *Virtual Reality Report*.

Kenneth Meyer has professional experience in the computer and entertainment industries. He was recently a principal and executive VP at Piltdown Inc. who developed products for the virtual reality market. Previously, he directed development at Quick Tally Systems where he was responsible for product design and implementation. He is a contributor to the *CyberEdge Journal* and editor of the *CyberEdge Journal*'s Special Business Edition.

Chapter 8

MULTIMEDIA AND FUTURE MEDIA

DAVID ROSEN
PRAXIS

MULTIMEDIA—A PUBLISHING MEDIUM

Interactive multimedia is the publishing medium for the new millennium. It represents a further extension of the electronic processes of personal and social discourse and creates a new medium of communications. Once one spoke and recalled; oration and memory were the modes of social discourse for reaching other people in "space" and in "time." Later one wrote and read; twenty-six letters could say nearly everything that needed to be known. Now one sees and hears and responds; the waves and particles of optical light cascade in a ceaseless stream of symbols and data, information and values that must be artfully managed by the user.

Multimedia is the next step in the social and technological evolution of publishing and sets the stage for even more profound means and experiences of communications. Multimedia is, in the simplest terms, the digital processing of binary-coded electronic signals. These signals could be of voice or data, text or images, music or video. With digitalization, they are rendered in a uniform identity.

While it is dangerous to prognosticate on the future, it seems clear from today's vantage point that the media world beyond 2001 will likely witness the expanded performance capabilities of digital media. Going further, it seems that this media will likely be transformed into an increasingly "plastic" media, fostering a communication experience that aspires to become quasi-organic in form and function.

During the preceding millennium, human civilization evolved an array of communications technologies, each providing a unique experience. As media, they allowed for the reproduction of letters, then images, then increasingly more exact renderings of images, their coloration, then the capture of sound, and, finally, the conveyance of motion sequences.

Over time, human labor was augmented by mechanical, steam and, as today, electrical forms of power. The media's technical capabilities have been matched with economic and social consequences, principally mass production (with lowered costs of manufacturing and distribution) and mass reception (with wide-scale literacy and product ownership).[1]

This process has created a communications media that is both "richer" in composition and more popular in usage: From books and magazines and newspapers, to lithographs, photography and phonographs, to home videos and CDs, to telegraphy and telephone and cable, to radio and television and satellite, computers and videogames. The electronic media appear to make the world smaller, people are more intimately connected yet more alone, more isolated. This media environment is in the process of further remaking itself, embodying a shift to digital from analog signal processing, and thus being transformed into a new form of communications, one not yet clearly or fully comprehended.

Electronic communications is a flow, the movement of light and electricity, of complex signals and subtle nuances, of sustained messages and discrete bites and bytes. It is the unity of form and content creating meaning. Shape the flow and you influence the meaning. This flow comes from wide and disparate sources: broadcast television and radio signals, cable and telephone lines, satellites and wireless, videotapes and compact discs (CDs), to name but a few. This flow is one-way and two-way, private and public, individual and shared, point-to-point and point-to-multipoint, fixed and mobile, original and copied, invaluable and worthless, empowering and oppressive. Electronic media is invisible and ubiquitous, a sea in which we swim or sink.

Today, Americans avail themselves of a diverse assortment of electronic media, including broadcast television and radio, wire-distributed cable television and telephone voice and on-line computing, and prerecorded music, home videos, and videogames, among others. These media serve the most private of purposes as well as forge a shared culture through the mass dissemination of information, images, and values.[2]

PACKAGED GOODS	CONDUIT/WIRE	WIRELESS
Print publications (books, magazines, newspapers, catalogs)	Telephone Cable television	Broadcast TV Broadcast radio Satellite TV
Prerecorded audio (CDs, cassettes, mini-Disc)		Microwave Cellular "Wireless" cable
Prerecorded video (home video, laserdisc)		
Videogames (cartridges, PC floppy disk)		
Multimedia (CD-ROM)		

Table 8-1   U.S Household Media: The Medium Is The Message

Each medium is based on a distinct technology and provides the user with a unique experience, whether it be watching, listening, speaking, messaging, computing or playing. Each clusters within one of the three domains of media distribution: wire-based, wireless, or packaged (see Table 8-1). Together, the media help fashion a modern sensibility having both economic, sociopolitical, and personal consequences. Each form of distribution is undergoing technological transformation and becoming a multimedia mode of communications.

Interactive multimedia is an all-digital technological innovation and is realized in three forms of signal distribution. It finds its most popular current form as a packaged product, such as a CD-ROM or videogame cartridge. In a wired form, multimedia is emerging slowly as network-distributed on-line services; it is a medium for which sound and still- and moving-image quality are quickly increasing to the level of alternative analog media. The gradual digitalization of wireless signal distribution (e.g., DBS satellites, and microwave) makes it a potentially powerful multimedia platform.

Media communications is based on a user's engaging content as either a self-contained, "closed-loop" experience or as an "open-loop" connection to libraries, databases, or other people. The content takes any number of forms, ranging from the dominant form of a preproduced program (e.g., a game, television show, reference work, or spreadsheet) to a telephone connection with someone a continent away. In all cases, the user receives a signal and responds to it, engages it, interacts with it—whether it is through a PC, videogame player, telephone, Personal Digital Assistant (PDA), or set-top converter box.

Multimedia advances publishing in two critical ways. First, digital signal processing breaks the continuous signal flow that defines analog media, thus creating the opportunity for interactivity; second, and equally important, with the radical reduction of the electronic signal to a numerical value, the inherent differences between existing media—be they audio, text, graphics, images, or video—are negated, creating the conditions for the emergence of a new media form, multimedia. Together, they set the stage for a new communications era.

THE NEXT WAVE

During this decade, packaged multimedia will move with slow, but steady, inevitability across from the business world of computer-peripheral usage into wide-scale consumer adoption. In time, it will likely achieve high levels of popular acceptance, not dissimilar to videogame or in-home computer penetration levels. The social adoption of multimedia will affect in-home leisure and productivity and make an important contribution to the creation of a new TV era, one of an all-digital communications media for 2001 and beyond.

Whole segments of today's print, cassette, floppy disk, and cartridge media will migrate to the multimedia CD format. Everything from early readers and encyclopedias, directories and catalogs, games and movies, how-tos and photo collections will be rendered as multimedia documents.

However, this innovative publishing medium will not completely replace the other media for one simple reason. Multimedia is a screen-dependent experience, involving active eye/hand engagement of content. In counter-distinction of print, prerecorded audio, and traditional television, multimedia does *not* encourage passivity. Failing to satisfy what may be a social (if not biological) need for passivity, one wonders whether multimedia can cultivate reflection, pondering, or patient consideration. Only the future will reveal the answer.

The magic of the multimedia experience is rooted in the "black box" player and the sophisticated microprocessors that determine its computer-like functions and performance capabilities. During the 1990s, the power of the signal processor, the CPU that is the player's brains and guts, will probably witness exponential growth. As is evident today, the move from 16-bit to 32-bit and now to 64-bit machines suggests the rapid developments that lie ahead.

The power of the Pentium chip, and the competitive challenge presented by the PowerPC chip, suggest where the line of development is going. Some analysts predicted that the Pentium, with 3.1 million transistors and running at 112 MIPS (million instructions per second), will give way by the year 2000 to more powerful processors running 50 million transistors at 700 MIPS.[3] Such computing capabilities will create enormously fast and breathtaking multimedia experiences.

YEAR	EVENT
1974	Philips begins optical media research, establishes 12 cm format
1976	Matshushita, Hitachi, others offer proposals
1977	CD player prototypes available
1979	Philips and Sony alliance and CD-DA standard proposed
1982	CD-Digital Audio introduced in Europe
	CDi development at Philips commences
1983	CD-DA introduced in United States
	Philips and Sony announce CD-ROM extensions
	CDi collaboration between Philips and Sony commences
	WORM systems introduced
1984	CD-Video prototypes available
	CD-ROM prototypes available
1985	CD-DA for cars introduced
	CD-DA portables introduced
	CD-ROM introduced
1986	CDi announced by Philips
	CD-PROM (a writable version of CD-ROM) announced by Philips
1987	DVI announced by GE/Sarnoff, later acquired by Intel/IBM
1988	CD-ROM standard set [ISO-9660]
1990	CDTV introduced by Commodore
1991	CDi introduced by Philips
1992	VIS introduced by Tandy
	Sega-CD introduced
	Sony DiscMan, MiniDisc, and MultiMedia players introduced
1993	3DO announced
	FM Towns player to be introduced
1995	Sega, Philips, and Sony introduce 32-bit CD games system
	2x drives become with MPEG-1 chips standard consumer WORM players introduced
1997	Quad-CD with full-motion NTSC/MPEG introduced
	Quad-CD mini-disc for games, etc., introduced
	HDTV-format enhanced disc developed
2000	Erasable optical discs
2005	HDTV makes 12 cm disc obsolete; new format

Table 8-2   Life History of the Evolving Compact Disc

These advances, however, come with some systemic problems. Today there are more than a half-dozen such players on the market, and more will shortly appear. They fall into four dominant categories:

- Computer peripherals for IBM/MS-DOS/Windows and Macintosh machines;
- Portable players with LCD screens and TV-set/monitor connectivity;
- Dedicated videogame peripherals attached to the TV set; and
- Dedicated stand-alone "black boxes" that attach to the TV set.

Not only are these players incompatible across categories but also among a category. No machine can play the titles from any other player. Software companies, out of sheer desperation over this intolerable condition, are beginning to incorporate header "readers" to allow for some cross-platform readability. These multiple multimedia platforms offer the consumer a similar interactive experience, but there are enough performance differences among the platforms to engender marketplace confusion and frustrate the average consumer (see Table 8-2).

If history of the electronic media during the 20th century has taught anything, it is that new, improved forms of communications will emerge. Thus one must ask: Among packaged media, what will supersede the current generation of CD-based multimedia? Today's CD, while a remarkable technological advance, is a flawed medium. It is a "narrowband" medium originally developed to replace the analog vinyl record and, due to its enormous storage capacity, it is uniquely appropriate for data publishing and archival purposes. However, the current CD system of player and disc is appropriate for neither full-motion video, nor for off-air recording. Thus, multimedia cannot meet the performance accomplishments of the technologically inferior VCR.

To overcome these deficiencies, manufacturers are committing an enormous amount of R&D investment to improve the format's overall performance capabilities. Among the defining issues that will shape innovation during the decade and beyond are as follows:

- Digital signal compression is a principal "gating" issue affecting overall capacity as well as still-image and full-motion video storage. Adoption of MPEG-1 provides an interim solution. Technical problems with the standard (problems that MPEG-2 fail to overcome) will likely lead to the standard being superseded by a more dynamic mathematical algorithm.

- Multispeed disc drives can increase the disc's throughput and generate higher-quality video (e.g., 4x player)—however, disc-drive speeds are set by the original audio standard ("red" book at 150 kilobits per second) and must be adhered to in order to ensure backward compatibility.

- The disc's storage capacity will likely double or even quadruple to reach the 1 and 2 gigabit range (e.g., Nimbus 2x disc, Denon's Quad-CD).

- An erasable or "rewriteable" optical disc system, that is becoming common in industry (as write-once/read-many, etc.) and in audio (Sony's MiniDisc) will extend to multimedia;

- There will be a shift from today's "red" lasers to higher-powered "blue" lasers (who knows what's beyond this) to read the even smaller pits that encode the binary data on the disc.

Assuming that these or similar developments are accomplished, the CD will be a higher-performance medium and better prepared to compete with the serious challenges from wired and wireless alternatives.

The CD system's inherent limitations, combined with the structural drive within the media industry to achieve higher storage levels at more cost-effective rates, are also pushing the development of alternative storage devices. Among these are:

- Advanced cartridge-based systems, like that being introduced by Nintendo and utilizing Silicon Graphics technologies, have faster access and performance time than the CD and could provide an alternative approach in the games market.

- Digital videotape, while effective for higher-quality off-air recording, suffers from the traditional limitations of tape (e.g., stretching, head-end friction) and fails to offer the CD's random-access capabilities; the introduction of DAT (digital audio tape) and DCC (digital compact cassette) are two attempts to extend tape into the digital media.

- Solid-state technologies, particularly the use of advanced crystal processing, represent the most likely long-term alternative as a publishing medium, especially when an entire movie can be placed on a single silicon chip.

These and other lines of development, while incorporating the accomplishments of past media, are driven by the more demanding requirements of video. Video is a broadband signal, a bandwidth "hog" compared with music or data/text. As we move toward the new millennium, video will likely become an even more defining media component than it is today. All modes of distribution will compete on the basis of their relative ability to distribute high-quality digital (eventually HDTV-level) full-motion video.

Perhaps the greatest challenge facing multimedia's long-term mass-market adoption is the development of an industry-wide user interface. This is the image that "greets" the user and establishes the starting point, mode of access, and means of maneuvering through the digital experience. It needs to be as simple and "friendly" as that which greets TV viewers when they turn on the "boob tube." Neither the excruciating tedium of MS-DOS nor the point-and-click drudgery of the Mac or Windows will satisfy the impulse-driven world of TV viewing. Equally troubling, the current evolution of the once-simple handheld remote control toward hyperfunctionality—resembling a palm-top computer—fosters user exhaustion. Something more personal—"smart" in the Artificial Intelligence (AI) sense—is likely to emerge as a magic wand for navigation through the information superhighway.

AN EXPRESSION OF COMMUNICATIONS INDUSTRY RESTRUCTURING

The 1980s was a tumultuous decade. It witnessed General Motor's takeover of Hughes satellites; the Time merger with Warner, and then Toshiba and US West taking stakes in the new company;

CapCities joining with ABC; Sony's acquisition of Columbia Pictures and CBS Records; Matsushita scooping up MCA/Universal; Murdoch gobbling up Fox and Harper & Row; Turner's chewing up Castle Rock and New Line; and AT&T swallowing NCR and McCaw. Year after year, the United States media landscape has been systematically reconfigured through mergers and acquisitions. The dice roll and the deals get bigger. What's after Viacom's merger with Blockbuster and (with Nynex) buyout of Paramount—Microsoft's acquisition of AT&T?

These deals signify the global reconfiguration of the communications media. They bear witness to mammoth businesses colliding with one another in trying to stake out a strategic position for 21st century media. Hollywood studios are being integrated into consumer electronics companies, phone companies are swallowing cablecasters, broadcasters are diversifying into print and electronic publishing, business software publishers are entering the games industry, and the list only gets longer.

These unlikely developments are more than isolated activities of individual companies; they represent structural linkages between much larger industrial sectors, and vast constellations of capital welding together dozens of associated hardware and software suppliers as well as the supporting financial institutions. Like titanic dinosaurs, the companies formed in the strategic mergers and bitter takeover battles are being recast into huge business combines. With bone-crunching tenacity, these huge industrial behemoths are breaking down historic lines of business and remaking the media landscape.

All aspects of the communications media are being transformed as a result of the combination of technological convergence and corporate collision. Television witnessed fundamental splintering as more networks were introduced from broadcast, cable, satellite, and microwave; new programming services (especially premium and pay-per-view) expanded, and advertising shifted from mass dissemination to targeted markets.

Telephony became more widespread and important for personal and business life, with increased service features such as speed dialing, memory, call waiting, and functions like picture-phones and videoconferencing; in addition, wireless (e.g., cellular, beepers) and network-based and on-line services expanded usage.

Even more important, the computing industry has been transformed along two complementary lines:

- At one extreme, the introduction of ever higher-performance computing systems, typified by the Sun workstation, Cray supercomputers and video servers, to be used in next-generation on-demand television systems; and

- At the other, the integration of lower-level performance microprocessors into a ubiquitous assortment of common products such as handheld calculators, watches, microwave ovens, and cars.

Taken together, increased performance, miniaturization, and cost reductions have created a computing environment for which the processing power of old-time mainframes is now available in desktop or laptop machines. The goal of tomorrow's computing is to place the power of a supercomputer onto a single chip!

For those media professionals who lived through the turbulent 1980s, a new watchword defines the industry. Nothing can be taken for granted. Technology has become as significant a factor in recasting the media industry as government regulation, financial clout, management savvy, and the fickle tastes of the American consumer.

Innovation is now recognized as an endemic, if not determining, characteristic of the communications media industries. By technologically remaking itself, by offering newer (and, hopefully, better) performance capabilities, the media business has been able to continue to grow and remain strongly profitable. The media's future is tied directly to its ability to continually reinvent itself.

This technological development is leading to the transindustry realignment that some have called "convergence." Traditionally distinct industries such as broadcasting and cable television, prerecorded audio and home video, gaming and consumer electronics are now colliding with print publishing, computing, and telecommunications. Convergence is fostering the creation of a new communications media industry. Out of this process new corporate entities will emerge, older ones will be reconfigured (if they survive!), and improbable alliances established.

It's still too early to foresee the outcome of this process. Nevertheless, current technological developments have contributed to the worldwide marketplace uncertainty and intensified corporate instability. Technology has wreaked havoc on the balance sheets of leading consumer electronics and computer companies, to name but two industry sectors undergoing tumultuous restructuring.

The absence of a popular breakthrough product such as the VCR, Walkman, or CD player in the late 1980s/early 1990s is a symptom of this phenomenon. Another symptom is the proliferation of incompatible CD-based multimedia players. These symptoms reveal the opportunist impulses of the individual platform vendors and the weakness of anyone (or even a consortia of the biggest) to stabilize or police the marketplace. This situation may be resolved by the year 2000, but failure to do so will only inhibit overall market development.

Goals Realizable and Unrealizable

During the 1980s, average American consumers began the dramatic process of integrating digital media into their daily lives. Up to then, nearly all home communications media were analog, be it radio, telephony, television, or home video. In the 1980s, the enormously popular acceptance of the compact disc and the videogame helped remake entire industries and create new standards of experience that redefined popular entertainment.

Until the 1980s, digital media had been experienced principally (if at all) in a consumer's work life. There, it was and still often is an expression of computer-based applications such as word processing, data-entry tasks, and spreadsheets. A user's experience of the applications, and its performance quality, were assessed on the basis of functionality. Thus, an application's success is a pragmatic issue. How well does it work?

With entry into consumer life, digital media faces a new and far more demanding set of experience standards based on aesthetic considerations. The performance quality or value of a particular program is measured by the pleasure it provides. The leading digital-media products of the 1980s set new aesthetic standards that excited consumers. The CD redefined audio recording and playback, and the videogame created an addictive frenzy among masses of youthful enthusiasts. "Digital" and "optical" became the watchwords of consumer progress.

In the 1990s, visually based digital media—multimedia—will face a far more difficult challenge: Adapting to the requirement of TV viewing. This medium has its own highly defined aesthetic. The socially accepted standard involves elements such as 30 frames per second full-motion, a color palette composed of 16 million colors and a pseudo-naturalistic or representational "reality." These elements help make TV viewing familiar and comfortable to viewers.

The TV aesthetic evolved in conformity with the technological requirements of the analog, NTSC television standard. It is characterized by a point-to-multipoint architecture and a linear-sequential coherence. These factors form the river of video information in which swim those elements popular with viewers, be it their favorite on-air celebrities, gruesome images of devastating catastrophes, or the nearly infinite variety of programming choices.

Multimedia grows out of a very different set of defining factors. First, it emerged out of computing and is an all-digital medium, with higher processing requirements. Second, it incorporates interactivity—the ability consciously to break linear coherence and maximize user input—as the defining aesthetic criterion. Third, in migrating from a computer monitor to an NTSC (television) screen, it witnesses a fundamental shift in user ergonomics, from an arms-length interface to an across-the-room viewing experience.

So far, the cartridge-based videogame has been the only all-digital medium to venture onto the TV screen, and it has done so quite poorly. While players might be enormously engaged (even captivated) by the game, the genre has no traditional aesthetic value—no reference to naturalistic or pseudo-realistic standards.

One could argue that videogames have, rather, an anti-aesthetic that turns traditional media standards on their head. They create an overstylized, antinaturalistic vivaciousness that undercuts the reflective aesthetic of traditional TV viewing. The introduction of CD-based videogames—especially Sega's CD for the Genesis system—offer more movielike representational characters and are finding strong consumer acceptance. However, the new "realism" offered by multimedia may undercut the very nonrepresentational appeal or game-play "magic" that has defined the genre up to now.

The few attempts to bring digital multimedia to the home TV screen in a multipurpose stand-alone device have been disappointing. Platforms introduced by companies such as Commodore (CDTV), Philips (CDi), Tandy (VIS), and Panasonic (3DO REAL machine) have met with cool marketplace reception. This can be attributed, in part, to the technological incompatibility of current-generation analog TV and all-digital CD-based entertainment and information programs running on it. Future players, especially ones built around 64-bit processors or integrated directly into a cable set-top converter box (the original 3DO plan), may fare better.

However different the multimedia formats may be on a technical level, they share two marketplace assumptions. First, they assume that consumers want to interact with their TV sets; and second, they assume that TV-based multimedia must conform to the requirements of CD-audio to be adopted. These assumptions may have taken the industry down the wrong road for mass-market acceptance.

No one speaks with more enthusiasm—verging on a religious conviction—about the appeal of interactivity than Trip Hawkins, chairman of Electronic Arts and the 3DO Company, which has announced the latest and most powerful (yet incompatible) multimedia format. "People want, and need, to interact," he passionately claims. "Brain scientists have proven that interaction is the single best way for a human being to increase their intelligence." His vision is of a high-performance home player that combines the best of a user-friendly computer and a videogame machine.

Others question whether interactivity is really appealing enough to draw a mass-market, adult following. Richard Bruno has a more sober perspective. "I was wrong," he says, reflecting on his experience as technical head of Philips interactive initiatives. "We thought that consumers were evolving from passive to active uses and wanted an 'interactive living room.' I've learned that people, and especially hard-working adults, relax and enjoy themselves in living rooms, they don't live in Skinner-boxes," he emphasizes.

His earlier outlook was based on the appeal of videogames and popularity in France of MiniTel. "The future [of multimedia] will be determined by digital video," he notes. In the West, this will take the form of CD home video, while in Japan it will extend out from Karaoke use.

Dr. Bruno goes further in rethinking the industry's multimedia market positioning. "The TV set and the stereo system are two separate and distinct aesthetic and ergonomic experiences," he states emphatically. "We tied them together, and in doing this we committed a major technological error. We required multimedia to be compatible with CD-audio," he adds. He further elaborates, "Consumers don't play their TV sets to listen to music, and both devices are often in separate rooms of the house or parts of the den or livingroom."

Having adopted this approach, hardware manufacturers have built multimedia players with data rates conforming to the low level of CD-audio requirements—rates insufficient for movies. "How many people use their CDi, CDTV or 3DO player to listen to music"? Bruno questions. Instead of creating two separate formats for CD-audio and CD-multimedia (such as cassette and videotapes), the current attempts to introduce multispeed disc drives are strategies that may well lead to a dead end.

While Bruno and others are at work devising higher-performance CD systems, much of the most creative work within multimedia is taking place among program developers working in conformity with the current CD format. As program development migrates into the consumer category, it is forming along two twin axes: by demographics for youth and adult markets, and by genre for play and learning.

Nolan Bushnell, the founder of the original Atari and one of the godfathers of the multimedia industry, calls multimedia programming a "continuum." "It all comes down to clicks per minute," he notes. "The youth market is defined by highly engaging, action-adventure, violent videogames with 30 to 60 or more clicks per minute," he reflects. "Adults," he adds, "tend to utilize a lower click rate, sometimes as low as one per minute, and they tend to want more fantasy or knowledge-based programs that show off their maturity."

A new multimedia aesthetic is taking shape and will increasingly define the market as the decade proceeds. It will be built on improved performance as higher processing power and full-motion video is actively incorporated into the programs. All popular media genres will be affected:

- *Movies.* A complete linear movie will be distributed on a single disc and will incorporate value-added information like many laserdiscs.

- *Interactive movies.* More "participatory" movies will emerge and will offer branching for multiple plot development paths.

- *Music videos.* Cutting-edge, MTV-like aesthetics will be combined with play-along MIDI music tracks to create an innovative Karaoke format.

- *Simulations.* High-engagement aviation, auto-racing, and other programs (with accompanying headsets and other visual stimulants) will achieve more life-like realism.

- *Edutainment.* Learning-defined programming will be "enhanced" with appealing entertainment elements to create popular learning titles along the lines of PBS shows for both adults and children.

- *Infotainment.* "Hard" information, news, and reference material will be "enlivened" with an entertainment component to achieve greater popular usage.

- *Interactive "strips".* Discs based on popular half-hour TV formats such as game shows, soap operas, sitcoms, sports programs, and other established genres that encourage user game-like participation will likely proliferate.

Multimedia is, first and foremost, a publishing medium, and the genres outlined above are likely to be among the initial core product lines—lines that build upon the high level of visual or video materials. Users are familiar with the video component that now define them, and the interactive dimension, if it promises ease-of-use and real benefits, will only enhance acceptance.

A host of other currently print-based product categories will likely migrate to the CD-multimedia format during the decade. This migration will be driven in major part by the cost efficiencies offered by the CD format. Not only is the cost of manufacturing or replication far more advantageous than that for print, but the disc is easier and cheaper to ship. Among the potential array of innovative multimedia product categories are:

- *Telephone books*. These can provide not only nearly instantaneous location of a White or Yellow Pages listing, but also provide for automatic dialing.

- *Catalogs*. These can provide not only full-motion product sequences, a palette of colors, and sizing adjustments, but also automatic ordering capabilities.

- *Directories*. These can provide database information on a wide variety of subject matter and be random-accessed based on price, location, and other factors.

Multimedia will also likely see usage growth and performance enhancement along two additional lines of development. One, dubbed "multiple-media," involves the active integration of multimedia with other media, particularly real-time information from on-line data/text or cable video services. An example of such an endeavor involves the use of a CDi player and programming as a complement to Discovery Channel shows as part of the GTE Cerritos, California, optical fiber trial.

The second, and probably the most important, development will involve the integration of advertising placements into multimedia titles. The most ambitious undertaking is *Newsweek*'s new quarterly CD service, but this is only the tip of the iceberg.

In-home media economics are based on two paradigms. At one extreme, advertising subsidizes media costs (e.g., TV, radio, and magazine/newspaper/catalog publishing) and, at the other, the consumer's out-of-pocket, discretionary spending drives purchasing (e.g., prerecorded audio, home video, videogames, books). During the early phases of multimedia evolution it has been defined as a discretionary spending business. During the rest of the decade and beyond, multimedia is likely increasingly to incorporate advertising as either an outright promotional offering or an indirect subsidy to reduce the purchase price.

A critical factor in CD-multimedia's growth is its ability to secure multiple revenue streams. Failure to accomplish this makes it extremely vulnerable to the challenges posed by the alternative distribution media, wired and wireless.

MULTIMEDIA—AN ACHILLES HEEL

All communications media are composed of three distinct, yet interdependent dimensions: document or program production, distribution, and reception. For a quarter-century and more, the dominant electronic media industries—prerecorded audio, radio, telephone, television, and computing (and, more recently, home video and videogames)—have existed as separate business sectors, with unique and often incompatible ways of producing, distributing, and receiving their respective messages or programming. The trans-industry convergence that is recasting today's media is rapidly putting an end to this separation.

Multimedia is first and foremost a distribution medium for the storage and playback of digital information. It is, like CD-audio and home video, a packaged good, a shrinkwrapped commodity bought and sold through an elaborate chain of retail distribution. Expensive marketing and sales campaigns—the classic "push/pull" strategies—are not only required to gain consumer awareness, but also to secure retail exposure. Without adequate "doors" (retail outlets) and shelfspace, a product dies, no matter how clever its advertising and promotional activities.

Packaged-goods retailing is, however, but one form of product distribution. While appropriate for toothpaste, carrots, and clothes, it may no longer be appropriate for electronic media signal distribution. Historically, a host of competitive distribution techniques have provided viable alternatives to retailing. These include terrestrial broadcasting of television and radio; cellular and wireless narrowcasting for data, audio, and video; satellite downloading of video, audio, and data; and wire-based conduits for two-way voice, data, and videoconferencing via telephony and one-way video and data via cablecasting. The same digital signal processing that makes possible CD-based multimedia is transforming these other forms of signal distribution.

Retailing is multimedia's Achilles' heel. Retailing is really two distinct experiences: purchasing and shopping, goods acquisition and getting out of the house, meeting a material need (whether real or imagined) and socializing. While both coexist, they are—from a phenomenological perspective—nevertheless distinct social and economic functions. And given today's high-pressure marketing efforts, the two activities all too often implode upon each other and create consumer disgust. No wonder that in-home purchasing services are proliferating, as evident from the phenomenal success of catalogs and other forms of direct marketing.

Technology-driven convergence adds velocity to the momentum pushing in-home purchasing. The increase of cable services (e.g., home shopping channels and pay-per-view), voice services (e.g., 800- and 900-numbers), and on-line computing networks (e.g., America Online, Prodigy) are leading the charge. The significant increases in capital spending on infrastructure and central-office/headend upgrades by cable system operators, and local- and long-line telephone companies are improving signal distribution capabilities, especially for two-way signaling. Transactional processing is becoming the media's watchword, a development duly noted by the career shift of media executive Barry Diller.

Nevertheless, for much of the 1990s, multimedia will remain predominantly a retail-distribution business. While a thorough discussion of the evolving structure of multimedia title distribution is outside the scope of this chapter, a broad picture of the shifting retail landscape can be suggested.

Retail sales are currently organized into three principal forms of distribution: retail channels, covering purchasing through traditional computer software outlets, mass-market outlets, and superstores; "bundles" offered by hardware manufacturers with new products or upgrade kits as promotional incentives; and direct sales of programs offered through mail-order catalogs or direct mail campaigns that bypass traditional retail outlets.

The retail channel for multimedia is structured along the following lines:

- *Traditional computer software outlets.* These include such national chains as Babbage's, Egghead, and Software, Etc. They have provided modest outlets for CD-ROM products since their emergence but are likely to grow in importance.

- *Mass-market software outlets.* As computer and videogame household penetration has increased, nontraditional media and other outlets have moved to take advantage of sell-through opportunities. The leaders include such video chains as Blockbuster, bookstores such as Crown and Barnes & Noble, and record stores such as Tower and J&R Records. They should become more aggressive.

- *Superstores.* In order to increase foot traffic and customer spending, traditional computer and consumer-electronics retailers are beginning to refashion themselves as both hardware and software outlets. Among the leaders of this trend are such computer retailers as Tandy/Radio Shack, CompUSA, and PC Warehouse and such consumer-electronics retailers as Circuit City and The Wiz. They should provide most distribution.

Changes in product distribution will likely have the most profound impact on the multimedia titles business. Retail changes are characterized by a number of factors:

- The entry of mass-market retailers (e.g., Blockbuster, Tower Records) and "superstores" will expand product distribution beyond the traditional forms of specialty-retail outlets (e.g., software, video, videogame, books, music), direct mail, and promotional bundling.

- Entry of high-volume distributors and rack-jobbers (e.g., Handleman, Merisel) will aggressively expand sell-through reach and challenge leading distributors (e.g., Compton's, Electronic Arts, and Broderbund).

- Title bundling as a hardware promotional strategy will gradually be eclipsed as title prices decline, except for new-product introductions or upgrade kits.

- There will be a gradual shift to a hit-driven/high-volume retailing landscape, with shelf space allocated on the bases of unit "turns," co-op support, and other retailing incentives.

- Mega-programming—music, video, books, etc.—companies (e.g., Sony, Time Warner, Polygram, MCA) will dominate shelf space.

The retail channel dominates sell-through—i.e., sale of products to consumers—of packaged goods, be it toothpaste, videogames, or home videos. For the near term, sell-through will account for the lion's share of CD multimedia title distribution. Smart direct marketers will take advantage of the highly focused appeal of individual titles and aggressively pursue retail bypass, direct-to-home sales initiatives. Targeted niche marketing makes the most sense in reaching highly selective early adopters, especially when price discounting and other incentives are offered.

But the near term is not the long term. As the performance capabilities of conduit- or networked-based signal distribution improve, it will pose a real alternative to retail sales. The network's near-impulse capabilities to access enormous databases offers a powerful appeal. With ever-increasing reach into more households, the adoption of sophisticated encryption procedures for capturing and erasing of distributed copyright programs, and the introduction of an affordable storage and playback device (e.g., a player with 8-plus megabytes of RAM), networked-based multimedia will become a social reality.

Such a development will likely lead to stalled retail sales of audio, video, gaming, and computing programs. Potentially, this development could transform the very nature of the multimedia product, creating an on-line experience that can be both private and open to multiple players located at different fixed points but interfacing through a nearly instantaneous network. This development is likely to define post-2000 media in America.

Advances in conduit signal distribution point to a deeper social dynamic that could profoundly affect long-term multimedia sales.

When such enhanced networks come into full bloom, society will be asked: Why own an electronic media program product? Why spend lots of money collecting music, movies, favorite TV shows, videogames or books that one tends to enjoy (for the most part) infrequently? If one extends by analogy the phenomenal success of home video (for which rentals account for approximately 60 percent of the nearly $9 billion market) to all other electronic media, significant opportunities exist not only for affordable rental but for affordable on-line pay-per-use as well.

Multimedia's very claim as an interactive or nonlinear media may, in fact, turn out to be its ultimate Achilles heel. The dominant in-home leisure or media experiences are linear; whether they be music, movies, TV shows, videogames or multimedia titles, they are used or enjoyed in sequential order. However much one tries, one can only truly enjoy leisure media as a series of discrete, consecutive experiences. One has to give each activity full attention, often to the exclusion of everything else.

But acquiring or collecting one's favorite movies, shows, CDs, games, or multimedia titles is nonlinear, randomly assembled as tastes change, and is arbitrarily organized and stored in one's home. The linear and nonlinear aspects of choice come together in the actual selection of a particular title or selection to play, either as an impulse or planned decision. This mix of linear and nonlinear calls into question the retail purchasing experience as a mode of acquisition of electronic signal-based products. Providing impulse ordering, especially on a very low-priced nonownership basis, where the option for ownership is always available, circumvents retail purchasing and represents the major long-term challenge to the CD-based multimedia business.

THE NATIONAL INFORMATION INFRASTRUCTURE

The remaking of the United States communications system—what Vice President Al Gore has dubbed the "national information infrastructure" (NII)—is a high priority of the Clinton Administration. Like NAFTA, GATT, and health care reform, its full impact on the life of the nation will likely not be evident until long after the Administration passes into history. Such foresight speaks of a bold vision long absent from previous administrations. But it also presents a challenge that must be clearly recognized: Today's decisions will determine the nation's destiny long into the next millennium.

The Vice President is not alone in appreciating this historic opportunity. Nearly all the leading U.S. and worldwide media, technology, and electronics companies share his perception. They are matching his call for vision with investments totaling tens of billions of dollars. Their investments—from the biggest mergers to fiber optic upgrades to the production of the simplest CD-ROM title—are strategic decisions, testaments to opportunistic initiatives to secure an advantageous position in the new media environment.

The establishment of an all-digital communications infrastructure—along with a complement of technical advances that include optical fiber conduits, 150:1 and higher rates of data compression, photon switches, video servers, and intelligent agents—is fostering a unified, video-defined media. This development is evident from the alternative upgrade strategies being implemented by the signal distributors, the cable and telephone industries:

- The telephone system, building on its switching capabilities, is upgrading from a narrowband voice and data network to a broadband network so that it can transport movies and other video programming; and

- The cable system, building on its ability to distribute video signals, is upgrading from a one-way pipe to a fully interactive network.

When rebuilt, these two networks will be nearly identical competitors with separate wires running into the home, offering essentially the same array of video, voice, and other services. Both will be two-way systems, allowing users to both receive and send messages.

However, there will likely be a profound difference between the signal being received and the one being sent. Like today's cable networks, tomorrow's "downstream" signal flowing from the file server or headend to the home will be broadband, providing an enormous (essentially unlimited) assortment of video and other programming options; like today's telephone networks, tomorrow's messages sent "upstream" will be narrowband, adequate for voice and slow-scan video communications, impulse ordering, and other services.

Initial versions of what can only be called the "private-market NII"—as distinct from a "public-market NII" suggested in skeleton form by the Internet—are taking shape in enhanced-service trials, upgrades being built by the big cable operators and telephone companies in Orlando, Florida, Loudon County, Virginia, and elsewhere.

However, this path of development is troubling for two important reasons. First, as the business history of media communications over this century suggests, redundant media systems lead to the killing off of the weakest or least capitalized one. However, the best one does not necessarily succeed. Second, the media distribution network that the telephone companies and cable operators are putting into place will likely fail to meet long-term citizen and marketplace needs and, in time, will have to be further rebuilt at enormous additional expense.

Discussion of the NII is framed by a set of two compelling concerns. One consists of the public policy issues associated with the establishment of a new media environment. The other involves the technological policy issues associated with deploying a new communications system. These concerns are distinct yet intimately intertwined and, together, define not only what is socially possible but the very character of the 21st century electronic culture.

Among the most critical public policy concerns involved with the new media are:

- Protecting constitutional safeguards relating to freedom of speech, "electronic" assembly, privacy, and copyright;

- Assuring a "free" marketplace in which competition—between products, services, and ideas—is encouraged and in which unfair, monopolistic practices are prohibited; and

- Fostering a "free" civil society in which the means of discourse are universally available and affordably priced, and/or subsidized so that all are encouraged to use them.

Public policy that realizes these goals will foster economic as well as social progress, diversity, and growth.

Among the most critical "technological issues" associated with the new media are:

- Assuring adoption of an all-digital, switched, two-way—with broadband upstream capabilities—system that seamlessly interconnects with all alternative modes of signal transport (e.g., wireless, DBS).

- Assuring interoperability among and between transport, content, and interface devices that will make up the NII system.

- Fostering de jure (as opposed to de facto) standards for critical features of the system, such as compression and encryption that help create a level playing field for providers and lower costs for users.

Technological policy that realizes these goals will create an "open architecture" environment that stimulates rapid implementation of the NII, increases efficient competition among diverse providers, and establishes a secure migration path for long-term growth.

The media exist so that people can communicate with one another and gain access to information in a variety of forms and from a variety of sources. Communications technologies facilitate this process in the easiest and most affordable means historically possible. Reconciling the apparent differences between the public policy and the technological concerns is the historical challenge facing the NII. A framework to address this challenge is suggested in the following set of principals that are likely to be adopted:

- Media distribution is a common carrier function. The historic model of the telephone industry will likely be extended to all signal distribution vehicles.

- Common carriage is a means to achieve interoperability and interconnectivity among distribution alternatives. It provides users with maximum utility and does not impose unnecessary burdens on manufacturers.

- A "base-case" package of programming content and user devices provides a means to achieve universal access and service as well as a clear migration path for user upgrades and system advances. This is an extension of a "common carrier" approach to content and interface equipment.

- A "base-case" model for the communications media would insure all users a level of performance capabilities that does not exclude them from the rapidly evolving civil society. This would satisfactorily address constitutional and equity concerns.

The apparent tension between public policy and technology policy concerns can be reconciled by establishing a "common carrier" network universally accessed by an affordable, "base-case" player. Users, particularly the least privileged (and the least technically savvy), would be able to easily access a variety of "functionalities" or performance capabilities and, in turn, specific services such as television, telephone, education, health care, police/judicial, employment, and others.

How would such a scenario work? How would it be paid for? It seems clear that the NII will be built on an optical fiber backbone running to the curb or pedestal. It will be to some extent a "switched" system and will carry multiple media in a digital form meeting some of the "common carrier" requirements.

Given this, the key question then arises as to what the "base-case" home device should be like. What level of performance capabilities are necessary? And does every household need a box on top of the TV set that performs like a 386-level PC with a built-in MPEG-1 decompression chip? Who decides whether you need it or not? Are there no alternatives? And, if this is the case, why should the box provider have a monopoly on local distribution?

These questions will have to be resolved in one form or other before network-distributed multimedia become a meaningful alternative to "packaged goods" multimedia. It appears that as the Federal Communications Commission (FCC) and Congress slowly move to implement the NII, the telephone companies and cable operators will undertake an increasing number of enhanced service trials, test-bed upgrades, and network deployments.

These developments, while important for technical as well as marketing purposes, set the stage for the creation of geographically isolated "pockets" of advanced communication technology and services. They should be watched carefully, for these "pockets" represent the future of interactive television.

CONFRONTING THE EVOLUTION OF TELEVISION

With the coming of the new millennium, America will welcome the introduction of next-generation television—High-Definition Television (HDTV). The FCC, in 1941, adopted the current television standard, National Television System Committee (NTSC). Since then, television signal transmission has remained remarkably homogeneous, even with the shift from black and white to color and the wide adoption of cable. However, the advent of HDTV will fundamentally change this half-century-old paradigm.

The original NTSC standard defined the basic technical specification of the signal, including the use of a monochrome analog signal, a frame rate of 30 frames per second with interlaced scanning, 525 scanning lines, the 4:3 aspect ratio, and FM sound. The FCC is finalizing the specifications for the new HDTV standard. Among the key features of this new standard are a color digital signal, a frame rate of 30 frames per second, 1025 scan lines and a 16:9 aspect ratio. When fully implemented, HDTV will create a new viewing experience and true "interactive" television.

"Higher-definition" TV had its origins nearly half a century ago with the pioneering work of Otto Schade, an RCA engineer, in the late 1940s. During the 1960s, the Japanese national broadcasting company, NHK, began the current phase of advanced TV development. After more than a decade of research, it demonstrated the first prototype analog MUSE system in 1981. Now, more than another decade and billions of yen later, the original HD analog format has been "leapfrogged" by United States digital technology.

The FCC's adoption of the Zenith HDTV system sets the stage not merely for a new television era, but also for the further evolution of the TV set as a home entertainment and information device. Since the late 1940s, as cable developed, and in the late 1970s with the introduction of the VCR, an increasing number of "peripheral" devices—including the cable box, videogame player, and camcorder—have begun to redefine TV set functionality and, with it, the viewer's usage habits. After decades of use as a passive play-through device for the reception and display of a broadcast signal, the TV set has been reconceived as a multifunctional appliance.

CD-based multimedia and HDTV are both all-digital media, but the amount of data that the planned HD system will transmit simply dwarfs today's—and tomorrow's—disc-carrying capacity. By analogy, today's NTSC TV provides a viewing experience similar to a 16mm movie; HDTV will offer one analogous to a 35mm movie. HDTV's overall expansion and enhancement of TV viewing will crush today's CD as a storage and distribution medium.

In fact, the current generation of CD-multimedia disc and player systems is simply incapable of meeting the high-performance demands of HDTV. The quantity of data transmission of HDTV is so enormous that even the most advanced CD formats, e.g., Quad-CD, which increases disc capacity fourfold to over 2 gigabytes, is still woefully inadequate. While a Quad-CD can store up to 105 minutes of S-VHS or High-8 quality video (thus accounting for about 85 percent of all movies), an HDTV movie would require a further quadrupling of the Quad-CD. In turn, this process would require still more powerful CD-multimedia players.

But this is only the most obvious problem that advanced TV poses for the future of disc-based multimedia. Another has to do with the set's functionality or performance capabilities. Clearly, a set's character (as defined by standard and enhanced features) often has more to do with marketing/sales decisions than technical factors. Nevertheless, the incorporation of a sophisticated central processor as the HDTV set's "brain" allows for functionalities never before imaged in a traditional boob tube.

The incorporation of an internal CPU will likely propel the TV set forward, achieving performance capabilities analogous to that of a computer. This allows for the development of "smart" TVs, which could incorporate sophisticated AI algorithms and thus permit the set to "know" the viewer's desires and program itself accordingly. This becomes critical in the next-generation TV universe of 500 channels, unlimited channels, or post-channels.

There is much talk of services with 500 channels, of Video-on-Demand, and of video dialtone. And they are all coming, slowly but inexorably. But in such a maze of programming options, what happens to the conventional channels that viewers are familiar with over the broadcast TV system, let alone the 35-plus channels available on most cable systems? Will viewers be forced to thumb through various directories or menus as computer users now do? Will this be a nightmare or a new modality of viewing requiring more than a smart viewer? Will we witness the introduction of a smart TV to help viewers navigate the video flood?

A smart TV assumes that the set has, in addition to a high-powered CPU, internal memory, the type of memory—RAM (random access memory)—found in computers, videogames, and multimedia players. This type of memory allows for the processing of operating commands such as a personalized AI programming profile. In addition, such a set will require the integration of a hard-disk memory device that can capture and play back down-loaded signals. Such a memory or internal-storage device is likely have a minimum 4-gigabyte capacity for capture/play of a HDTV movie.

As important as memory, the next-generation HDTV set will probably have two-way communications capabilities, either as built-in or add-on features via a set-top converter box. This communication could take any of a number of forms, including upstream signals over a telephone or cable wire (which by then would likely be one and the same) or feed through a bypass via a wireless or microwave signal. In any case, communications capabilities will empower the set to perform more transactional and real-time network functions.

While development of next-generation HDTV takes up most resources and will likely have the greatest social impact, other developments that will help to further redefine the communications media should not be lost sight of. Among the most critical are:

- *Flat-panel television*. Considerable effort is being put into flat-panel technologies, especially in Japan and Korea. How this develops (and whether it can meet the performance requirements of HDTV) will be important to the further proliferation of screen-based communications.

- *Electronic picture frames.* New genres of visual display are likely to emerge, further challenging traditional paper-based presentation media, including replacement of posters, paintings, photos, and other printed displays.

- *Ubiquitous television.* TVs are all around us, an evergrowing number of screen-based devices for personal communications, both portable and stationary. Such general- and special-function "sets" will provide an increasing number of alternative modes of communications.

- *Virtual Reality (VR).* This is a potentially powerful simulation and performance medium, representing a real challenge to multimedia. With "smart" VR systems, creating self-modeled "replicants" that play or do battle with one another, how will flat, two-dimensional multimedia compete?

- *3DTV.* An attempt to translate a movie-theater experience into the living room, with special goggles and screen enhancers seems to be suffering the same fate.

- *Holography.* This technology has long suggested a different way to render media, for instead of flat, two-dimensional representations, why not three-dimensional and in the round?

The changes sketched out here are years—some would say light years—away. Many are nearly real; some are being hotly pursued in research and development laboratories around the world; still others are merely part of more esoteric techno-futurist "blue sky" discussions. Nevertheless, taken together, they foreshadow a fundamentally redefined media environment and landscape. As an environment, it will be defined by a digital media that saturates all forms of communications, neutralizing the historical differences between print, radio, audio, telephony, and television and creates something new: multimedia. As a landscape, it will be populated by a varied assortment of high-powered, handheld and stand-alone devices, gizmos, and gadgets with enormous capabilities to enhance personal and social communications.

VISUAL LITERACY FOR 21ST CENTURY COMMUNICATIONS

During the first two centuries of United States history, the most critical social issue was the guarantee of universal education. Literacy was clearly understood by nearly everyone as something more than a privilege, even more than a right. It was recognized by politicians and business leaders, publishers and preachers, professionals and skilled workers, educators and immigrants as a defining personal and social attribute of modern life. For them as well as for us today, literacy is more than the ability to read; it is the ability to reason and make informed decisions.

To ensure universal literacy, the nation as a whole subjects itself to a social tax to underwrite the cost of education. That the definition of "literacy" has changed over the last two centuries is a testament to the modernizing propensity that defines all institutions. Once the study of Latin and Greek, mastery of the Bible and Newtonian physics, and rhetoric and diction were considered essential elements of a sound education. Those days are long past. Not only have new subject matter and new modes of pedagogy replaced the older, traditional forms of study, but exhaustive memorization (exemplified by mathematical times tables) has been replaced by the use of the handheld calculator; long hours devoted to the practice of penmanship have given way to a computer in every school, if not every classroom—and in over one-third of all households.

During the first half-century of the era of electronic communications, a period principally defined by telephone and television service, mass print-based literacy was critical not only to United States democracy, but to mass-market advertising and sales. Today, this model is changing. A new era of video or image-based "media literacy" is beginning to eclipse print; as print superseded the oral tradition, graphic-user interfaces, icons, mocons, and symbolic images are slowly gaining ascendancy as vehicles of instantaneous communication, social discourse, and coherence.

The emerging "video literacy" is something more fundamental in character and consequence than the recurring complaints about the "MTV generation," "sound bytes," and "TV violence." It portends a gradual extension of video imaging as the defining feature of electronic communications. From the most sophisticated scientific research and industrial automation initiatives to the most down-skilled keypunch operation or retail clerk function, video images permeate all discourse. The digital transformation of both programming (as multimedia documents) and distribution (stored on CDs or sent over powerful fiber-optic networks) sets the stage for the reconfiguration of a host of accepted social functions and ways of doing business.

The evolving video literacy is being engendered by the multimedia environment that is now taking shape. This new environment is marked by fundamental changes in both the quantity and quality of the new media experience. The anticipated explosion of available programming is clearly one of the great forces driving corporations into the interactive television business; all expect to win in the coming video "gold rush." Everything that has ever been produced or will be produced will be easily accessible at one's fingertips, creating a supersaturated video environment. But the more profound changes will be in the quality of the video experience.

Next-generation video literacy—a multimedia consciousness—will be based on nonlinear forms of coherence. It will foster a literacy that incorporates and thus supersedes the print-defined literacy of the past. But it will also be fundamentally different. It will likely replace the traditional universe of twenty-six letters and an ordered, linear sequence that establishes coherence and meaning with something profoundly revolutionary. The eye—and thus consciousness—will be greeted by an instantaneous flood of symbols and sounds, the cascade of familiar and foreign representations, the stunning assembly of color and jump-cuts, or text and data and photos and their magical collage into ever-newer forms of expression. A new intellectual skill or consciousness will be needed to master this flood of symbolic representations. This will be the challenge of the new literacy.[4]

The NII sets the stage for a new age of social literacy. A profound historical mistake is likely to occur if the NII is not recognized as playing this broader social role. To limit the NII conceptually to being merely an "infrastructure"—such as a sewer system with pipes of social creation and waste pumping through it—would miss the true historic opportunity that this momentous development signifies.

America will invest billions in the creation of this new multimedia "highway" system of the mind. However much private investment goes into its creation, the NII—as the Vice President insists—will not be reduced to a toll road. More to the point, the corporations that build the NII will receive subsidies through tax breaks, favorable depreciation allowances, and other financial incentives. These subsidies are part of a larger process of favorable treatment that the government extends to corporate America to facilitate technological and business development. In addition to favorable federal corporate tax rates, the lowest in American history, federal R&D grants and outright tax abatements serve to lessen corporate risks. Together, these subsidies will build the NII and, thus, make it a social investment.

In time, as NII usage increases, costs will decline. This will help transform video carriage to much more than an entertainment medium. Schools, colleges, universities, libraries, hospitals, and government agencies are likely to take advantage of the NII; while much of their video communications will be encrypted and private, a good proportion will be accessible by ordinary viewers. Such transmissions will be cheaper to send and will serve as marketing materials. Businesses of all types and sizes, from the smallest mom-and-pop corner store to the biggest corporations, are also likely to use the system, mixing protected and open programming, and helping to further drive down usage costs.

In addition, with the service introduction and price decline in consumer digital video and multimedia equipment (especially for "prosumer" camcorders, scanners, MIDI products, compilers, and editors), a whole new industry of personal videos (from videos of the kids for grandma to pornography), video bulletin boards (e.g., video mail, messages, etc.), and a host of other innovative programs are likely to emerge. These will be complemented by an equally diverse assortment of multimedia documents

The introduction of this post-2000 media world is not only quite feasible but actually very likely. It would take shape in the analogous way that desktop publishing and garage bands have, and will likely do so with equally profound consequences. A multimedia explosion is likely in the not-too-distant future.

How will this take place? What decisions—especially public policy initiatives—must be made that anticipate and facilitate this new media era? We must not forget that popular literacy resulting from public education helps publishers to secure a readership and thus blossom as private businesses. Had publishers been responsible for educating the public, it is doubtful whether universal literacy would have occurred or, if it did, it would have remained limited to only a small segment of the population. If such a policy had been followed, it would have embodied the purest form of "private-market" initiative and been a disaster not only for American democracy, but for private-market business as well. The business community is as much dependent on the social investment in literacy as are publishers. The Clinton Administration's role in creating the NII, the backbone of America's next-generation communications literacy and the future of multimedia, must be guided by the broadest vision of long-term consequences; failing to do so will fail the American public.

Notes

1. Steven Lubar, *InfoCulture: The Smithsonian Book of Information Age Inventions*, Boston: Houghton, Mifflin, 1993.

2. Raymond Williams, *Communications Technologies and Social Institutions*, in *Contact: Human Communications and Its History*, Raymond Williams, ed., London: Thames and Hudson, 1981.

3. P. Gelsinger et al., *2001: A Microprocessor Odyssey*, in *Technology 2001: The Future of Computing and Communications*, Derek Leebaert, ed., Cambridge: MIT Press, 1993.

4. William J. Mitchell, *The Reconfigured Eye: Visual Truth in the Post-Photographic Era*, Cambridge: MIT Press, 1993.

BIOGRAPHY

David Rosen is managing director of *Praxis*. With twenty years' professional experience, he is a nationally recognized authority on entertainment, consumer electronics, and the new interactive media. He uniquely combines senior-level corporate experience with ground-breaking critical analysis and awarding-winning media production.

Praxis is a consulting service providing expert assistance to many of the world's leading corporations and nonprofit organizations such as Ameritech, BellSouth, GTE, Home Box Office, and Matsushita/Panasonic. Among its nonprofit clients are Benton Foundation, MacArthur Foundation, KQED New Ventures (San Francisco), and the Rockefeller Foundation.

Mr. Rosen served as Commodore International's director of international marketing, responsible for the worldwide introduction of CDTV, the first consumer CD-ROM system of player, titles, and accessories. Previously, he served as Vice President, Entertainment Services, LINK Resources, a leading market planning and consulting firm. His practice area included film, television and home video, audio, and the new media (e.g., HDTV, multimedia, fiber optics).

He is the author of *Off-Hollywood: The Making & Marketing of Independent Films* (Grove Press), commissioned by the Sundance Institute; *Optical Fiber & the Future of Television* (Rockefeller Foundation/NVR); and other publications. His television credits include the Emmy-Award winning PBS series *The American City*, and the six-hour ABC miniseries *The Trial of Lee Harvey Oswald*.

Glossary

COMPILED BY MARKET VISION
SANTA CRUZ, CALIFORNIA

3D Sound	Sound that is produced so that it seems to come from various spatial locations.
6DOF	Six Degrees of Freedom are used to describe movement in a three-dimensional space.
ADSL	Asymmetric Digital Subscriber Line technology was developed by Bellcore to increase the bandwidth capability of existing twisted-pair copper wiring to the home. Telephone companies intend to use the increased bandwidth to deliver enhanced services to residential subscribers.
ATM	Asynchronous Transfer Mode is an international standard being developed by CCITT for the transport of voice, data, image, and video that is independent of rate, media, and services. ATM provides a simple, fixed-length packet or cell composed of destination address, priority, and service type to self-route packets through the network. ATM will operate at T1, T3, FDDI, and SONET rates.

Audio quality	Measures of audio quality include voice (8-bit), CD-quality (16-bit), master-quality (18-bit), and multi-track (stereo).
Audiographics	Collaborative work where only voice and graphics are shared across a network.
Authoring tool	User application programs that allow for the creation of courseware combining text, graphics, video, and audio for playback and interaction in a training environment. Generally this involves use of CD-ROM or laserdiscs.
Bandwidth	A measure of the capacity of a transport medium to carry digital data (e.g., megabytes per second).
BISDN	Broadband Integrated Services Digital Network is an integrated services digital network operating at bandwidths of 1.5 megabits per second and above. Three data rates will be available to Broadband ISDN subscribers: Full duplex services at 155 and 600 megabits per second; asynchronous service at 155 megabit per seconds from the subscriber to the network; and 600 megabits per second from the network to the subscriber. Information will be transferred across the network using the Asynchronous Transfer Mode on SONET transmission facilities.
Bit	The smallest unit of information defined by a zero or one (on or off).
Bitmapped	An image formed by a grid of pixels.
Broadcast-quality	A subjective measure of video and audio quality that conforms to the limitations of NTSC, PAL, or SECAM television carrier standards.
Broadcatch	The ability to select and repackage information at the receiving end of programmed broadcasts.

Browsing	Scanning a large body of information with no particular target in mind.
Business television	Primarily a "broadcast" application where a central source transmits corporate, sales, training and marketing communications to several remote sites simultaneously.
Byte	A unit of measure of information equal to 8 bits (2^3). (See *megabyte, kilobyte,* and *gigabyte*.)
CATV	Cable television as in the Cable Television Assoucation.
CBT	Computer-Based Training.
CD-ROM/XA	Microsoft's extension to CD-ROM that interleaves audio with data.
CD-ROM	Compact Disc Read-Only Memory—The ISO 9660 standard medium used by most companies.
CDi	Compact Disc Interactive—home entertainment compact disc standard introduced by Philips.
Cinematic game	A game that employs a large amount of film and video footage and may permit the audience to participate.
Clip art	A collection of 2D and 3D images, backgrounds, audio, video, and animation data files that are sold with reuse rights.
Codec	A device that converts an analog signal into a compressed digital stream and sends it as a digital signal as used in teleconferencing.
Collaborative work	Exchange and sharing of data between two or more workers in real-time. This extends the desktop visual communications to allow work on common

documents or scratch pads (white boards). Applications include screen sharing and videoconferencing.

Communication

Productivity software and supporting hardware that permits the sending, receiving, and management of voice, data, fax, and video. Applications include audio messaging, fax, e-mail, and video mail.

Convergence

The process of cross-industry realignment in which many corporations with a specialized business focus are taking advantage of digital signal processes to diversify into allied industries.

CPU

Central Processing Unit—microprocessor responsible for system control.

CRT

Cathode Ray Tube—output device that streams electrons to activate a screen coated with phosphor dots.

Cybersex

The act of sex between two or more people using technology and communication networks.

DAT

Digital Audio Tape.

Dataglove

Trademark of VPL Research Inc. for their input glove.

DBS

Direct Broadcast Satellite, a wireless mode of digital signal distribution.

Dedicated professional

A full-time user of computer-aided tools for specific technical, scientific, or manufacturing applications.

Desktop video

The creation of videotape presentations using desktop computers and video editing software.

Distance learning	One or two-way exchange of information for instructional purposes accessible from remote sites. May or may not involve the assistance of an instructor.
DOS	An operating system supported on most IBM-compatible platforms.
dpi	Dots per inch.
DSP	Digital Signal Processor used with specialized computer used with sound and other signal and math-intensive tasks.
DVR	Digital Video Recorders.
Edutainment	Educational or instructional materials that employ a large amount of entertainment content.
Electronic mail	Text and still images that are created and distributed electronically to one or more locations.
Entertainment	A suite of consumer entertainment services delivered to the home, displayed on a television or computer display, employing interactive navigation and using a return data path. Applications include movies, video, sports, special events, and guides.
Eye tracking systems	Hardware capable of following the motions of the human eye to direct the actions of user interfaces.
FCC	United States Federal Communications Commission.
Fiber optic networks	Local area networks that use fiber instead of copper twisted-pair transmission lines.
Field of view	The area seen when using a head mounted display.

File servers	A dedicated processor on a LAN with sufficient storage capacity and management software to serve as a central repository for shared data files.
Flat-panel displays	A thin, light-weight computer monitor employing display technologies such as active matrix LCD.
Force-feedback	The simulation of weight or resistance in a virtual world. FFB requires a device that produces a force on the body equivalent to that of a real object.
Frame	A single video image formed by interlacing two field scans.
Full-motion video	Supporting 30 frames per second for NTSC and SECAM and 25 frames per second for PAL broadcast standards.
Gigabyte	1,000 megabytes or one million kilobytes of digital information.
GPS	Global Positioning Satellites.
Grazing	Absorbing information with no attempt at selectivity.
GUI	Graphical User Interface—usually a graphical window system.
HDTV	High-Definition Television based on twice the vertical and horizontal resolution of standard NTSC.
headend	A cable industry term referring to the office where the local signal distribution equipment is housed.
Hertz (Hz)	The number of cycles that occurs over a period of one second. Normal hearing is in the range of 20–20,000 Hz.

HMD	Head Mounted Display, a device that is fastened to the head and is used to display a computer-generated image.
Home entertainment	The combination of consumer electronics equipment such as stereo players, VCRs, CD-audio, videogames, and large-screen televisions.
Home learning	Interactive multimedia software supporting casual exploration.
Home shopping	A consumer information service that permits the shopper to browse product catalogs and information. Ordering can be done by mail, by telephone or on-line including interactive multimedia software that supports buyer services such as on-line catalogs.
Home video market	The market that distributes, sells, and rents videotaped movies to consumers.
Hypermedia	Navigational access software in which text, graphics, audio, images and video are structured to allow for key association searches.
IICS	International Interactive Communications Society.
IMA	Interactive Multimedia Association—a nonprofit organization to promote multimedia technologies and markets.
Immersion	The degree to which a virtual environment immerses the perceptual system of the user. The more the system blocks out stimuli from the physical world and captures the senses, the greater the immersion.
Information Services	Delivering multimedia data over local or wide area networks not in real-time. Applications include audiographics and workflow.

Instruction	Any teaching activity, with or without the assistance of an instructor, that uses digital media in the form of courseware.
Integrated telephony	Productivity software and supporting hardware that permits the sending, receiving, and management of voice, data, fax, and video within a single application.
Intellectual property	Ownership of original work copyrighted or patent protected.
Interactive training	Software and reference information that supports the learning of specially designed tasks.
Interactive video	The ability to randomly access video sequences.
Interactive	The user's ability to interrupt, direct, and navigate within a multimedia environment. (See *multimedia*).
Internet	A global network of networks initially servicing university and government facilities and now being expanded for commercial and private uses.
ISDN	Integrated Services Digital Network—Planned foundation for telecommunication service using digital transmission and switching technology to provide voice and data communications.
ISO	International Standards Organization.
Karaoke	A popular Japanese sing-along form of entertainment.
LAN	Local Area Networks.
Laserdisc	Optical media containing 30 minutes of analog video or up to 54,000 individual frames of still video.

LATA	Local Access and Transport Area. With the AT&T consent decree, 164 court-approved LATAs were established. Local calls within the serving area of a Bell Operating Company (BOC) are also referred to as intraexchange, intra-LATA calls.
LBE	Location-Based Entertainment.
Media-rich	Computing environments that combine text, graphics, animation, audio, music, and video.
MIDI	Musical Industry Digital Interface, a worldwide standard for digital audio production.
MIPS	Millions of Instructions Per Second, a measure of computing power in terms of CPU speed.
MPC	Multimedia Personal Computer.
MPEG	Motion Picture Experts Group.
MSO	Multiple System Operators.
Multimedia	Computer control of the combination of text, graphics, audio, video, and animation data.
Multimedia networking	Distribution of digital media over a local or wide area network.
Multimedia platforms	Computer hardware designed with integrated media capabilities.
Multimedia titles	Presentation, training, educational, and entertainment software intended for commercial distribution.
Multiplayers	A consumer device capable of playing interactive titles, videogames, video, and audio compact discs.
NAB	National Association of Broadcasters.

Near-Video-on-Demand	The delivery of digital movies via cable, telephone, or wireless where the user has the ability to start the movie on 15-minute intervals.
Networking	The ability to connect two or more computers locally or remotely located for the purpose of communicating or sharing resources.
NREN	National Research and Education Network.
NTSC	National Television Systems Committee's standard for U.S. color broadcast using 525 horizontal lines per frame at 30 frames per second with interlaced scans.
PAL	Phase Alternating Line—the European television standard, which uses 25 frames per second.
PCS	Personal Communications Services.
PDA	Personal Digital Assistant is a hand-held device used for data input and two-way cellular communications, as well as a host of specialized applications (e.g., word processing, gaming, etc.).
Performance support	Computer-based on-site information delivery systems to assist in the performance of specific work tasks.
PhotoCD	A digital image format standard developed by Eastman Kodak that specifies five levels of photographic resolution.
Pixel	Picture Element, the basic building block of a 2D graphic display and the unit in which display resolution is usually expressed. The smallest location on a display.

POI   Point-of-Information—a computer kiosk system used to display information on a range of topics including site location, exhibit information, and catalog items.

POS   Point-of-Sales—a computer kiosk system used to display and sell consumer products.

Position tracker   An electronic system that measures the position and orientation of a head, arm, or object in space.

Postproduction   That portion of the video production work when the final assembly is performed, and audio and other special effects are added.

POTS   Plain Old Telephone Service.

Powerglove   A gauntlet-like input device for Nintendo games. Players pull the glove over their hands and control the game with gestures and finger movements. The Powerglove has become a popular component of garage VR systems.

PPV   Pay-per-view is a broadcast cable television service that delivers movies and special presentations on a two-hour schedule for an additional subscriber fee.

Presence   The perceptual illusion of being actively present in another place, sometimes called "being there." The sensation of presence is influenced by three factors: the intensity, sensory range, and sensory resolution of the mediated experience; the amount of interactive control; and the ability to modify the environment with your actions.

Producers   Anyone involved in the process of multimedia authoring, including writers, graphic artists, and directors, regardless of whether or not the materials are for commercial distribution.

Product sales	Software and supporting hardware (i.e., kiosks) that advertises and informs a buyer about products. It may involve the actual purchasing process or may only involve product information.
Production	The stage of the video work where the actual material is generated.
Proprioception	Refers to sense of space through limbs and body.
Public networks	The distribution of digital information over publicly owned communication systems.
QuickTime	Extensions to Apple Macintosh system software and APIs to perform media integration and synchronization of time-dependent information.
QVC	The name of a company and home shopping network seen on cable television.
RAM	Random Access Memory—Semiconductor memory that can be read and changed during microcomputer operation.
RBOC	Regional Bell Operating Company. Under the AT&T consent decree, ownership and control of about 80% of the Bell System's assets was assumed by seven regional Bell holding companies. Bell companies are prohibited from providing "information services," manufacturing telecommunications equipment, and engaging in long-distance communications between and among 164 court-delineated "local access and transport areas" (LATAs). The seven RBOCs are Ameritech, Bell Atlantic, Bell South, Nynex, Pacific Telesis, Southwestern Bell, and US West.
Reference	Interactive multimedia software supporting reference information, such as dictionaries and encyclopedia.

ROM	Read-Only Memory—Semiconductor memory that can be read but not changed during micro-computer operation.
S-VHS	Super VHS—a high-resolution video recorder with 400 horizontal lines.
SECAM	Sequential Color with Memory—a broadcast standard developed in France and adopted by the former USSR and parts of the Middle East and North Africa.
SIGs	Special Interest Groups.
SONET	Synchronous Optical Network (Synchronous Digital Hierarchy) is a fiber optic transmission system based on multiples of a 51.84 megabit per second building block that will be used to transport SMDS and BISDN services. Speeds will range from 51.84 megabit per second to more than 13 gigabit per second. The SONET standards developed by the CCITT provide for basic compatibility between different optical-line systems and define the parameters for setting up a local fiber network and enabling it to interconnect with similar networks via optical links.
Speech recognition	The ability to compare voice input with previously recorded digital patterns of speech to identify and direct computer functions.
STB	Set-Top-Box, a residential device normally located on top of a television set; used by cable television industry for household "addressibility," decryption of scrambled signals, and other purposes.
Storyboard	An artist's rendition of the major elements of a film or video script.

Sync	Synchronization is the portion of the video signal that indicates the end of a field or line. Used to insure that the video stream is delivered at a constant rate of 30 frames per second in the case of NTSC.
Tactile feedback	Sensation applied to the skin typically in response to contact or other actions in a virtual world.
Tactile systems	Computers with the ability to convey a sense of touch.
Telephony	Relating to the use of telephones and the communications industry.
Telepresence	The feeling of being in some distant physical location with the ability to act and interact in a thorough cybernetic technology. The electronic analog to an out-of-body experience.
Training	Providing interactive training and information support in the field or office. Applications include training, mobile reference data, distance learning, and performance support .
VAR	Value-Added Reseller.
VCR	Video Cassette Recorder—generally refers to a consumer videotape recorder.
VESA	Video Electronics Standards Association.
VHS	Video Home System is a one-half-inch videotape cassette format originally developed and standardized by JVC .
Video server	A magnetic or optical storage system that records digital video signals for playback.

Video-on-Demand	The delivery of digital movies via cable, telephone, or wireless where the user has the ability to start and stop the movie at any time.
Videoconferencing	Use of video cameras and displays at two or more locations to replace face-to-face meetings.
Virtual reality	An advanced user interface that connects the visual and sensory human processes to 3D graphical computer systems.
Visualization	The use of specialized software to calculate and display processes difficult to describe or display on paper.
VTR	Video Tape Recorder.
VUI	Video User Interface.
Walkthroughs	Computer 3D animation that allows the viewer to move through an architectural 3D model as if viewed in person.
WAN	Wide-Area Data Networks.
Wireless	The transmission of analog or digital signals without the use of a physical connection.
Wire services	The distribution of news through telephone systems.
Yellow pages	A directory of addresses, telephone numbers, or on-line network addresses. May contain advertising and other self-promotions.

Index